WORKING WOMEN
ON THE HOLLYWOOD SCREEN

GARLAND REFERENCE LIBRARY
OF THE HUMANITIES
(VOL. 469)

This book is dedicated to the memory and the spirit of Carolyn Galerstein, who died on 27 March 1988, shortly before it was due to be finished. Although her graduate degree was in Spanish literature, Dr. Galerstein had become interested in American film and taught several courses in it at the University of Texas at Dallas. The idea for this book came from her interest in film and a deep commitment to women's issues and, despite her progressing illness, she worked intensively on it until her final hospitalization. Because of her dedication to the project, all that remained after her death was to coordinate its final presentation.

WORKING WOMEN
ON THE
HOLLYWOOD SCREEN
A Filmography

Carolyn Galerstein

GARLAND PUBLISHING, INC. • NEW YORK & LONDON
1989

Library of Congress Cataloging-in-Publication Data

Galerstein, Carolyn L., 1931–88
    Working women on the Hollywood screen : a filmography / Carolyn L.
Galerstein.
        p. cm. — (Garland reference library of the humanities ; vol.
469)
        ISBN 0–8240–5642–6 (alk. paper)
        1. Working women in motion pictures—Catalogs. 2. Motion
pictures—United States—Catalogs. I. Title. II. Series.
PN1995.9.W6G34 1989
016.79143'09'093—dc19   88-29218
                                                                    CIP

Cover design by Valerie Mergentime

Printed on acid-free, 250-year-life paper
Manufactured in the United States of America

CONTENTS

ILLUSTRATIONS

PREFACE

This filmography lists approximately 4500 American feature films released between 1930 and 1975, in which the leading female role is that of a working woman. The films, which were culled from some 12,000 films of the period, are categorized by occupation and, within each category, by year. Each entry includes the title of the film, the name of the leading actress, the studio and the director.

No such list of films exists and the method used to identify them for this study consisted primarily of examining the approximately 9200 reviews of American films published in *The New York Times* during those years. Not every American film was reviewed in the *Times*, however, and reviewers may not have mentioned the fact that the leading actress portrayed a working woman. Therefore, other sources, such as *Variety*, American Film Institute directories and television listings were also consulted. Many of them I have viewed directly.

The study and categorization of such a large number of films has allowed me to make certain observations about the way working women have been depicted in the movies. Some of these are contained in the Introduction and some are in annotations to selected films within each category. These annotations are not plot summaries but, rather, comments on the manner in which the film portrays the working woman. The films annotated have been chosen both because of intrinsic interest and as exemplars of some of the typical features of the category.

This time period was selected as a significant and distinctive period, set between the era of silent films, in which a lack of subtlety tended to stereotype all characters male and female, and the full advent of the women's movement, with its revolutionary impact on the participation of women in the workforce and the portrayal of working women in the mass media.

ACKNOWLEDGMENTS

Several people contributed time and expertise to this project and deserve thanks. Margaret Hanson was a tireless researcher, who tidied up many loose ends. Becky Rice also helped with research. With the persistence and skill of Cynthia Keheley, hundreds of pages of notes and manuscript would not have been transformed into the present format; Donald Hanson also lent his computer knowledge to this task. UTD Administrative Assistant J. C. Tupper was a constant and faithful source of help in innumerable ways. At Garland, Editor Marie Ellen Larcada was always ready with information, advice and enthusiasm, especially in the book's final stages of preparation. And George Galerstein provided the love and support that made it possible.

INTRODUCTION

American films during the period 1930-1975 portrayed women
working at numerous and diverse occupations, from domestic
servant to queen and including both female-dominated jobs
such as secretary and male-dominated jobs such as doctor.
Despite this diversity, however, the employed woman was in a
distinct minority as compared with the great majority of
women shown in non-working roles as sweethearts, wives and
mothers. Not only was filmdom's working woman in the
minority during this entire period, but her number actually
decreased over the years, in direct opposition to the
increase in numbers of women in the actual work force.[1] The
lack of correlation between Hollywood's fictional and
America's real work force is illustrated by the inordinately
high percentage of women, about 30 percent, shown in films as
entertainers - actresses, singers, dancers, chorus girls and
the like - a percentage that has no parallel in the real
world of work.

The second most populous category is secretary or other
office worker. In this case, the movies were reflecting a
reality of the workplace, where an average of 25 percent of
employed women were working as clerical and other office
workers. In fact, the majority of women portrayed in the
movies work in sex-segregated jobs, mirroring the situation
in the real world since the end of the nineteenth century.[2]
In some other instances there is a wide discrepancy between
the reality of the work force and the celluloid portrayal of
working women. For example, for much of the period a sizable
proportion of women were employed as domestic workers, but
very few movies feature a maid. Notable exceptions are
Loretta Young in *The Farmer's Daughter* and Patricia Neal in
Hud (and Ethel Waters in the very important secondary role in
The Member of the Wedding). Similarly, although many women
were employed in manufacturing, they are not seen as factory
workers except in the Rosie-the-Riveter movies of World War
II, but those are quite unrealistic and treat women factory
workers as a strictly temporary phenomenon. A more realistic
treatment is, surprisingly, a musical, *The Pajama Game*,
because it shows women involved in union activities.

Factory work, as we all know, is dull and housework even duller, so why, Hollywood filmmakers undoubtedly reasoned, would women go to the movies to escape the drudgery of their own lives, merely to watch the drudgery of others? It's only worthwhile if the payoff is the rescue of the woman from drudgery by a Prince Charming. Loretta Young marries the Congressman and even gets elected to Congress herself. Joseph Cotton carries her over the threshold, but the threshold is the Capitol building. This convention is still flourishing as recently as 1982, when Debra Winger is rescued and literally carried out of the factory in *An Officer and a Gentleman*.

One large category that was difficult to define is businesswoman. There are a great many businesswomen in the movies if you count every widow who turns her home into a boardinghouse, every woman who runs the family ranch while the husband is off prospecting for gold or every madam. Madam is included here as a manager, not as a prostitute, another very popular film occupation. It has always been nearly impossible to count the number of prostitutes in the United States, but their proportion in the movies is surely way out of proportion to their contribution to the American economy. There are small shopkeepers in the movies but no women executives in corporations. One exception is Ruth Hussey in a 1957 film, *Woman of the North Country*. She owns an iron ore mining company, having wrested control from her brothers. She is so ruthless in dealing with her competition that she tries to have him murdered. When that doesn't work, she marries him.

The categories of nurse and teacher are also quite large. Nurses are shown as loving, caring, self-sacrificing and teachers often stereotypically repressed. But the cinematic portrayal of women journalists, the only one of the most popular categories that is not sex-segregated, is particularly revealing. The most memorable of the newspaper films are *Mr. Deeds Goes to Town* and *Front Page Woman* from the 30s and *Meet John Doe*, *His Girl Friday* and *Woman of the Year* from the 40s. At first glance, you might think that Hollywood, using such big stars as Bette Davis, Jean Arthur, Barbara Stanwyck, Rosalind Russell and Katharine Hepburn, was glorifying women journalists. It is true that these characters are shown as competent professionals, but that is their problem. By taking on a man's role, they have overstepped the boundaries and the newspaper world really is not the right place for them. In *Front Page Woman*, Davis sets out to prove that she is as good a newspaperman as her boyfriend, George Brent. He asserts, "I'm going to teach her

once and for all that a woman's place is in the home." After
a journalistic coup by Davis, Brent is forced to admit she is
a good reporter. "That's being a good newspaperman," he
compliments her. "That's all I wanted to hear you say," she
replies. They kiss and make up, conveying the clear message
that now she will behave appropriately and give up this
rough, tough business and settle down to be a respectful and
respectable wife.

In *Mr. Deeds Goes to Town*, Arthur is ashamed of the
subterfuge she has used in order to get some good stories out
of Gary Cooper. Only after he forgives her for her deceit
can she be happy and fulfilled. He carries her out of the
courtroom and away to a bucolic life in Vermont where she can
be Mrs. Deeds and never again have to worry about scrounging
for an extra journalistic buck. Cooper also ends up carrying
a journalist in his arms in *Meet John Doe*. Here again the
newspaperwoman is deceitful, but the scenario is more
insidious because Stanwyck is innocently controlled by
sinister forces. The hapless Doe is led and controlled by
her, emotionally and politically, until she repents her
wicked desire for power and begs his forgiveness. Hepburn's
sin in *Woman of the Year* is that she is much more of a
celebrity than her sportswriter husband. Tracy expects her
to do those womanly things like pay attention to him on their
wedding night, care for an adopted child, even have a child
of their own. After her hilarious failure at cooking, there
are compromises, but they are all hers. She gives up her
officious male secretary, adds her husband's name to hers,
and moves into his apartment, while he goes on doing just
what he did before. So does Cary Grant in *His Girl Friday*.
It's Russell who make the compromises, giving up marriage to
an insurance salesman (hardly a sacrifice) for the excitement
of a profession she claims she deplores because it's so dirty
and for remarriage to her boss. In one sense, then,
journalism is romanticized: women are shown in the thick of
activity, doing exciting things, but their roles as women are
always the dominant factor and this forces them to leave the
business or make other adjustments.

Therefore, the way journalists are portrayed is not much
different from the way all working women are shown. It is
glamorous to be an actress, but even the distinguished Margo
Channing in *All About Eve* grows unhappy over her career and
happiness can be reclaimed only by the love of a good man.
Either the men serve to rescue the women from the drudgery of
work or they provide the women the opportunity to leave an
environment in which they really do not belong.

Regardless of the social or economic status of the
occupation, films consistently express certain attitudes
toward women as wage-earners. Professional accomplishments
are viewed only as stepping stones to romantic success as
sweetheart and personal fulfillment as wife and mother.
Keith Reader's penetrating observation on journalist Hildy
Johnson in *His Girl Friday* can be applied to all of the
cinema's working women:

> Whether the news story is sacrificed or merely
> subordinated to the resolution of the woman's story
> through romantic union, the result is substantially
> the same. Her independent career comes to be read
> retrospectively as a staging-post on the road to
> love and marriage, and the search for news and
> information - her life in the public domain - has
> been but an alibi for the deeper search for "good
> news" in the private domain.[3]

With few exceptions, women are rescued from the drudgery of
work or the inappropriateness of their profession so that
they can enter into a conventional family life. Women's
work, therefore, is seldom taken seriously. It is the men
who make important decisions about money, justice, life and
death; women decide whom to marry. Unlike a man, a woman is
not defined by her career. Rather, work is either explicitly
or implicitly a temporary and secondary involvement, with the
major emphasis on romance. Although a woman's working life
may sometimes appear exciting and glamorous, it is only a
substitute for the pleasures and rewards of the wifely role.

Women who step outside of prescribed sex-defined boundaries
and compete with men are punished for their transgressions.
The punishment may be failure in their career or failure of a
marriage or romantic relationship. Those who assume roles
that have traditionally been the male domain are punished
more severely than those who operate in a more permissible
field. Independence is shown as incompatible with femininity
and the few independent, successful career women are depicted
as oddities. Most "independent" women are simply waiting for
the right men upon whom to rely for guidance and protection.
In the world created by Hollywood, a real woman is caring and
nurturing, concerned with affairs of the heart rather than
matters of the mind.

In general, Hollywood films portray ability and
aggressiveness as masculine traits, unsuitable for emulation
by women. As Mike says in *Pat and Mike*: "I like for a he to
be a he and a she to be a she." In order to be feminine, a

woman must shed her assertiveness and capability and be seductive. The gender confusion is often symbolized by clothing. For example, Pat is criticized for wearing slacks on the golf course and, in the end, compromises with a long tunic over culottes.

In the movie workplace, women are usually regarded as sex objects and possessions by the men for whom they work, as well as by the other men in their lives. In the cinematic world, men and women cannot be friends and colleagues and they cannot be competitors; the only valid relationship is a romantic one. Perhaps the only working women who escape these stereotypes are queens, prostitutes and nuns, all of whom stand outside conventions of romantic love, home and family. Even in these cases, however, love sometimes conquers all.

Although the numbers of employed women and the fields in which they participated are not accurately reflected in the movies of this period, these films do truly reflect the attitudes toward working women that prevailed in American society. They embodied, for example, the general belief that married women should not work outside the home unless forced by economic necessity or wartime patriotism. A working woman might jeopardize her marriage by her independence and consequent threat to her husband's primacy. If the marriage is to be saved, she must make all necessary compromises and sacrifices.

Just as American women were deterred from entering the work force (except for a brief period during World War II) and, particularly, from challenging the male-dominated professions and the executive elite, so too did the movies discourage such activity, making it appear unattractive, inappropriate and emotionally unrewarding. No matter how glamorous a career might seem when painted in a movie, the glamor is soon shown to be superficial, less satisfying than a woman's traditional role. Celluloid women are ready and willing to give up their careers for romance, thus fortifying the notion that career and love are incompatible. Career-woman movies usually bear a stamp of disapproval, if not downright condemnation, of the woman in the non-traditional role.

It would be misleading to say that the movie industry decided on roles for women, which then affected the public consciousness. Rather, filmmakers simply made films they believed the public wanted to see. To the moviegoer of this period, all was right with the world when the woman gave and received love and found, perhaps after some picturesque indecision, her rightful place as wife and mother.

[1] In 1930, the *New York Times* reviewed 316 American feature films, almost as many as they reviewed in any subsequent year, except for a high of 321 in 1938. In 1975, there were reviews of 127 American films, almost an all-time low, except for 111 the previous year. Of the 1930 films, 112 (over one-third) featured working women in the leading female role, 48 of them as actress/entertainer. In 1975, only 34 films (a bit over one-fourth) featured the leading female as a working woman, 8 as actress/entertainer. Compare this decline in Hollywood representations of working women with the extraordinary growth in the percentage of actual adult women who work, from less than 20 percent in 1930 to 56 percent in 1975. See Gaye Tuchman, "The Impact of Mass Media Stereotypes upon the Full Employment of Women," in *Women in the U.S. Labor Force*, ed. Anne Foote Cahn (New York: Praeger, 1979), p. 249.

[2] See Valerie Kincade Oppenheimer, *The Female Labor Force in the United States* (Berkeley: University of California Press, 1970), pp. 64-104.

[3] Keith Reader, *Cultures on Celluloid* (London: Quartet Books, 1981), p. 38.

KEY TO STUDIO ABBREVIATIONS

AA	Allied Artists
AE	Avco-Embassy
AIP	American International Pictures
AMER REL	American Releasing Corporation
ARTCLASS	Art Classics
ASSOCFILM	Associated Film Releasing Corporation
BOREALIS&D	Borealis and Dorad Pictures
BV	Buena Vista
CHESTERF	Chesterfield Pictures
CINC	Cinema Center
COL	Columbia Pictures
CP	Continental Pictures
CR	Continental Releasing
CUE	Commonwealth United Entertainment
DISTCORP	Distributors Corporation of America
D SELZNICK	David O. Selznick
EL	Eagle Lion Classics
FADSIN/PAL	Fadsin/Palomar
FD	First Division
FILMCLASS	Film Classics
FM	Filmmakers
FN	First National Pictures
GN	Grand National Pictures
IA	Independent Artists
IFP	International Film Producers
II	Independent International
INDEP	Independent
IP	International Pictures
IRC	International Releasing Corporation
LCSDIST	LCS Distributing
MAURICE MC	Maurice McEndree
METROPOLTN	Metropolitan
MGM	Metro-Goldwyn-Mayer, Inc.
MILDOLLAR	Million Dollar
MONO	Monogram Pictures
MORALREARM	Moralrearmament
MPC	Motion Picture Corporation of America
NG	National Grand Pictures

NW	New World Pictures
PANAV	Panavision
PARA	Paramount Pictures
PD	Producers Distributing Corporation
PP	Pleasant Pastures
PRC	Producers Releasing Corporation
PRESSBERGE	A. Pressberger
PRODPIC	Producers Pictures
PROG	Progressive Pictures
REP	Republic Pictures
RIALTO PRO	Rialto Productions
RKO	RKO Radio Pictures
SALOONPROD	Saloon Productions
SAWW	Sono Art-World Wide
SCREENGUIL	Screenguild
SELMUR/ROB	Selmur/Robertson
S GOLDWYN	Samuel Goldwyn Studios
SOLTERS/SA	Solters and Sabinson
SPECFEAT	Special Features
SU	Studio Unknown
TAP	Trans America Pictures
TAYLORLAUG	Taylor/Laughlin
TCF	20th-Century Fox Film Corporation
UA	United Artists
UI	Universal International
UNIV	Universal Pictures
WB	Warner Brothers Pictures
WE	World Entertainment

WORKING WOMEN
ON THE HOLLYWOOD SCREEN

ADVERTISING

Women have long been important and noticeable in the creative side of advertising, but apparently Hollywood filmmakers were not so impressed with their accomplishments, as evidenced in the relative paucity of films showing women in the advertising game.

| 1930 | *Divorcee, The* | | NORMA SHEARER |
| | MGM | Robert Z. Leonard | |

| 1931 | *Big Business Girl* | | LORETTA YOUNG |
| | FN | William A. Seiter | |

| 1933 | *Jimmy and Sally* | | CLAIRE TREVOR |
| | TCF | James Tinling | |

| 1934 | *Housewife* | | BETTE DAVIS |
| | WB | Alfred E. Green | |

| 1936 | *Trapped by Television* | | MARY ASTOR |
| | COL | Del Lord | |

| 1937 | *Love on Toast* | | STELLA ARDLER |
| | PARA | E. A. Dupont | |

| 1938 | *Danger on the Air* | | NAN GREY |
| | UNIV | Otis Garrett | |

| | *Women Are Like That* | | KAY FRANCIS |
| | WB | Stanley Logan | |

| 1941 | *H. M. Pulham, Esq.* | | HEDY LAMARR |
| | MGM | King Vidor | |

| 1942 | *Lady Bodyguard* | | ANNE SHIRLEY |
| | PARA | William Clemens | |

| 1943 | *All By Myself* | | EVELYN ANKERS |
| | UNIV | Felix Feist | |

3

1944 *Laura*   GENE TIERNEY
      TCF   Otto Preminger

The story of Laura's career is told by her mentor, who
recognized her talent and claims her career began with
his endorsement. At first her appearance is rather
ordinary, but as she becomes more successful, she
looks more sophisticated. She takes charge and
becomes a good employer. Refusing a proposal of
marriage from one of her employees, she says she has
her work, "beautiful work." But she claims she has
been working too hard and needs to get away. In
response to surprise that she can cook, she explains,
"My mother always listened sympathetically to my
dreams of a career and then taught me another recipe."
Once the flashback outlining her career is over, the
film is only concerned with the mystery of who is
trying to kill her.

1946 *Cuban Pete*   JOAN FULTON
      UNIV   Jean Yarbrough

1947 *Ladies' Man*   VIRGINIA FIELD
      PARA   William D. Russell

1948 *Manhattan Angel*   GLORIA JEAN
      COL   Arthur Dreifuss

1951 *Callaway Went Thataway*   DOROTHY MCGUIRE
      MGM   Norman Panama/Melvin Frank

1955 *It's Always Fair Weather*   CYD CHARISSE
      MGM   Stanley Donen/Gene Kelly

1956 *Toy Tiger*   LARAINE DAY
      UNIV   Jerry Hopper

A small boy is left at a boarding school and receives
no visits from his mother. Halfway through the
picture we finally meet the mother, an advertising
executive who wears a hat in the office and is tough
on her employees. Her art director has unknowingly
become close to her son and claims the boy "had to
invent a father, with a button-pusher like you for a
mother." He berates her for failing her son, but she
explains she was widowed, pregnant, and penniless and
so had to go to work to support her son. She has
worked hard to move up to executive vice president of
the agency just so she could sell her stock and have

enough money to quit the agency and be with her son full-time. She and the art director fall in love, so it is evident she will once again fulfill her duties as a mother and a woman, and society can forgive as an abberation her temporary stint as an executive.

1957   *Slim Carter*   JULIE ADAMS
        UNIV   Richard H. Bartlett

1958   *The Deep Six*   DIANNE FOSTER
        WB   Rudy Mate

        Mardi Gras   SHEREE NORTH
        TCF   Edmund Goulding

1962   *Lover Come Back*   DORIS DAY
        UI   Delbert Mann

Day is immediately identified specifically as a "worker," while her male rival (Rock Hudson) is considered a "drone." Knowledgeable, professional, aggressive and full of ideas, she is shown as an important person, giving orders pleasantly. She enjoys the creative challenge of advertising, but she is a prude and does not like social obligations. Posing as a client, Hudson insults her by telling her she is like a man. "Of course you're not married," he says; "you could only stand to have one man in the house." "I don't use sex to sell," she asserts. "It figures," is his reply and she is offended at being accused of being undersexed. When she wears a golf outfit that shows off her figure, her secretary approves: "Today you are a woman." When Hudson offers to help her with the dishes, she says, "I wouldn't think of it; that's a woman's job." Day insists on her right to have a baby, claiming, "It's my baby, and I'll have what I want; and I want a girl." Her ambivalence toward work and a woman's role is thus resolved, and her role as wife and mother is considered more important.

        Madison Avenue   ELEANOR PARKER
        TCF   Bruce Humberton

1963   *The Thrill of It All*   DORIS DAY
        UNIV   Norman Jewison

1966   *The Glass Bottom Boat*   DORIS DAY
        MGM   Frank Tashlin

1973   *Frasier, the Sensuous Lion*   KATHERINE JUSTICE
       LCSDIST   Pat Shields

AGENT

This is to some extent a catchall category which includes primarily talent and literary agents. Press agents are included if it seemed more appropriate to put them here than under Advertising. Secret agents are not included; they're under Spy.

1938	*The First 100 Years* MGM Richard Thorpe	VIRGINIA BRUCE
	Garden of the Moon WB Busby Berkeley	MARGARET LINDSAY
1941	*Second Chorus* PARA H. C. Potter	PAULETTE GODDARD
	Two Latins From Manhattan COL Charles Barton	JOAN DAVIS
1942	*Call Of The Canyon* REP Joseph Stanley	RUTH TERRY
1943	*What A Woman* COL Irving Cummings	ROSALIND RUSSELL
1944	*Beautiful But Broke* COL Charles Barton	JOAN DAVIS
	The Girl From Monterey PRC Wallace Ford	ARMIDA
	Sensations Of 1945 UA Andrew Stone	ELEANOR POWELL
1946	*Gay Blades* REP George Blair	JEAN ROGERS
1949	*Alias the Champ* REP George Blair	BARBARA FULLER

1950 *Right Cross*   JUNE ALLYSON
      MGM   John Sturges

1957 *Jailhouse Rock*   JUDY TYLER
      WB   Richard Thorpe

      Loving You   LIZABETH SCOTT
      PARA   Hal Kanter

1959 *The Big Circus*   RHONDA FLEMING
      AA   Joseph M. Newman

      Career   CAROLYN JONES
      PARA   Joseph Anthony

      The Perfect Furlough   ELAINE STRITCH
      UI   Blake Edwards

1963 *Wives and Lovers*   MARTHA HYER
      PARA   John Rich

1964 *Man's Favorite Sport?*   PAULA PRENTISS
      UNIV   Howard Hawks

1973 *The Last Of Sheila*   DYAN CANNON
      WB   Herbert Ross

      Tales That Witness Madness   KIM NOVAK
      PARA   Freddie Francis

AIRLINE STEWARDESS

Airline Stewardess (very few films were made featuring this occupation after they came to be called flight attendants) is one female-dominated occupation that appears to have received about the appropriate amount of attention from Hollywood filmmakers. Earlier films concentrated more on the glamour and adventure of flying, but later films tend to view the stewardesses more as sex objects.

1933	*Air Hostess*		EVALYN KNAPP
	COL	Al Rogell	
1934	*Murder in the Clouds*		ANN DVORAK
	WB	D. Ross Lederman	
1936	*Flying Hostess*		JUDITH BARRETT
	UNIV	Murray Roth	ELLA LOGAN
	Without Orders		SALLY EILERS
	RKO	Lew Landers	
1937	*Fugitive in the Sky*		JEAN MUIR
	WB	Nick Grinde	
	Love Takes Flight		BEATRICE ROBERTS
	GN	Conrad Nagel	
	Reported Missing		JEAN ROGERS
	UNIV	Milton Carruth	
1939	*Flight At Midnight*		JEAN PARKER
	REP	Sidney Salkow	
	Nick Carter, Master Detective		RITA JOHNSON
	MGM	Jacques Tourneur	

	Sky Patrol MONO	Howard Bretherton	MARJORIE REYNOLDS
1940	*Flight Angels* WB	Lewis Seiler	VIRGINIA BRUCE
1947	*Dragnet* SCREENGUIL	Leslie Goodwins	MARY BRIAN
1949	*Skyliner* SCREENGUIL	William Berke	PAMELA BLAKE
1951	*Three Guys Named Mike* MGM	Charles Walters	JANE WYMAN
1952	*Geisha Girl* REALART	G. Breakston/C.R. Stahl	MARTHA HYER
1954	*The High And The Mighty* WB	William A. Wellman	DOE AVEDON
1957	*Calypso Joe* AA	Edward Dein	ANGIE DICKINSON
1960	*The Crowded Sky* WB	Joseph Pevney	ANNE FRANCIS
1963	*Come Fly With Me* MGM	Henry Levin	DOLORES HART
1964	*Fate Is The Hunter* TCF	Ralph Nelson	SUZANNE PLESHETTE
	Quick, Before It Melts MGM	Delbert Mann	ANJANETTE COMER
1965	*Boeing-Boeing* PARA	John Rich	DANY SAVAL
1967	*The Big Mouth* COL	Jerry Lewis	SUSAN BAY
1968	*The Odd Couple* PARA	Gene Saks	MONICA EVANS
1970	*Airport* UNIV	George Seaton	JACQUELINE BISSET
	The Stewardesses SHERPIX	Alf Silliman Jr.	CHRISTINA HART

1972	*Skyjacked*		YVETTE MIMIEUX
	MGM	John Guillermin	
1974	*Airport 1975*		KAREN BLACK
	UNIV	Jack Smight	

THE SANDPIPER

ARTIST/PHOTOGRAPHER

Women artists are rarely portrayed in Hollywood films as the obsessive creator, ready to sacrifice everything for their art. They do not pursue dedicated and successful careers, and there are no film biographies of women artists.

1932	*The Animal Kingdom* RKO Edward H. Griffith	ANN HARDING
1933	*Cocktail Hour* COL V. Schertzinger	BEBE DANIELS
	Design For Living PARA Ernst Lubitsch	MIRIAM HOPKINS
	Ex-Lady WB Robert Florey	BETTE DAVIS
1934	*Affairs of a Gentleman* UNIV Edwin L. Marin	PATRICIA ELLIS
	Paris Interlude MGM Edwin L. Marin	UNA MERKEL
	Personality Kid, The WB Alan Crosland	CLAIRE DODD
1935	*Biography of a Bachelor Girl* MGM Edward H. Griffith	ANN HARDING
1937	*Man-Proof* MGM Richard Thorpe	MYRNA LOY
1939	*In Name Only* RKO John Cromwell	CAROLE LOMBARD
1940	*My Son, My Son!* UA Charles Vidor	MADELEINE CARROLL

13

1942   *A Gentleman At Heart*   CAROLE LANDIS
       TCF   Ray McCarey

1943   *The Sky's the Limit*   JOAN LESLIE
       RKO   Curtis Bernhardt

Leslie is known even to the bartender of a fancy night
club as a photographer for a high-class magazine, so
she's a bit of a celebrity herself. But she does not
want to take pictures of celebrities; she asks her
boss to send her overseas. "I have a brain and
talent," she maintains. "And beauty, don't forget
that," chimes in the boss. She persists, asking why
he doesn't send her to London or some other place
where there is excitement. "Because you are a girl,"
is his answer, whereupon she points out the exploits
of Margaret Bourke-White. Finally the boss agrees to
send her to Russia, thinking she is too dumb or lazy
to learn Russian. After she falls in love with a Navy
flier, the boss sends her to photograph bombers being
flown to Australia just so she can have a reunion with
her boyfriend. Although she also does some nightclub
singing and dancing, she is portrayed as someone
serious about her career.

1946   *A Stolen Life*   BETTE DAVIS
       WB   Curtis Bernhardt

Davis is an artist who uses her desire to paint the
portrait of a lighthouse keeper as an excuse to
develop a relationship with his assistant. She loses
her lover to her twin sister, and to assuage her
disappointment, she says she will keep busy and paint.
An exhibit of her paintings elicits the criticism of a
young artist, who claims her work is stiff because she
is too inhibited. "You probably are not even a
woman," he says, hating her because she is rich. "You
are dabbling away at being an artist." The young
artist agrees to teach her, but she finally admits she
is a third-rate artist and always will be; then the
major concern of the plot becomes her attempt to get
her lover back.

1948   *The Bride Goes Wild*   JUNE ALLYSON
       MGM   Norman Taurog

Allyson plays an elementary school teacher who is also
an artist. She wins a contest to illustrate a
children's book, and she sees this as an opportunity

to launch a new career. The "lovable" author of the
book is a lush and a womanizer, so she refuses to work
with him, but he gets her drunk and tricks her into
changing her mind. The author calls her a frustrated,
narrow-minded Vermont spinster; "I bet you haven't
even been kissed." She is insulted. "A spinster, am
I," she says, and then mentions her fiance, a fellow
teacher. But, she adds, "He has his work and I have
mine." She cuts her hair and dresses more glamorously
to show him she is more "womanly." Meanwhile he sees
that she is really talented, and of course they fall
in love.

1949   *Adventure In Baltimore*   SHIRLEY TEMPLE
       RKO   Richard Wallace

As an art student in 1905, Temple wants to paint the
human figure from "unclothed models." This shocks her
teacher, who says china painting is most appropriate
for a woman. Expelled from school because of her
women's suffrage activities, she returns home to her
understanding family, which thinks she should not be
punished for wanting to paint. She continues
sketching and painting, and her unconventional
activities get her and the boy next door in trouble,
as well as nearly ruining her minister-father's
chances of becoming a Bishop. When she brings a
painting to enter in a competition, she is told no
woman has ever entered before, and no woman has ever
painted a great painting; but she insists that there
is no rule against it and that they have no right to
bar her painting. She wins first prize, and although
she claims she wants to study in Paris, it looks as
though marriage to the boy next door is going to put
an end to that ambition.

1952   *The Light Touch*   PIER ANGELI
       MGM   Richard Brooks

1954   *Monster From The Ocean Floor*   ANNE KIMBALL
       LIPPERT   Wyott Ordung

1958   *Curse of the Faceless Man*   ELAINE EDWARDS
       UA   Edward L. Cahn

1962   *Hatari*   ELSA MARTINELLI
       PARA   Howard Hawks
Here is another one of those trite situations where
everyone is surprised when the professional person
turns out to be a woman because the letter was signed

with initials. In this case the woman is a
photographer for a Swiss zoo, sent to Africa to
photograph animal catchers as they go about their job.
The head of the animal outfit, Sean (John Wayne) does
not want her around, and she pouts, "Because I am a
girl, you think I cannot do the job." At first she is
a nuisance, but then she becomes more proficient at
taking pictures of the action. Sean complains about
being stuck with a woman photographer and chides his
men, "Next time you write to a zoo, check what the
initials mean." But they fall in love, and her
photographs never get developed.

1964   *The Night of the Iguana*   DEBORAH KERR
        MGM   John Huston

Deborah Kerr earns her living doing quick character
sketches in charcoal and occasionally selling one of
her watercolors. She and her grandfather are
traveling around Mexico, earning their keep at hotels
by drawing sketches of the guests. She admits she is
not very talented, but she is a proud New Englander
and says she will set up her easel in the town plaza
and peddle watercolors to tourists rather than stay
where she is not wanted. Kind, gentle, and celibate,
she is obviously the "lady" the alcoholic "defrocked"
minister cum tour guide calls her.

1965   *The Sandpiper*   ELIZABETH TAYLOR
        MGM   Vincente Minnelli

In the first scene Laura (Taylor) is painting, and is
thus shown immediately as a serious artist. To
emphasize the seriousness of her work, she explains
how she lives: "I am an artist; I paint, but nobody
buys. I turn out water colors when I need groceries."
A bohemian and a feminist, she is rearing her son
alone, having refused to marry his father; but she did
allow a man to "keep" her and pay her way through art
school. Throughout the course of her affair with her
son's headmaster, she paints during conversations and
sketches while they picnic on the beach. He buys a
painting, commissions her to create stained glass
windows for the school chapel, and helps launch her
career. Laura even paints while her friends are
partying on her beach, and in the last scene she is
painting a portrait of her son. This is her way of
being something, because, to her, "A man is a husband
and a father and a something, but a woman is a wife
and a mother and a nothing."

1965	*These Are The Damned*		VIVECA LINDFORS
	COL	Joseph Losey	
1968	*Double-Stop*		MIMI TORCHIN
	WE	Gerald S. Sindell	
	More Dead Than Alive		ANNE FRANCIS
	UA	Robert Sparr	
1973	*The Hero*		ROMY SCHNEIDER
	AVCO	Richard Harris	
1975	*The Stepford Wives*		KATHARINE ROSS
	FADSIN/PAL	Bryan Forbes	

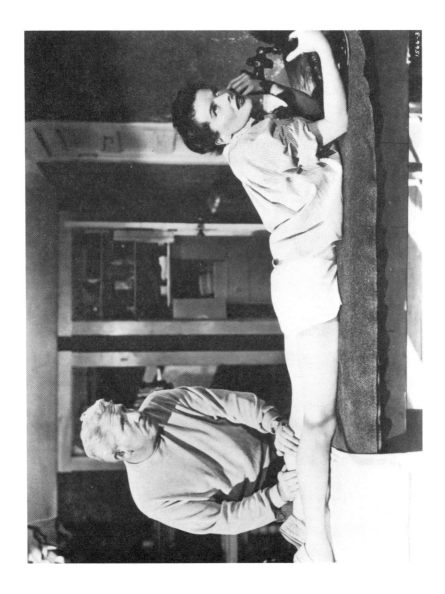

ATHLETE

Generally, women athletes are more entertainers than athletes in the movies, as exemplified by the aqua shows graced by Esther Williams and ice skating demonstrations which feature Sonja Henie. The exceptions are the biographies of famous athletes and the ever wonderful *Pat and Mike*.

| 1930 | *Follow Thru* | | NANCY CARROLL |
| | PARA | Laurence Schwab | |

| 1938 | *Happy Landing* | | SONJA HENIE |
| | TCF | Roy Del Ruth | |

| 1941 | *Ice-Capades* | | DOROTHY LEWIS |
| | REP | Joseph Santley | |

| 1942 | *Danger In The Pacific* | | LOUISE ALLBRITTON |
| | UNIV | Lewis D. Collins | |

| | *Two-Faced Woman* | | GRETA GARBO |
| | MGM | George Cukor | |

| 1944 | *Lake Placid Serenade* | | VERA RALSTON |
| | REP | Steve Sekely | |

| 1945 | *It's A Pleasure* | | SONJA HENIE |
| | RKO | William A. Seiter | |

| 1946 | *Suspense* | | BELITA |
| | MONO | Frank Tuttle | |

| 1949 | *Daughter of the Jungle* | | LOIS HALL |
| | UA | George Blair | |

| 1951 | *Hard, Fast, and Beautiful* | | SALLY FORREST |
| | RKO | Ida Lupino | |

| 1952 | *Million Dollar Mermaid* | | ESTHER WILLIAMS |
| | MGM | Mervyn LeRoy | |

1952   *Pat And Mike*   KATHARINE HEPBURN
        MGM   George Cukor

Hepburn plays a college basketball coach who decides
to become a professional golfer and tennis player, not
so much to prove that she can be successful as a pro
as to become independent of her overpowering fiancee,
whose criticism and lack of confidence in her athletic
abilities cause her performance to suffer. He thinks
of her only as "the little woman" and demands that she
quit work so that he can take charge of her life.
She, however, determines to take charge of herself and
reaches   self-determination   through   professional
achievement   and   personal   acclaim.   Her   manager's
(Spencer   Tracy)   initial   estimation   of   her   is   the
classic "There ain't much meat on her, but what there
is   is   cherce,"   but   she   is   able   to   establish   a
relationship with Tracy based on equal ability and
mutual   respect   ("five-o,   five-o").   Hepburn
embarrasses Tracy when she decks the hoods who are
after him: "I like for a he to be a he and a she to
be a she," he opines. The film also parades a bevy of
well-known   professional   women   athletes,   including
Alice   Marble,   Gussie   Moran,   and   Babe   Didrickson
Zaharias, who are realistically depicted as capable
women pursuing their careers. Professional athletics
is shown as hard work for women.

1953   *Dangerous When Wet*   ESTHER WILLIAMS
        MGM   Charles Walters

        Easy To Love   ESTHER WILLIAMS
        MGM   Charles Walters

1959   *Born Reckless*   MAMIE VAN DOREN
        WB   Howard W. Koch

1967   *Fathom*   RAQUEL WELCH
        TCF   Leslie Martinson

1968   *The Wicked Dreams of Paula Schultz*   ELKE SOMMER
        UA   George Marshall

1969   *Impasse*   ANNE FRANCIS
        UA   Richard Benedict

1972   *Kansas City Bomber*   RAQUEL WELCH
        MGM   Jerrold Freedman

1973	*The Neptune Factor* TCF Daniel Petrie	YVETTE MIMIEUX
	Unholy Rollers AIP Vernon Zimmerman	CLAUDIA JENNINGS
1975	*The Other Side Of The Mountain* UNIV Larry Peerce	MARILYN HASSETT

BEAUTICIAN

The majority of beauticians in leading roles are not hairdressers, a job that would put them in contact primarily with other women. Instead, they are manicurists, presumably so that they can work in barbershops and thus meet men.

1930	*The Big Fight* SAWW James Cruze	LOLA LANE
	The Devil's Holiday PARA Edmund Goulding	NANCY CARROLL
1932	*Beauty Parlor* CHESTERF Richard Thorpe	BARBARA KENT
1933	*Beauty For Sale* MGM R. Boleslavsky	MADGE EVANS
	Don't Bet On Love UNIV Murray Roth	GINGER ROGERS
1934	*Kansas City Princess* WB William Keighley	JOAN BLONDELL
1935	*Hands Across The Table* PARA Mitchell Leisen	CAROLE LOMBARD
	Public Menance COL Erle C. Kenton	JEAN ARTHUR
1936	*Big Brown Eyes* PARA Raoul Walsh	JOAN BENNETT

A manicurist in a barber shop wisecracks with customers but does not let them touch her because she has a boyfriend, a cop. Sore at the boyfriend, she quits her job, but refuses an offer from a customer to set her up in an apartment, with a cynical, "And all I have to do is manicure your nails?" She accepts an offer to work on a newspaper and is immediately a terrific reporter who helps her boyfriend solve a case. When the criminal is found innocent, she quits the paper in disgust and goes back to manicuring. By recognizing a customer's thumb, she is able to pinpoint the head of the crime ring and now happily quits to marry the cop.

Here Comes Trouble		ARLINE JUDGE
TCF	Lewis Seiler	
Lady From Nowhere		MARY ASTOR
COL	Gordon Wiles	
Lady Luck		PATRICIA FARR
CHESTERF	Charles Lamont	
1937	*She Loved A Fireman*	ANN SHERIDAN
	WB	Johnny Farrow	
1938	*Sally, Irene And Mary*	ALICE FAYE
	TCF	William A. Seiter	
1939	*Beauty For The Asking*	LUCILLE BALL
	RKO	Glenn Tryon	
1940	*Laughing At Danger*	JOY HODGES
	MONO	Howard Bretherton	
1946	*Two Guys From Milwaukee*	JOAN LESLIE
	WB	David Butler	
1969	*Eye Of The Cat*	GAYLE HUNNICUT
	UNIV	David Lowell	

BOARDINGHOUSE KEEPER

Often a woman had no way of earning her living other than at home. Hollywood films depicted older women, especially widows, who had no choice but to turn their homes into their business and thus survive by taking in boarders.

| 1930 | *Caught Short* | | MARIE DRESSLER |
| | MGM | Charles F. Reisner | |

| | *Min And Bill* | | MARIE DRESSLER |
| | MGM | George Hill | |

Dressler won an Oscar for her portrayal of the rough and tough owner of a bar and hotel for sailors. She also gives an occasional shave. Min prides herself on running a "decent joint" and beats up the sailors who misbehave. Min's method of bookkeeping is to take money out of the cash drawer and put it in her sock, but she pays her taxes, and is saving to go back to her home, Seattle. She refuses to let a prostitute operate out of her place and is careful not to do anything that would give the cops an excuse to close her down. In the end she sacrifices all her money so her ward can get an education, proudly stating, "I ain't never gonna leave this joint and I ain't never gonna live on charity." While Min is made to look as old and ugly as possible, she's still a romantic temptation for Wallace Beery.

| | *One Night At Susie's* | | HELEN WARE |
| | FN | John F. Dillon | |

| 1931 | *Laugh And Get Rich* | | EDNA MAY OLIVER |
| | RKO | Gregory LaCava | |

| | *Women Go On Forever* | | CLARA KIMBALL YOUNG |
| | TIFFANY | Walter Lang | |

| 1935 | *Bad Boy* | | LOUISE FAZENDA |
| | TCF | John Blystone | |

| 1937 | *Thoroughbreds Don't Cry* | | SOPHIE TUCKER |
| | MGM | Alfred E. Green | |

| 1941 | *Pot O' Gold* | | MAY GORDON |
| | UA | George Marshall | |

| | *The Wild Man Of Borneo* | | BILLIE BURKE |
| | MGM | Robert B. Sinclair | |

| 1945 | *She's a Sweetheart* | | JANE DARNELL |
| | COL | Del Lord | |

| 1949 | *Chicken Every Sunday* | | CELESTE HOLM |
| | TCF | George Seaton | |

| 1950 | *Bright Leaf* | | LAUREN BACALL |
| | WB | Michael Curtiz | |

| 1954 | *About Mrs. Leslie* | | SHIRLEY BOOTH |
| | PARA | Daniel Mann | |

| | *The Raid* | | ANNE BANCROFT |
| | TCF | Hugo Fregonese | |

| 1959 | *Ten Seconds To Hell* | | MARTINE CAROL |
| | UA | Robert Aldrich | |

| 1965 | *Sons of Katie Elder* | | MARTHA HYER |
| | PARA | Henry Hathaway | |

| 1966 | *This Property is Condemned* | | KATE REID |
| | PARA | Sidney Pollack | |

| 1973 | *Killing Kind* | | ANN SOTHERN |
| | MEDIATREND | Curtis Harrington | |

| | *One Little Indian* | | VERA MILES |
| | BV | Bernard McEveety | |

BUSINESS

Businesswoman is a very difficult category to define. If we are limiting this list to women who work outside the home, can we include a woman who keeps a boarding house as a businesswoman? Is a madam a businesswoman or a prostitute (retired)? Is the manager of a saloon who also sings for the guests a businesswoman or entertainer? Is a newspaper publisher a businesswoman or a journalist? These issues are not always clearcut, but I have tried to fit women into the appropriate categories can on the basis of their primary activities in the film.

Most of the businesswomen we see in films of this era are entrepreneurs; like Mildred Pierce they create and run their own businesses. Very few move up in the corporate world. If they hold power in a corporation they did not create themselves, it is usually because they inherited the mantle from a father or husband. And whatever power or position they may hold, we often find them giving it up for a man.

1930	*Be Yourself* UA	Thornton Vreeland	FANNY BRICE
	The Big House MGM	George Hill	LEILA HYAMS
	The Czar Of Broadway UNIV	W. Craft	BETTY COMPSON
	Hook Line And Sinker RKO	Eddie Cline	DOROTHY LEE
	The Man Hunter WB	Ross Lederman	NORA LANE
	Rain or Shine COL	Frank Capra	JOAN PEERS

Silver Horde		EVELYN BRENT
RKO	George Archainbaud	
Trigger Tricks		SALLY EILERS
UNIV	Reaves Eason	
True To The Navy		CLARA BOW
PARA	Frank Tuttle	
Women Everywhere		FIFI D'ORSAY
TCF	Alexander Korda	

1931 *Caught*   LOUISE DRESSER
      PARA   Edward Sloman

      Manhattan Parade   WINNIE LIGHTNER
      WB   Lloyd Bacon

      Mother and Son   CLARA KIMBALL YOUNG
      MONO   J. P. McCarthy

      Once a Lady   RUTH CHATTERTON
      PARA   Guthrie McClintic

      Reducing   POLLY MORAN
      MGM   Charles F. Riesner

      The She-Wolf   MAY ROBSON
      UNIV   James Flood

      Silence   MARJORIE RAMBEAU
      PARA   Louis Gasnier

      Suicide Fleet   GINGER ROGERS
      RKO-PATHE   Albert Rogell

      Westward Bound   ALLENE RAY
      STATERIGHT   Harry Webb

      The Woman Between   LILI DAMITA
      RKO   V. Schertzinger

1932 *Hell Fire Austin*   IVY MERTON
      WORLDWIDE   Forrest Sheldon

      Lady and Gent   WYNNE GIBSON
      PARA   Stephen Roberts

Man Wanted		KAY FRANCIS
WB	William Dieterle	
Midnight Lady		SARAH PADDEN
CHESTERF	Don Thorpe	
Prosperity		MARIE DRESSLER
MGM	Sam Wood	
The Shanghai Gesture		ONA MUNSON
PRESSBERGE	J. Von Sternberg	
Silver Dollar		ALINE MACMAHON
WB	Mervyn LeRoy	
Trouble In Paradise		KAY FRANCIS
PARA	Ernst Lubitsch	
Week-end Marriage		LORETTA YOUNG
FN	Thorton Freeland	

1933	*Blood Money*		JUDITH ANDERSON
	UA	Rowland Brown	
	Female		RUTH CHATTERTON
	WB	Michael Curtiz	
	A Lady's Profession		ALISON SKIPWORTH
	PARA	Norman McLeod	
	My Mother		PAULINE FREDERICK
	MONO	Phil Rosen	
	No Marriage Ties		DORIS KONGON
	RKO	J. Walter Ruben	
	Only Yesterday		MARGARET SULLAVAN
	UNIV	John M. Stahl	
	Reunion In Vienna		MAY ROBSON
	MGM	Sidney Franklin	
	The Secret of Madame Blanche		IRENE DUNNE
	MGM	Charles Brabin	
	She Done Him Wrong		MAE WEST
	PARA	Lowell Sherman	

Sitting Pretty PARA Harry Joe Brown		GINGER ROGERS
Strictly Personal PARA Ralph Murphy		MARJORIE RAMBEAU
Tugboat Annie MGM Mervyn LeRoy		MARIE DRESSLER
Walls Of Gold TCF Kenneth McKenna		SALLY EILERS

1934 *Heat Lightning*   ALINE MCMAHON
      WB   Mervyn LeRoy

      Hip, Hips, Hooray   THELMA TODD
      RKO   Mark Sandrich

      Imitation Of Life   CLAUDETTE COLBERT
      UNIV   John M. Stahl

      The Life Of Vergie Winters   ANN HARDING
      RKO   Alfred Santell

      Meanest Gal in Town   ZASU PITTS
      RKO   Russell Mack

      No More Women   SALLY BLANE
      PARA   Albert Rogell

      The Personality Kid   GLENDA FARRELL
      WB   Alan Crosland

      The Quitters   EMMA DUNN
      FD   Richard Thorpe

      Side Streets   ALINE MCMAHON
      FN   Alfred E. Green

      The World Moves On   MADELEINE CARROLL
      TCF   John Ford

1935 *Home On the Range*   EVELYN BRENT
      PARA   Arthur Jacobson

      Mary Jane's Pa   ALINE MACMAHON
      WB   William Keighley

Orchids To You   JEAN MUIR
TCF   William A. Seiter

Redheads On Parade   DIXIE LEE
TCF   Norman McLeod

Smart Girl   IDA LUPINO
PARA   Aubre Scotta

Times Square Lady   VIRGINIA BRUCE
MGM   George B. Seitz

1936 *Colleen*   RUBY KEELER
      WB   Alfred E. Green

      Come Closer, Folks   MARIAN MARSH
      COL   D. Ross Lederman

      Comin Round the Mountain   ANN RUTHERFORD
      REP   Mack Wright

      Dizzy Dames   MARJORIE RAMBEAU
      LIBERTY   William Nigh

      Doughnuts and Society   LOUISE FAZENDA
      REP   Lewis B. Collins

      The Girl On The Front Page   GLORIA STUART
      UNIV   Harry Beaumont

      Ladies in Love   LORETTA YOUNG
      TCF   Edward H. Griffith

      A Son Comes Home   MARY BOLAND
      PARA   E. A. DuPont

      Speed   UNA MERKEL
      MGM   Edward L. Marin

      White Fang   )   JEAN MUIR
      TCF   David Butler

1937 *Behind the Mike*   JUDITH BARRETT
      UNIV   Sidney Salkow

      Double Wedding   MYRNA LOY
      MGM   Richard Thorpe

Duke Comes Back REP Irving Pichel	GENEVIEVE TOBIN
A Girl With Ideas UNIV S. Sylvan Simon	WENDY BARRIE
God's Country and the Women WB William Keighley	BEVERLY ROBERTS
Life Begins With Love COL Raymond B. McCarey	JEAN PARKER
My Dear Miss Aldrich MGM George B. Seitz	MAUREEN O'SULLIVAN
Outcast PARA Robert Florey	ESTHER DALE
Roaring Timber COL Phil Rosen	GRACE BRADLEY
The Shadow COL C. C. Coleman, Jr.	RITA HAYWORTH
What Price Vengeance RIALTO PRO Del Lord	WENDY BARRIE
Woman Chases Man S GOLDWYN John Blystone	MIRIAM HOPKINS

1938   *Arkansas Traveler*   FAY BAINTER
        PARA   Alfred Santell

        Call of the Rockies   IRIS MEREDITH
        COL   Allan James

        Daredevil Drivers   BEVERLY ROBERTS
        WB   B. Reeves Eason

        The Girl Of The Golden West   JEANETTE MACDONALD
        MGM   Herbert Stothart

        Hawaiian Buckaroo   EVALYN KNAPP
        TCF   Ray Taylor

        I'm From the City   KATHRYN SHELDON
        RKO   Ben Holmes

Partners of the Plain PARA	Les Selander	GWEN GAZE
Service Deluxe UNIV	Rowland V. Lee	CONSTANCE BENNETT
Slander House PROG	Charles Lamont	ADRIANNE AMES
Under the Big Top MONO	Karl Brown	MARJORIE MAIN
Wide Open Faces COL	Kurt Neumann	JANE WYMAN

1939 *Bridal Suite* ANABELLA
MGM   William Theile

Cowboy Quarterback MARIE WILSON
WB   Noel Smith

Newsboys' Home WENDY BARRIE
UNIV   Harold Young

Outside These Walls DOLORES COSTELLO
COL   Ray McCarey

The Phantom Stage MARJORIE REYNOLDS
UNIV   George Waggner

Stand Up And Fight FLORENCE RICE
MGM   W. S. Van Dyke II

Unmarried HELEN TWELVETREES
PARA   Kurt Neumann

Whispering Enemies DOLORES COSTELLO
COL   Lewis D. Collins

1940 *East Of The River* MARJORIE RAMBEAU
WB   Alfred E. Green

Millionaire Playboy LINDA HAYES
RKO   Leslie Goodwins

New Moon JEANETTE MACDONALD
MGM   Robert Z. Leonard

Orphans Of The North		MARY JOYCE
MONO	Norman Dawn	
Pier 13		LYNN BARI
TCF	Eugene Forde	
Queen Of The Yukon		IRENE RICH
MONO	Phil Rosen	
The Ranger And The Lady		JACQUELINE WELLS
REP	Joseph Kane	
Rangers Of Fortune		PATRICIA MORISON
PARA	Sam Wood	
Tugboat Annie Sails Again		MARJORIE RAMBEAU
WB	Lewis Seiler	

1941

Arizona		JEAN ARTHUR
COL	Wesley Ruggles	
Arizona Bound		LUANA WALTERS
MONO	Spence Bennet	
Blossoms In The Dust		GREER GARSON
MGM	Mervyn LeRoy	
Riders Of The Purple Sage		MARY HOWARD
TCF	James Tinling	
Road Show		CAROLE LANDIS
UA	Hal Roach	
Shadows On The Stairs		FRIEDA INESCOURT
WB	D. Ross Lederman	
Six Lessons From Madame La Zona		LUPE VELEZ
UNIV	John Rawlins	
The Stork Pays Off		ROCHELLE HUDSON
COL	Lew Landers	
Sundown		GENE TIERNEY
UA	Henry Hathaway	
Under Age		NAN GREY
COL	Edward Dmytryk	

Wide Open Town   EVELYN BRENT
PARA   Lesley Selander

1942   *Bells Of Capistrano*   VIRGINIA GREY
       REP   William Morgan

       Ghost Town Law   VIRGINIA CARPENTER
       MONO   Howard Bretherton

       Ice-Capades Revue   ELLEN DREW
       REP   Bernard Vorhaus

       Jackass Mail   MARJORIE MAIN
       MGM   Norman Z. McLeod

       Lady For A Night   JOAN BLONDELL
       REP   Leigh Jason

       Blondell is half-owner with her lover of a gambling
       boat on the Mississippi. She is an efficient boss and
       good businesswoman, and she also sings as part of the
       club's entertainment. In order to break into Memphis
       society, she marries an aristocrat who owes the club
       money and spends the rest of the film trying to become
       accepted by his family and social class. When she is
       accused of murdering her husband, newspaper headlines
       call her "former gambling queen." After her acquittal
       she goes back into business with her former partner,
       changing the name of his King's Club to the Queen's
       Club.

       Romance On The Range   LINDA HAYES
       REP   Joseph Kane

       The Spoilers   MARLENE DIETRICH
       UNIV   Ray Enright

       Strictly In The Groove   MARY HEALY
       UNIV   Vernon Keays

       Take A Letter Darling   ROSALIND RUSSELL
       PARA   Mitchell Leisen

       They All Kissed The Bride   JOAN CRAWFORD
       COL   Alexander Hall

1943   *The Desperadoes*   CLAIRE TREVOR
       COL   Charles Vidor

Johnny Come Lately		GRACE GEORGE
W. CAGNEY	William K. Howard	
Pistol Packin' Mama		RUTH TERRY
REP	Frank Woodruff	
Silver Skates		PATRICIA MORISON
MONO	Leslie Goodwins	
Smart Guy		VEDA ANN BORG
MONO	Lambert Hillyer	
What's Buzzin' Cousin?		ANN MILLER
COL	Charles Barton	

1944

Barbary Coast Gent		BINNIE BARNES
MGM	Roy Del Ruth	
Jamboree		RUTH TERRY
REP	Joseph Santley	
Lady in the Dark		GINGER ROGERS
PARA	Mitchell Leisen	

The presentation of Liza, autocratic head of a fashion magazine, exemplifies Hollywood's contention that women who step outside the traditional boundaries must be punished. In this case, the punishment is psychic, as Liza suffers a nervous breakdown and her psychiatrist convinces her the only solution is a man who will dominate her. Although she runs a fashion magazine, she dresses in very severe suits, in fact of the same fabric and cut as her advertising manager, Charley, who accuse her of being uninterested in sex because she is married to her desk. "She shouldn't be top man," he complains; "she isn't built for it. It's flying in the face of nature." Too emotional to be a good executive, she refuses to marry a movie star who wants her to run his life, and allows Charley, to take over her job and her heart.

Laura		GENE TIERNEY
TCF	Otto Preminger	
None But The Lonely Heart		ETHEL BARRYMORE
RKO	Clifford Odets	
Shake Hands With Murder		IRIS ADRIAN
PRC	Albert Herman	

Three Is A Family UA Edward Ludwig		FAY BAINTER
Trocadero REP William Nigh		ROSEMARY LANE
1945	*Frontier Gal* UNIV Charles Lamont	YVONNE DE CARLO
	Gangs Of The Waterfront REP George Blair	STEPHANIE BACHELOR
	The Lost Trail MONO Lambert Hillyer	JENNIFER HOLT
	Mildred Pierce WB Michael Curtiz	JOAN CRAWFORD

Mildred turns her talents as a cook and homemaker to profit when she leaves her husband, gets training as a waitress, then opens a restaurant and develops a successful chain. Her success is punished by the death of one daughter and the loss of the other. Her final punishment is the loss of her business, as well as of her second husband, because she has been naive in business matters and dependent upon men, who have taken advantage of her. Thus, she is punished for having left her first husband and home.

	Road To Utopia PARA Mitchell Leisen	DOROTHY LAMOUR
1946	*The Bride Wore Boots* PARA Irving Pichel	BARBARA STANWYCK
	Faithful In My Fashion MGM Sidney Salkow	DONNA REED
	Roll On Texas Moon REP William Witney	DALE EVANS
	The Strange Love Of Martha Ivers PARA Lewis Milestone	BARBARA STANWYCK

Young Martha murders her aunt, the head of a large company, inherits the company and marries one of the witnesses to the murder. Years later the other witness, Sam, returns and finds Martha a seductive woman, the kind always described in the movies as a man-eater. She now owns the hotel, saying that owning it gives her a sense of power. With Sam's return, she fears blackmail because of her new power and wealth. When Sam comes to her office at her behest, they have the following exchange: Sam: "You should have kept me waiting; big executives do." Martha: "Good executives don't." Sam: "I bet you are good." Martha: "I am. I was twenty-one when I took [the company] over; now it has three thousand employees. I did it all by myself." She has extended the company without the help of her husband, and she dominates him completely, on economic grounds. Her domination over Sam is sexual, but in the end both men consider her insane, unable to tell right from wrong, and she dies rather than lose her power.

Talk About A Lady		JINX FALKENBERG
COL	George Sherman	
To Each His Own		OLIVIA DE HAVILLAND
PARA	Mitchell Leisen	
Tugboat Annie		JANE DARWELL
REP	Phil Rosen	
1947	*The Exile*	PAULA CROSET
	UNIV Max Opuls	
	Range Beyond The Blue	HELEN MOWERY
	PRC Ray Taylor	
	Spoilers Of The North	EVELYN ANKERS
	REP Richard Sale	
	Stallion Road	ALEXIS SMITH
	WB James V. Kern	
1948	*Appointment With Murder*	CATHERINE CRAIG
	FILMCLASS Jack Bernhard	
	River Lady	YVONNE DE CARLO
	UI George Sherman	
	Silver River	ANN SHERIDAN
	WB Raoul Walsh	
1949	*Bride For Sale*	CLAUDETTE COLBERT
	RKO William D. Russell	

Impact		ELLA RAINES
UA	Arthur Lubin	

The Judge Steps Out		ANN SOTHERN
RKO	Boris Ingster	

The Lady Takes A Sailor		JANE WYMAN
WB	Michael Curtiz	

Take Me Out To Ball Game		ESTHER WILLIAMS
MGM	Busby Berkeley	

Tulsa		SUSAN HAYWARD
EL	Stuart Heisler	

When an oilman, Tanner, tries to buy rancher Hayward's oil leases, she refuses because she does not like the way oilmen operate. She decides to drill for oil herself, telling Tanner, "You have no monopoly on brains or luck," and his retort is, "And I'm not as pretty as you are." She takes on geologist Brady as a partner, but clearly makes him understand she is the boss. She wins at the crap table, obviously experienced, having learned how to shoot craps in the ranch bunkhouse. When her well comes in, she works with the shovel to control the gusher. Despite her status as an adult woman, the newspaper headline screams "Girl Wildcatter Gets Gusher," and she is dubbed the Oil Queen to Tulsa. Originally she agrees to marry Brady, but her methods become as ruthless as Tanner's, and Brady complains, "You don't want a husband; you want a trained seal you can pull around on a leash." Smart, ambitious, hard as a driller's fist, she decides in the end to do the right thing in terms of conservation, and of course, she marries the right guy.

1950	*Comanche Territory*	MAUREEN O'HARA
	UNIV	George Sherman	

Double Deal		MARIE WINDSOR
RKO	Abby Berlin	

Mystery Street		ELSA LANCHESTER
MGM	John Sturges	

The Showdown		MARIE WINDSOR
REP	D. S. McGowan	

Singing Guns		ELLA RAINES
REP	R. G. Springsteen	
There's A Girl In My Heart		ELYSE KNOX
AA	Arthur Dreifuss	
Under My Skin		MICHELINE PRESLE
TCF	Jean Negulesco	
The Whipped		GALE STORM
UA	Cyril Endfield	

1951   *Belle Le Grand*   VERA RALSTON
         REP   Allan Dwan

         The Big Gusher   DOROTHY PATRICK
         COL   Lew Landers

         Father Takes The Air   M'LISS MCCLURE
         MONO   Frank McDonald

         Frenchie   SHELLEY WINTERS
         UI   Louis King

         Inside Straight   MERCEDES MCCAMBRIDGE
         MGM   Jerry Mayer

         The Mating Season   THELMA RITTER
         PARA   Mitchell Leison

         Whistle At Eaton Falls   DOROTHY GISH
         COL   Robert Siodmak

1952   *Deadline - USA*   ETHEL BARRYMORE
         TCF   Richard Brooks

         Lovely To Look At   KATHRYN GRAYSON
         MGM   Mervyn LeRoy

         Oklahoma Annie   JUDY CANOVA
         REP   R. G. Springsteen

         Outlaw Women   VIVIAN BLAINE
         LIPPERT   R. Ormond/S. Newfield

         Park Row   MARY WELCH
         UA   Samuel Fuller

The Redhead From Wyoming MAUREEN O'HARA
UNIV   Lee Sholem

Rodeo   JANE NIGH
MONO   William Beaudine

Stage To Blue River   PHYLLIS COATES
MONO   Lewis Collins

Tropic Zone   RHONDA FLEMING
PARA   Lewis R. Foster

Woman Of The North Country   RUTH HUSSEY
REP   Joseph Kane

Christine Powell wrests control of the family iron-ore
mining business from her brothers. When a potential
rival appears on the scene, she tries to scare him
off; then she tries to have him murdered. When that
doesn't work, she marries him! She deceives both her
husband and her banker. Ruthless in business,
domineering as she swallows up men, not above
employing "feminine" seductive wiles to get what she
wants, she enjoys power but loses everything,
including her life, in the end.

1953 *The Beggar's Opera*   ATHENE SEYLER
      WB   Peter Brook

      City Beneath The Sea   MALA POWERS
      UNIV   Budd Boetticher

      Fast Company   POLLY BERGEN
      MGM   John Sturges

      Great Sioux Uprising   FAITH DOMERGUE
      UNIV   Lloyd Bacon

      Hannah Lee   JOANNE DRU
      J.BRODER   John Ireland

      Off Limits   MARILYN MAXWELL
      PARA   George Marshall

      Powder River   CORINNE CALVERT
      TCF   Louis King

      Rebel City   MARJORIE LORD
      AA   Thomas Carr

Vice Squad UA Arnold Lavin		PAULETTE GODDARD
1954	*The Americano* RKO William Castle	URSULA THEISS
	Border River UI George Sherman	YVONNE DE CARLO
	Casanova's Big Night PARA Norman Z. McLeod	JOAN FONTAINE
	Green Fire MGM Andrew Marton	GRACE KELLY
	Johnny Guitar REP Frank Borzage	JOAN CRAWFORD
	Make Haste To Live REP William A. Seiter	DOROTHY MCGUIRE
	Pride of the Blue Grass AA William Beaudine	VERA MILES
	Rails Into Laramie UNIV Jesse Hibbs	MARI BLANCHARD
	Three Ring Circus PARA Joseph Pevney	JOANNE DRU
1955	*Escape To Burma* B.BOGEAUS Allan Dwan	BARBARA STANWYCK
	The Far Country UI Anthony Mann	RUTH ROMAN
	Flame Of The Islands REP Edward Ludwig	YVONNE DE CARLO
	The Girl Rush PARA Robert Pirosh	ROSALIND RUSSELL
	Lucy Gallant PARA Robert Parrish	JANE WYMAN

The love triangle here is a woman, a man and her
store. Stranded in a small Texas town, Wyman sells
her unneeded trousseau, then decides to open a dress
shop, believing there is no reason why women should

not take advantage of the local oil boom. "I'm going
to give the women an opportunity to celebrate the way
they like to, buying clothes." Although she knows
nothing about business, she convinces the banker to
back her and even makes a deal with the madam-dance
hall owner for the right property. The oilman
(Charlton Heston) has difficulty courting her because
of the time devoted to the store, which becomes a big
success. He wants to marry her but lets her play out
the store idea first, thinking she'll get over it, and
they'll marry, with "me taking care of you, the way we
both want it." She insists the store comes first.
Heston, unable to understand, complains "You are out
to prove something. You are too independent. You and
that store." When he joins the Army, he sends a
farewell message to Lucy, "Tell her to mind the store
for me." On his return, Lucy Gallant Incorporated has
prospered, and a big new modern store is an obvious
symbol of the town's prosperity. When she tells
Heston to call her sometime, she coyly says, "You know
where." At the same time she agrees to marry him, she
talks about a bigger store. When he asks who's going
to run it, she of course replies "I am." "I thought
being married was a full time job," is Heston's
rejoinder. "What about kids? How are you going to
manage that? Move the maternity ward into the store?"
She will not give up on the store, so he gives up on
the relationship. Her friend warns her she will wind
up a rich old lady, but alone; it's better to have a
man. When Lucy goes out to Heston's land to
congratulate him on striking oil, he only asks
bitterly, "Who's minding the store?" But when the
store burns down, he lends her the money to rebuild it
because he admires her nerve. When her general
manager "cold decks" her in a board meeting, she is
about to lose control of the store, but once again he
saves her by paying off her bank note. Finally she
tells him she wants marriage, and he asks, "Who'll
mind the store?" "What store?" is her final line.
Kiss.

Man With The Gun   JAN STERLING
UA   Richard Wilson

One Desire   ANNE BAXTER
UI   Jerry Hopper

The Spoilers   ANNE BAXTER
PARA   Jesse Hibbs

Tennessee's Partner RKO Allan Dwan		RHONDA FLEMING
Texas Lady RKO Tim Whelan		CLAUDETTE COLBERT
Timberjack REP Joe Kane		VERA RALSTON
Top Of The World UA Lewis R. Foster		EVELYN KEYES
1956	*Death of a Scoundrel* RKO Charles Martin	YVONNE DE CARLO
	Glory RKO David Butler	MARGARET O'BRIEN
	Great Day In The Morning RKO Jacques Tourneur	VIRGINIA MAYO
	Murder On Approval RKO Bernard Knowles	DELPHI LAWRENCE
	The Oklahoma Woman AMER REL Roger Corman	PEGGY CASTLE
	The Solid Gold Cadillac COL Richard Quine	JUDY HOLLIDAY
	These Wilder Years MGM Roy Rowland	BARBARA STANWYCK
	Thunder Over Arizona REP Joe Kane	KRISTINE MILLER
1957	*The Badge of Marshall Brennan* AA Albert Gannaway	ARLEEN WHELAN
	Drango UA Hall Bartlett	JULIE LONDON
	Peyton Place TCF Mark Robson	LANA TURNER
	Spoilers of the Forest REP Joe Kane	VERA RALSTON

| 1958 | *Bell, Book And Candle* | KIM NOVAK |
| | COL   Richard Quine | |

Bullwhip   RHONDA FLEMING
AA   Harmon Jones

Separate Tables   WENDY HILLER
UA   Delbert Mann

Wind Across The Everglades   GYPSY ROSE LEE
WB   Nicholas Ray

| 1959 | *The Best of Everything* | JOAN CRAWFORD |
| | TCF   Jean Negulesco | |

Crawford gets special billing and a juicy role as the tyrannical executive of a publishing house. However, her role is secondary to the secretary, played by Hope Lange, who rises in the publishing world. One interesting feature of the film is the number of women in executive positions in the company.

It Happened To Jane   DORIS DAY
COL   Richard Quine

The Miracle of the Hills   BETTY LOU GERSON
TCF   Sidney Lumet

Pillow Talk   DORIS DAY
UNIV   Michael Gordon

The Wasp Woman   SUSAN CABOT
FILMGROUP   Roger Corman

Cabot is the chairman of the board of a cosmetics firm she established and built on her image as a beauty. But, she is no longer young and beautiful, and sales are declining. More to save the company than out of personal vanity, she insists on being the guinea pig for experimental injections of enzymes from queen wasps which a scientist believes can restore beauty and youth. It works, and she looks terrific, but it turns her into a terrible, man-stinging monster.

| 1960 | *The Big Gamble* | JULIETTE GRECO |
| | TCF   Richard Fleischer | |

Cimarron   MARIA SCHELL
MGM   Anthony Mann

The Fugitive Kind   ANNA MAGNANI
COL   George Sidney

Magnani is married to a depraved Southerner who owns a
general store, but she refers to it as "my" store.
She ran it while her husband was away in the hospital,
and continues to run it while he is upstairs in bed,
recuperating but shouting orders to her. Her husband,
who claims she is good for nothing, demands nursing
care from her, but she is too busy running the store,
which she considers a "going thing." She hires a good
looking man as a clerk, and this improves business,
but her husband reminds her he still owns the store by
asking, "How much am I paying him?" She bosses the
young man around, but when she gives in to her desire
for him, everything leads downhill to destruction.
Just as she realizes her dream of adding a
confectionary on to the store, her husband sets fire
to her confectionary and then shoots her.

Ice Palace   CAROLYN JONES
WB   Vincent Sherman

The Secret Of The Purple Reef   MARGIA DEAN
TCF   William N. Whitney

1961   *Bachelor In Paradise*   LANA TURNER
       MGM   Jack Arnold

1962   *The Man Who Shot Liberty Valance*   JEANETTE NOLAN
       PARA   John Ford

1963   *Hot Horse*   MARTHA HYER
       UNIV   Hal Kanter

       Palm Springs Weekend   CAROLE COOK
       WB   Norman Taurog

       The Wheeler Dealers   LEE REMICK
       MGM   Arthur Hiller

Remick is a stockbroker on Wall Street, and her boss
wants to fire her to cut expenses. He wouldn't dream
of firing one of the "boys" but "taking on that girl
was just an experiment," and he doesn't want her
around. So he gives her the impossible assignment of
selling stock in a company which does not exist. She
wants to be taken seriously, and considered bright,
instead of pretty. She insists, "The man I marry is

going to have to want more than a chief cook and
bottle washer. I like Wall Street; I like my job, and
I am good at it." The Texas oilman she tries to sell
the stock to thinks she's clever; but he is the one
who comes up with the ideas to push the stock and make
money. And it's off to Texas in the end. For the
most part, the film treats the woman stockbroker
seriously, especially by showing how appalled the
stuffy old New England lawyer is when he learns there
are now women on Wall Street. Although Remick
occasionally wears nice suits to work, she also wears
inappropriately large bows on her dresses and suits
and there's plenty of cleavage when she is out to
dinner with the male customer. Also, at the meeting
of the Women Securities Analysts, the women get very
emotional when they complain that men consider women
too emotional to be on Wall Street. Everyone's ego is
poked a bit.

Who's Minding The Store?		JILL ST. JOHN
PARA	Frank Tashlin	

1964   *He Rides Tall*   MADLYN RHUE
        UNIV   R. G. Springsteen

        Law Of The Lawless   YVONNE DE CARLO
        PARA   William F. Claxton

        Mail Order Bride   MARIE WINDSOR
        MGM   Burt Kennedy

        The Night Of The Iguana   AVA GARDNER
        MGM   John Huston

As the owner of a seedy hotel in Mexico, Ava Gardner
shares the female lead with Deborah Kerr as the
artist. A widow, Gardner is an old friend of the
"defrocked" minister cum tourguide, and resents being
incorrectly called his paramour; she prefers to play
around with the beach boys. Though her guests are an
unlikeable bunch, she tries to be nice to them; she
eats with them and is otherwise very informal. When
the cook doesn't want to work, she does the cooking.
She is shown as a free-spirited, good-humored,
outspoken woman, and the hotel, which was left to her
by her husband, provides a comfortable setting and
apparently just enough income for her to live the way
she wants to. However, she says the first rule of
hotel administration is that there must be a man

around to attract the female customers; so she ends up
with the minister.

Roustabout HAL WALLIS	John Rich	BARBARA STANWYCK
Viva Las Vegas MGM	George Sidney	ANN-MARGRET

1965   *Double-Barrelled Detective Story*   GRETA THYSSEN
       SALOONPROD   Adolfos Mekas

       The Train   JEANNE MOREAU
       UA   J. Frankenheimer

1966   *Johnny Reno*   JANE RUSSELL
       PARA   R. G. Springsteen

       Namu, The Killer Whale   LEE MERIWETHER
       UA   Laslo Benedek

1967   *El Dorado*   CHARLENE HOLT
       PARA   Howard Hawks

       Guess Who's Coming To Dinner   KATHARINE HEPBURN
       COL   Stanley Kramer

In a preachy film about interracial marriage, the
mother's business is hardly important (though the fact
that the father has been a crusading, liberal
newspaper editor is). Even so, the first thing we
hear from the daughter is about her mother's art
gallery, and that is the first place she takes her
fiancee. She brags that, although the assistant
really runs the gallery now, her mother is the one
with all the ideas and that her idea of putting
originals in hotel rooms was brilliant. The other
reference to her business is when her assistant comes
to the house out of curiosity about the black fiancee
and is appalled. Hepburn fires her, telling her to
write a check for $5000 and get permanently lost.
Hepburn tells her husband that the most wonderful
thing for a wife is to be able to help her husband,
that the best time for her was when they were first
married and struggling and she felt she was a help to
him (presumably before she had the gallery). This
role was another Oscar-winner for Hepburn, this time
for portraying a mother primarily and wife
secondarily; businesswoman had nothing to do with it.

The Last Challenge MGM Richard Thorpe	ANGIE DICKINSON
Rough Night In Jericho UNIV Arnold Laven	JEAN SIMMONS
Those Fantastic Flying Fools AIP Don Sharp	HERMIONE GINGOLD
The Tiger Makes Out COL Arthur Hiller	RUTH WHITE
Waterhole No. 3 PARA William Graham	JOAN BLONDELL
You're A Big Boy Now WB Francis F. Coppola	JULIE HARRIS

1968

Angels From Hell AIP Bruce Kessler	ARLENE MARTEL
Chubasco WB Allen H. Miner	ANN SOTHERN
Five Card Stud PARA Henry Hathaway	INGER STEVENS
The Horse in the Grey Flannel Suit BV Norman Tokar	DIANE BAKER
Kona Coast WB Lamont Johnson	JOAN BLONDELL
With Six You Get Eggroll CINC Howard Morris	DORIS DAY

Widowed with three sons, Day runs a lumber yard.
Although it is not stated, the implication is that it
was originally her husband's business. She wears a
hard hat and is obviously very knowledgeable and
efficient; she is respected by her employees. One
customer calls her "sir," and her son, who also works
there, calls her "boss." Unable to attend another
son's baseball game, her excuse is that she could not
get away from the yard. When her sister tries to find
her a man, she insists that she does not need one: "I
have a business to run; I am doing just fine."
However, the majority of the film is taken up with her
romance with a widower and their marriage and attempt

to merge their families. During the courtship he comments, "I am trying to imagine you running that lumber yard," and she retorts that she is a whiz at a band saw. In addition to the opening, there are two more scenes in which she is shown at work and nothing is said about her giving up the business after the marriage.

| 1969 | *Alice's Restaurant* | PAT QUINN |
| | UA   Arthur Penn | |

| | *Death of a Gunfighter* | LENA HORNE |
| | UNIV   Allen Smithee | |

| | *Eighty Steps To Jonah* | DIANA EWING |
| | WB   Gerd Oswald | |

| | *Heaven With A Gun* | CAROLYN JONES |
| | MGM   Lee H. Katzin | |

| 1971 | *Blood And Lace* | GLORIA GRAHAME |
| | AIP   Philip Gilbert | |

| | *Fool's Parade* | ANNE BAXTER |
| | COL   Andrew McLaglen | |

| 1973 | *The Harrad Experiment* | TIPPI HEDREN |
| | CINERAMA   Ted Post | |

| | *Oklahoma Crude* | FAYE DUNAWAY |
| | COL   Stanley Kramer | |

| | *Rivals* | JOAN HACKETT |
| | AE   Krishna Shah | |

| | *Terror in the Wax Museum* | ELSA LANCHESTER |
| | CINERAMA   George Fenady | |

| 1974 | *Golden Needles* | ANN SOTHERN |
| | AIP   Robert Clouse | |

| | *Harry and Tonto* | ELLEN BURSTYN |
| | TCF   Paul Mazursky | |

| 1975 | *The Strongest Man In The World* | EVE ARDEN |
| | DISNEY   Vincent McEveety | |

CRIMINAL

Most of the women criminals in Hollywood films are thieves; the attempt here has been to identify those who are professional thieves, rather than those who steal on impulse. There are gun molls, too, but they seem to be more kept women than murderers themselves.

1930   *Alias French Gertie*   BEBE DANIELS
      RKO   George Archainbaud

      Double Cross Roads   LILA LEE
      SU   Alfred Warker

      One Night At Susie's   BILLIE DOVE
      FN   John F. Dillon

      Outside the Law   MARY NOLAN
      UNIV   Tod Browning

      Slightly Scarlet   EVELYN BRENT
      PARA   Gasnier/Knopf/Ober

      The Unholy Three   LILA LEE
      MGM   Tod Browning

      Wide Open   PATSY RUTH MILLER
      SU   Archie Mayo

1931   *The Lady Who Dared*   JUDITH VOSSELLI
      FN   William Beaudine

      The Maltese Falcon   BEBE DANIELS
      WB   Roy Del Ruth

      Man Of The World   CAROLE LOMBARD
      PARA   Richard Wallace

1932   *Beast of the City*   JEAN HARLOW
      MGM   Charles Brobin

51

Docks of San Francisco		MARY NOLAN
ACTION	George B. Seitz	

False Madonna   KAY FRANCIS
PARA   Stuart Walker

Madam Racketeer   ALISON SKIPWORTH
PARA   Alexander Hall

The Miracle Man   SYLVIA SIDNEY
PARA   Norman McLeod

Sally of the Subway   DOROTHY REVIER
ACTION   George B. Seitz

Trouble In Paradise   MIRIAM HOPKINS
PARA   Ernst Lubitsch

Hopkins and her male partner and lover masquerade as
European aristocrats and steal any way they can,
including shoplifting and picking pockets. When he
gets a job as secretary to a female perfume company
owner in order to steal her jewels as well as embezzle
company funds, Hopkins becomes jealous and is willing
to sacrifice the loot in order to keep her lover.

1933   *Blondie Johnson*   JOAN BLONDELL
       FN   Ray Enright

       Ladies They Talk About   BARBARA STANWYCK
       WB   Howard Bretherton

1934   *One Exciting Adventure*   BINNIE BARNES
       UNIV   Ernest L. Frank

       Sophie Lang   GERTRUDE MICHAEL
       PARA   Ralph Murphy

1935   *The Girl Who Came Back*   SHIRLEY GREY
       FD   Charles Lamont

1936   *Desire*   MARLENE DIETRICH
       PARA   Frank Borzage

       Nobody's Fool   GLENDA FARRELL
       UNIV   A. G. Collins

       The Return Of Sophie Lang   GERTRUDE MICHAEL
       PARA   George Archainbaud

Satan Met a Lady WB William McGann	BETTE DAVIS
Whipsaw MGM Sam Wood	MYRNA LOY
Yours For the Asking PARA Alexander Hall	IDA LUPINO

1937 *Federal Bullets*   ZEFFIE TILBURY
      MONO   Karl Brown

      The Last of Mrs. Cheyney   JOAN CRAWFORD
      MGM   Richard Boledowski

      Midnight Taxi   FRANCES DRAKE
      TCF   Eugene Forde

      Sophie Lang Goes West   GERTRUDE MICHAEL
      PARA   Charles Reisner

1938 *The Amazing Dr. Clitterhouse*   CLAIRE TREVOR
      WB   Anatole Litvak

      Arsene Lupine Returns   VIRGINIA BRUCE
      MGM   George Fitzmaurice

      Stolen Heaven   OLYMPE BRADNA
      PARA   Andrew L. Stone

      Tarnished Angel   SALLY EILERS
      RKO   Leslie Goodins

      Tip-Off Girl   EVELYN BRENT
      PARA   Louis King

1939 *Daughter Of The Tong*   EVELYN BRENT
      METROPOLTN   Raymond K. Johnson

      The Housekeeper's Daughter   JOAN BENNETT
      UA   Hal Roach

      Persons In Hiding   PATRICIA MORISON
      PARA   Louis King

      The Saint Strikes Back   WENDY BARRIE
      RKO   John Farrow

1940   *Adventure In Diamonds*   ISA MIRANDA
       PARA   George Fitzmaurice

       I Was An Adventuress   ZORINA
       TCF   Gregory Ratoff

       Queen Of The Mob   BLANCHE YURKA
       PARA   James Hogan

1941   *Belle Starr*   GENE TIERNEY
       TCF   Irving Cummings

       Lady Scarface   JUDITH ANDERSON
       RKO   Frank Woodruff

       They Met In Bombay   ROSALIND RUSSELL
       MGM   Clarence Brown

1942   *Lady Gangster*   FAYE EMERSON
       WB   Florian Roberts

       Man From Cheyenne   SALLY PAYNE
       REP   Joseph Kane

       Quiet Please, Murder   GAIL PATRICK
       TCF   John Larkin

       Sin Town   CONSTANCE BENNETT
       UNIV   Ray Enright

       Wildcat   ARLINE JUDGE
       PARA   Frank McDonald

1944   *Main Street After Dark*   SELENA ROYLE
       MGM   Edward Cahn

       Spider Woman   GALE SONDERGAARD
       UNIV   Roy William Neill

1945   *Dangerous Partners*   SIGNE HASSO
       MGM   Edward L. Cahn

       Gentle Annie   MARJORIE MAIN
       MGM   Andrew Martin

       Hold That Blonde   VERONICA LAKE
       PARA   George Marshall

Mama's Shotgun
MGM   Andrew Martin   MARJORIE MAIN

1946   *Heartbeat*
RKO   Sam Wood   GINGER ROGERS

Two Smart People
MGM   Jules Dassin   LUCILLE BALL

1947   *Calcutta*
PARA   John Farrow   GAIL RUSSELL

Framed
COL   Richard Wallace   JANIS CARTER

Intrigue
UA   Edwin L. Marin   JUNE HAVOC

Second Chance
TCF   James S. Tinling   LOUISE CURRIE

1948   *The Argyle Secrets*
FILMCLASS   Cyril Endfield   MARJORIE LORD

The Hawk Of Powder River
EL   Ray Taylor   JENNIFER HOLT

Madonna Of The Desert
REP   George Blair   LYNNE ROBERTS

Remember The Night
PARA   Mitchell Leisen   BARBARA STANWYCK

The Sainted Sisters
PARA   William D. Russell   JOAN CAULFIELD / VERONICA LAKE

Station West
RKO   Sidney Lanfield   JANE GREER

1949   *Belle Starr's Daughter*
TCF   Lesley Selander   RUTH ROMAN

Calamity Jane And Sam Bass
UI   George Sherman   YVONNE DE CARLO

Deadly Is The Female
UA   Joseph H. Lewis   PEGGY CUMMINS

Hellfire
REP   R. G. Springsteen   MARIE WINDSOR

Post Office Investigator   AUDREY LONG
REP   George Blair

South Of St. Louis   ALEXIS SMITH
WB   Ray Enright

The Story of Molly X   JUNE HAVOC
UI   Crane Wilbur

The Younger Brothers   JANIS PAIGE
WB   Edwin L. Marin

1950   *The Blonde Bandit*   DOROTHY PATRICK
REP   Harry Keller

Barricade   RUTH ROMAN
WB   Peter Godfrey

Blonde Dynamite   ADELE JERGENS
MONO   William Beaudine

Dakota Lil   MARIE WINDSOR
TCF   Lesley Selander

Windsor is a forger and counterfeiter and the brains
behind a gang of train robbers. For cover she works
as a singer in a club in Mexico, where she has many
admirers.

The Damned Don't Cry   JOAN CRAWFORD
WB   Vincent Sherman

Federal Agent At Large   DOROTHY PATRICK
REP   George Blair

Good Time Girl   JEAN KENT
FILMCLASS   David MacDonald

I Was A Shoplifter   MONA FREEMAN
UI   Charles Lamont

Lonely Hearts Bandits   DOROTHY PATRICK
REP   George Blair

Southside 1-1000   ANDREA KING
AA   Boris Ingster

Whirlpool   GENE TIERNEY
TCF   Otto Preminger

1951   *Anne Of The Indies*   JEAN PETERS
       TCF   Jacques Tourneur

       Cry Danger   JEAN PORTER
       RKO   Robert Parrish

       Hurricane Island   MARIE WINDSOR
       COL   Lew Landers

       The Law and the Lady   GREER GARSON
       MGM   Edwin H. Knopf

       My True Story   HELEN WALKER
       COL   Mickey Rooney

       Outlaws of Texas   PHYLLIS COATES
       MONO   Thomas Carr

       Two Dollar Bettor   MARIE WINDSOR
       REALART   Edward L. Cohn

1952   *Against All Flags*   MAUREEN O'HARA
       UI   George Sherman

       Captain Black Jack   AGNES MOOREHEAD
       W.GOULD   Julien Duvivier

       Confidence Girl   HILLARY BROOKE
       UA   Andrew L. Stone

       Duel at Silver Creek   FAITH DOMERGUE
       UNIV   Don Siegel

       The Golden Hawk   RHONDA FLEMING
       COL   Sidney Salkow

       Montana Belle   JANE RUSSELL
       RKO   Allan Dwan

       Outlaw Women   MARIE WINDSOR
       LIPPERT   R. Ormond/S.Newfield

       Son Of Paleface   JANE RUSSELL
       PARA   Frank Taslin

       This Woman Is Dangerous   JOAN CRAWFORD
       WB   Felix Feist

1953   *Great Diamond Robbery*   CARA WILLIAMS
       MGM   Robert Z. Leonard

1954	*Drive A Crooked Road* COL Richard Quine	DIANNE FOSTER
	The Miami Story COL Fred F. Sears	ADELE JERGENS
1955	*Return of Jack Slade* AA Harold Schuster	MARI BLANCHARD
1956	*The Come On* AA Russell Birdwell	ANNE BAXTER
	Francis In The Haunted House UNIV Charles Lamont	VIRGINIA WELLES
	The Scarlet Hour PARA Michael Curtiz	CAROL OHMART
1957	*The Dalton Girls* UA Reginald LeBorg	MERRY ANDERS
	Hell Bound UA William J. Hale, Jr.	JUNE BLAIR
	My Gun Is Quick UA G. White/P. Victor	WHITNEY BLAKE
1958	*The Bonnie Parker Story* AA William Witney	DOROTHY PROVINE
	The Buccaneer PARA Anthony Quinn	CLAIRE BLOOM
	Diamond Safari TCF Gerald Mayer	BETTY MCDOWALL
	Girl On The Loose UNIV Paul Henreid	MARA CORDAY
1960	*Cage of Evil* UA Edward L. Cahn	PAT BLAIR
	Psycho SHAMLEY Alfred Hitchcock	JANET LEIGH
	Seven Thieves TCF Henry Hathaway	JOAN COLLINS
	Valley of the Redwoods TCF William N. Witney	LYNN BERNAY

Why Must I Die   DEBRA PAGET
AIP   Roy Del Ruth

Young Jesse James   MERRY ANDERS
TCF   William Claxton

1961 *Twenty Thousand Eyes*   MERRY ANDERS
TCF   Jack Leewood

1962 *The Happy Thieves*   RITA HAYWORTH
UA   George Marshall

Who's Got The Action?   LANA TURNER
PARA   Daniel Mann

1964 *Marnie*   TIPPI HEDREN
UNIV   Alfred Hitchcock

A compulsive thief gets jobs in offices, where she
performs clerical duties efficiently, and then helps
herself to the contents of the safe. She sends most
of the money to her mother. One boss sees what she is
and decides to marry her, rather than send her to
jail, and discover the psychological reasons for her
behavior. Considering men "filthy pigs," she will not
let her husband touch her. Hitchcock's usual misogyny
shows how abnormal her rejection of men is, even
though she also believes that women are stupid and
feeble. An oversimplified psychological explanation
clears up the reasons for her stealing.

Robin and the Seven Hoods   BARBARA RUSH
WB   Gordon Douglas

Topkapi   MELINA MERCOURI
UA   Jules Dassin

Mercouri introduces herself to the audience with, "I
am a thief. Honest." Well, it's a living. And,
besides, she is sexually excited by the thought of the
emerald-encrusted dagger in the Topkapi Museum. She
masterminds the elaborate plan to steal the dagger,
but her part of the plan is to keep the lighthouse
keeper distracted while her confederates are in the
museum. They all end up in prison, where she is
planning the next fabulous heist.

1965 *Cat Ballou*   JANE FONDA
COL   Elliott Silverstein

1966   *Assault on a Queen*   VIRNA LISI
        PARA   Jack Donohue

        Gambit   SHIRLEY MACLAINE
        UNIV   Ronald Neame

        How To Steal A Million   AUDREY HEPBURN
        TCF   William Wyler

        A Man Could Get Killed   MELINA MERCOURI
        UNIV   Ronald Neame

        Penelope   NATALIE WOOD
        MGM   Arthur Miller

1967   *Bonnie And Clyde*   FAYE DUNAWAY
        WB   Arthur Penn

Dunaway was nominated for an academy award for her
portrayal of the restless Bonnie Parker. When Clyde
first meets Bonnie, he guesses correctly that she is a
waitress. She hates her job because of the pink
uniform and the customers who are dumb and want to get
in her pants. No wonder she is attracted by the
adventure of armed robbery. Clyde maintains that
Bonnie can find herself a lover boy: "They don't care
whether you're waiting tables or picking cotton. You
got something better than being a waitress." He
offers her fancy cars and clothes as well as
adventure. When next she introduces herself and
Clyde, it is with "We rob banks."

        Jack of Diamonds   MARIE LAFORET
        MGM   Don Taylor

1968   *The Biggest Bundle of Them All*   RAQUEL WELCH
        MGM   Ken Annakin

        The Mini-Skirt Mob   DIANE MCBAIN
        AIP   Maury Dexter

        The Shakiest Gun in the West   BARBARA RHOADES
        UNIV   Alan Rafkin

1969   *Butch Cassidy and the Sundance Kid*   KATHARINE ROSS
        TCF   George Roy Hill

        The Great Train Robbery   KIM NOVAK
        WB   Hy Averback

	Midas Run		ANNE HEYWOOD
	STROSS/MPI	Alf Kjellin	
	The Wrecking Crew		ELKE SOMMER
	COL	Phil Karlson	
1970	*Bloody Mama*		SHELLEY WINTERS
	AIP	Roger Corman	
1971	*Bunny O'Hare*		BETTE DAVIS
	AIP	Gerd Oswald	
	Dollars ($)		GOLDIE HAWN
	COL	Richard Brooks	
	Skin Game		SUSAN CLARK
	WB	Paul Bogart	
1972	*Boxcar Bertha*		BARBARA HERSHEY
	AIP	Martin Scorsese	
	Every Little Crook & Nanny		LYNN REDGRAVE
	MGM	Cy Howard	
1973	*Badlands*		SISSY SPACEK
	COL	Terrance Malick	
	Cleopatra Jones		SHELLEY WINTERS
	PANAV	Jack Starrett	
	Harry In Your Pocket		TRISH VAN DEVERE
	UA	Bruce Geller	
	Lady Ice		JENNIFER O'NEILL
	PANAV	Tom Gries	
	Little Cigars		ANGEL TOMPKINS
	AIP	C. Christenberry	
	The Outfit		KAREN BLACK
	MGM	John Flynn	
	The Sting		EILEEN BRENNAN
	UNIV	George Roy Hill	
1974	*The Bank Shot*		JOANNA CASSIDY
	UA	Gower Champion	
	Big Bad Mama		ANGIE DICKINSON
	NW	Steve Carver	

Sugarland Express   GOLDIE HAWN
UNIV   Steven Spielberg

Thomasine And Bushrod   VONETTA MCGEE
COL   Gordon Parks Jr.

1975   *Crazy Mama*   CLORIS LEACHMAN
       NW   Jonathon Demme

       Diamonds   BARBARA SEAGULL
       AE   Menahem Golan

       Lucky Lady   LIZA MINNELLI
       TCF   Stanley Donen

DETECTIVE

Usually female cinematic sleuths are amateurs, helping out their boyfriend or husband, or perhaps, like Miss Marple, assisting the police in solving a crime. One might expect to find *The Thin Man* series in this category, but Nick is the detective in this series; Nora participates as an amateur only occasionally. She is a commentator, sometimes helpful, sometimes not. In *After the Thin Man* Nick locks her in a closet so she cannot accompany him when he goes searching for the criminal.

1933	*Dangerously Yours* TCF	Frank Tuttle	MIRIAM JORDAN
1934	*Jimmy The Gent* WB	Michael Curtiz	BETTE DAVIS
	Murder on the Blackboard RKO	George Archainbaud	EDNA MAY OLIVER
	Their Big Moment RKO	James Cruze	ZASU PITTS
1935	*Murder on A Honeymoon* RKO	Lloyd Corrigan	EDNA MAY OLIVER
	Mr. Dynamite UNIV	Alan Crosland	JEAN DIXON
1936	*Killer at Large* COL	David Selman	MARY BRIAN
1938	*Romance on the Run* REP	Gus Meins	PATRICIA ELLIS
	There's Always A Woman COL	Alexander Hall	JOAN BLONDELL

1939	*Private Detective* WB Noel Smith	JANE WYMAN

1940	*The Girl In 313* TCF Richard Cortez	FLORENCE RICE

Honeymoon Deferred   MARGARET LINDSAY
UNIV   Lew Landers

1942   *This Gun For Hire*   VERONICA LAKE
PARA   Frank Tuttle

1944   *Leave It To The Irish*   WANDA MCKAY
MONO   William Beaudine

1945   *Having A Wonderful Crime*   CAROLE LANDIS
RKO   Eddie Sutherland

She Gets Her Man   JOAN DAVIS
UNIV   Erle C. Kenton

1946   *Invisible Informer*   LINDA STIRLING
REP   Philip Ford

1947   *Exposed*   ADELE MARA
REP   George Blair

1949   *Mary Ryan, Detective*   MARSHA HUNT
COL   Abby Berlin

1955   *The Crooked Web*   MARI BLANCHARD
COL   Nathan Hertz Juran

1957   *Affair In Reno*   DORIS SINGLETON
REP   R. G. Springsteen

1962   *Murder She Said*   MARGARET RUTHERFORD
MGM   George Pollock

The first of the Miss Marple series, MGM films made in England.

1968   *The Thomas Crown Affair*   FAYE DUNAWAY
UA   Norman Jewison

Dunaway is a "specialist" brought in by an insurance company to solve a bank robbery. Her methods are unorthodox; she operates on intuition, and has some clever ideas, but some of her gambits are unethical and even illegal. She also does not balk at seducing the man she is investigating, which leads the insurance executive to consider her a whore. She admits she is immoral, but she does her job, and she makes no bones about doing it for the money.

| 1971 | *Are You There?* | | BEATRICE LILLIE |
| | TCF | Hamilton MacFadden | |

| 1972 | *The Abductors* | | CHERI CAFFARO |
| | SOLTERS/SA | Don Schain | |

| 1973 | *Girls Are For Loving* | | CHERI CAFFARO |
| | CR | Don Schain | |

| 1975 | *Sheba, Baby* | | PAM GRIER |
| | AIP | William Girdler | |

DOCTOR/PSYCHOLOGIST

Psychologists are included here because the movies make no distinction between psychologists and psychiatrists in terms of their training or their treatment of patients. Psychiatrists dominate the woman doctor roles, and the majority of these doctors are foreign, as though nice American girls should not grow up to be doctors. Except for psychiatrists, there is always surprise when the doctor turns out to be a woman.

| 1931 | *Sit Tight* WB | Lloyd Bacon | WINNIE LIGHTNER |

| 1933 | *Mary Stevens, M.D.* WB | Lloyd Bacon | KAY FRANCIS |

The Right To Romance
RKO   Alfred Santell   ANN HARDING

1934 *Dr. Monica*
WB   William Keighley   KAY FRANCIS

1935 *The Flame Within*
MGM   Edmund Goulding   ANN HARDING

Private Worlds
PARA   Gregory LaCava   CLAUDETTE COLBERT

1936 *The Crime Of Dr. Forbes*
TCF   George Marshall   SARA HADEN

White Legion
GN   Karl Brown   TALA BIRELL

1937 *Prescription For Romance*
UNIV   S. Sylvan Simon   WENDY BARRIE

1938 *The Crime of Dr. Hallet*
UNIV   S. Sylvan Simon   JOSEPHINE HUTCHINSON

1939	*King Of Chinatown* PARA Nick Grinde	ANNA MAE WONG
	King Of The Underworld WB Lewis Seiler	KAY FRANCIS
	Woman Doctor REP Sidney Salkow	FRIEDA INESCOURT
1940	*Dr. Cyclops* PARA Ernest Schoedsack	JANICE LOGAN
1941	*Appointment For Love* UNIV William A. Seiter	MARGARET SULLAVAN
	Kathleen MGM Harold S. Bucquet	LARAINE DAY
	You Belong To Me COL Wesley Ruggles	BARBARA STANWYCK
1942	*Drums Of The Congo* UNIV Christy Cabanne	ONA MUNSON
1943	*Corregidor* PRC William Nigh	ELISSA LANDI
1944	*Three Men In White* MGM Willis Goldbeck	MARILYN MAXWELL
1945	*Bedside Manner* UA Andrew Stone	RUTH HUSSEY
	China Sky RKO Ray Enright	RUTH WARRICK
	Spellbound AA Alfred Hitchcock	INGRID BERGMAN

Dr. Peterson is a competent psychiatrist but is accused by her male colleagues of being a human glacier. "A woman like you can never fall in love," she is told. She wears sensible clothes, a plain hairdo and glasses. Still, the director considers her the best assistant he has ever had. "Women make the best psychiatrists," he maintains, "until they fall in love; then they make the best patients." When she does fall in love, he accuses her, "a promising psychoanalyst," of behaving like a schoolgirl. "You

are an excellent analyst, but a stupid woman" is his
summation; but if she puts love behind her, she can
have a great career and find happiness in hard work.
Since the plot revolves around the mystery of her
lover's identity and actions, and it is her ability as
a psychiatrist which effects the solution, the film
does indeed focus on her profession, rather than
merely on the love story.

1946	*She Wouldn't Say Yes* COL Mitchell Leisen	ROSALIND RUSSELL
1947	*High Wall* MGM Curtis Bernhardt	AUDREY TOTTER
1948	*Angel On The Amazon* REP John H. Auer	CONSTANCE BENNETT
	The Intruders TCF Ray McCarey	VIRGINIA GREGG
	Let's Live A Little EL Richard Wallace	HEDY LAMARR
1949	*Canadian Pacific* TCF Edwin L. Marin	JANE WYATT
	The Cowboy and the Indians COL John English	SHEILA RYAN
1950	*Emergency Wedding* COL Edward Buzzell	BARBARA HALE
	Shadow On The Wall MGM Patrick Jackson	NANCY DAVIS
1951	*Saddle Legion* RKO Leslie Selander	DOROTHY MALONE
1952	*The Girl In White* MGM John Sturges	JUNE ALLYSON
	Kisenga, Man Of Africa IRC Thorold Dickinson	PHYLLIS CALVERT
1953	*I, The Jury* UA Harry Essex	PEGGY CASTLE

Invaders From Mars TCF William C. Menzies	HELENA CARTER
Money From Home PARA George Marshall	PAT CROWLEY
Savage Mutiny COL Spencer C. Bennet	ANGELA STEVENS

1954 *Jungle Man-Eaters*   KARIN BOOTH
      COL   Lee Sholem

      Knock On Wood   MAI ZETTERLING
      PARA   N. Panama/M. Frank

1955 *Love Is A Many Splendored Thing*   JENNIFER JONES
      TCF   Henry King

      The Private War Of Major Benson   JULIE ADAMS
      UI   Jerry Hopper

      The Shrike   KENDALL CLARK
      TCF   Jose Ferrer

      Strange Lady In Town   GREER GARSON
      WB   Mervyn LeRoy

This film directly states the case for the ability of
women doctors and condemns the prejudice against them.
Dr. Garth (like many women in male occupations, she
uses her initials) comes to Santa Fe in the latter
part of the nineteenth century because she could not
make a living in Boston. After graduation from
Philadelphia Women's Medical College and study in
London and Paris, her Boston male colleagues exhibited
nothing but disdain, unable to tolerate the fact that
a woman would dare to practice medicine, "dare to
break down the gates of a man's world." Everyone in
Santa Fe comes to see her because "a lady doctor is a
very strange thing, like a chicken with two heads."
The other doctor in town rejects the new medical
knowledge she brings from the East and accuses her of
stealing his patients, trying to discredit him in
order to get her revenge on male doctors. He wonders,
"If she's all she's supposed to be, why isn't she
married? What man would want to come home to a woman
who has been rolling pills all day?" When he asks why
she doesn't get married, her reply is, "Because I have
more important things to do." Although she is very

capable and her cures lead the poor people to consider her a saint, the community "leaders," who call her "Miss" Garth, try to run her out of town. She is saved by the other doctor, who marries her, and it looks as though they are going to practice together.

| 1956 | *Emergency Hospital* | | MARGARET LINDSAY |
| | UA | Lee Sholem | |

| 1957 | *The Sad Sack* | | PHYLLIS KIRK |
| | PARA | George Marshall | |

| | *Twenty Million Miles To Earth* | | JOAN TAYLOR |
| | COL | Nathan Juran | |

| 1959 | *The Perfect Furlough* | | JANET LEIGH |
| | UI | Blake Edwards | |

| 1961 | *Voyage To The Bottom Of The Sea* | | JOAN FONTAINE |
| | TCF | Irwin Allen | |

| | *Wild In The Country* | | HOPE LANGE |
| | TCF | Philip Dunne | |

| 1963 | *Drums Of Africa* | | MARIETTE HARTLEY |
| | MGM | James B. Clark | |

| 1964 | *The Disorderly Orderly* | | GLENDA FARRELL |
| | PARA | Frank Tashlin | |

| | *Sex And The Single Girl* | | NATALIE WOOD |
| | WB | Richard Quine | |

| | *Shock Treatment* | | LAUREN BACALL |
| | WB | Denis Sanders | |

Bacall has impeccable credentials: Fellow of the American College of Psychiatry, Assistant Director of the State Psychiatric Hospital, author of two books on psychiatry and crime. Thoroughly professional, she teaches residents, is expert at treating patients, testifies in court cases; her work is her entire life. Her problem is that she is obsessed with obtaining money for her research, and this obsession leads to sinister behavior, Gestapo-like tactics, and eventually to total insanity.

| | *The Troublemaker* | | ADELAIDE KLEIN |
| | JANUS | Theodore Flicker | |

1965   *Brainstorm*   VIVECA LINDFORS
        WB   William Conrad

        Dead Heat On A Merry-Go-Round   MARIAN MOSES
        COL   Bernard Girard

        Harvey Middleman Fireman   HERMIONE GINGOLD
        COL   Ernest Pintoff

        Return From The Ashes   INGRID THULIN
        UA   J. Lee Thompson

        A Very Special Favor   LESLIE CARON
        UNIV   Michael Gordon

When a Frenchman has a daughter who prefers practicing
clinical psychology to marriage, what's a father to
do? Find her a lover, of course. Imagine a father's
horror at realizing his unmarried daughter is almost
30! "At 30, when a woman looks around, the only thing
coming is 40!" "I saw a thirty-year-old spinster, a
woman who has never tasted life." So he looks for
someone to seduce her, so she will have experience,
will have been through a romantic adventure, from
whose flames she will "emerge as a woman." He admits
she is skinny, flat-chested and buck-toothed, but he
begs the would-be seducer to "save" her. Caron does
plan to marry, but education and building a practice
have taken time, and there will be no children; she
has her career to think of. She dresses
conservatively but beautifully in Dior suits, is
professional in all ways, makes all the decisions for
her fiance, but is not naive when it comes to men.
Although the seducer claims "She's hopeless, a virgin;
this one has been left in the toaster too long; she'll
never pop up," they engage in a battle of the sexes
and predictably end up married, with a family of five
daughters.

1966   *Three On A Couch*   JANET LEIGH
        COL   Jerry Lewis

The sign on the door says "M.D., Ph.D." but the first
shot of the psychiatrist is her legs. She is engaged
to an artist who thinks she is the best psychiatrist
in the world. Professional and dedicated to her
patients, she nevertheless understands when an
obstetrician friend tells her, "After you have been in
practice longer, you will realize there are other

things in life, like being a person as well as a
doctor; you have to decide whether you want to be a
doctor or a woman or both." Not sexually repressed,
she has no trouble being both and is very loving with
her fiance (they wear suits made out of the same
fabric); but she does get angry with him when her
sense of ethics is outraged.

Fantastic Voyage		RAQUEL WELCH
TCF	Richard Fleischer	

Johnny Tiger		GERALDINE BROOKS
UNIV	Paul Wendkos	

Seven Women		ANNE BANCROFT
MGM	John Ford	

It is 1935 and a group of missionaries in China has
asked for a doctor to be assigned to the mission.
Expecting a man because the telegram does not give the
doctor's first name, only initials, they are appalled
at the appearance of a woman. "Are you the doctor?
But you're a woman," complains the pregnant wife of
the only man in the mission. "Don't worry," he
replies, "she's as good as any man." "Better!" is
Bancroft's retort. Bancroft does not wish to be
bothered with the religious aspects of the mission: "I
am dedicated to the practice of medicine... and you
are damn lucky to get me." She is rebellious, will
not obey mission rules, smokes and cusses, and the
woman who heads the mission considers her immoral.
She has worked in the worst slum hospitals of New York
and Chicago and seen everything. Wearing jodphurs,
she orders people around, takes care of sick refugees
fleeing from a warlord, quarantines the mission and
immunizes everyone when she diagnoses cholera. When
the warlord attacks the mission, she is unafraid, and
socks a warrior who tries to hold her. When she tries
to retrieve her medical bag so she can deliver the
baby, the warlord says she can do her work, but in
return he wants her. "Tell him it's a deal," is her
tough decision. Thus, she is able to get milk for the
baby and food for the captives, and finally secures
their release. Understanding what she has traded for
all this, the mission head calls her "harlot, whore of
Babylon, scarlet woman." Dressed in an elegant
Chinese robe, looking beautiful and feminine with a
flower in her hair, she calmly awaits as the warlord
comes to take possession of his spoils. But she has

kept a vial of poison from her bag. After serving it to him, with a "So long, you bastard," she too drinks the poison.

1968 *Charly*   LILIA SKALA
      SELMUR/ROB   Ralph Nelson

      Panic in the City   LINDA CRISTAL
      SU   Eddie Davis

1969 *Hornet's Nest*   SYLVA KOSCINA
      UA   Phil Karlson

1971 *Guess What We Learned At School Today*   YVONNE MCCALL
      CANNON   John G. Avildsen

      They Might Be Giants   JOANNE WOODWARD
      UNIV   Anthony Harvey

A man who believes he is Sherlock Holmes is taken to a psychiatrist named Watson (Woodward). Holmes had always expected to meet his Dr. Watson, and he is not surprised when she turns out to be a woman. Watson is serious about her work, and not afraid to tell the head of the clinic to stick to his fundraising and leave her to her patients. She has published, has three degrees and has had Guggenheim and Rockefeller grants and is a dedicated doctor; but she is soon captivated by Holmes's peculiar brand of insanity. Knowing that she is not beautiful, she is friendless and has never been loved. Her apartment is a mess; she cannot cook, and there is a trite scene where she is making fruitless attempts at cooking while also trying to get dressed and put on makeup, crying, "Some women do this every day." Woodward looks frumpy and appears as a stereotypical spinster-professional, but Holmes loves her and she is not afraid of danger as long as he is with her.

1972 *Superbeast*   ANTOINETTE BOWER
      UA   George Schenck

1974 *Man On A Swing*   ELIZABETH WILSON
      PARA   Frank Perry

      The Terminal Man   JOAN HACKETT
      WB   Mike Hodges

DOMESTIC SERVANT/MAID

The maid was a staple character in films before the 1970s, as a second lead, as a comic figure, as someone in the background in every middle or upper-class home. The starring roles for maids are usually Cinderella stories; she is rescued from this drudgery or lowly position by marriage to the family's son, or the widowed father, or a rich family friend.

Maids were almost the only roles available to black actresses, and although there are some memorable performances, such as Hattie McDaniel's Academy Award-winning Mammy in *Gone With the Wind*, they are almost invariably not the lead roles.

1930	*Alias French Gertie*		BEBE DANIELS
	RKO	George Archainbaud	
	The Cat Creeps		HELEN TWELVETREES
	UNIV	Rupert Julien	
	Common Clay		CONSTANCE BENNETT
	TCF	Victor Fleming	
	Free Love		ZAZU PITTS
	UNIV	Hobart Henry	
	The Grand Parade		HELEN TWELVETREES
	SU	Fred Newmeyer	
	Honey		NANCY CARROLL
	PARA	Wesley Ruggles	
	Liliom		ROSE HOBART
	TCF	Frank Borzage	
	Lummox		WINNIFRED WESTOVER
	UA	Herbert Brenon	

The Matrimonial Bed		BERYL MERCER
WB	Michael Curtiz	
Monte Carlo		ZASU PITTS
PARA	Ernst Lubitsch	
Numbered Men		BERNICE CLAIRE
SU	Mervyn LeRoy	
Once A Gentleman		LOIS WILSON
SU	James Cruze	
Passion Flower		ZASU PITTS
SU	William DeMille	
Runaway Bride		MARY ASTOR
RKO	Donald Crisp	
Second Wife		MARY CARR
PATHE	Russel Mack	
Seven Days Leave		BERYL MERCER
PARA	Richard Wallace	
The Squealer		ZASU PITTS
SU	Harry Brown	
Sweethearts and Wives		BILLIE DOVE
FN	Clarence Badger	

1931	*Alice In Wonderland*		LILLIAN ARDELL
	UNIQUE	Bud Pollard	
	Bad Sister		ZASU PITTS
	UNIV	Hobart Hensley	
	The Black Camel		SALLY EILERS
	TCF	Hamilton McFadden	
	Blonde Crazy		JOAN BLONDELL
	WB	Roy Del Ruth	
	Compromised		ROSE HOBART
	FN	John Adolfi	
	Daddy Long Legs		JANET GAYNOR
	TCF	Alfred Santell	

East Lynne		BERYL MERCER
TCF	Frank Lloyd	
It's A Wise Child		MARIE PREVOST
MGM	Robert Z. Leonard	
The Man In Possession		CHARLOTTE GREENWOOD
MGM	Sam Wood	
Merely Mary Ann		JANET GAYNOR
TCF	Henry King	
Murder at Midnight		ALICE WHITE
TIFFANY	Frank Strayer	
Personal Maid		NANCY CARROLL
PARA	Lothar Mendes	

1932 *The Crash*   BARBARA LEONARD
      FN   William Dieterle

      Cross-Examination   SARAH PADDEN
      WEISS BROS.   Richard Thorpe

      Emma   MARIE DRESSLER
      MGM   Clarence Brown

      The Greeks Had A Word For Them   JOAN BLONDELL
      UA   Lowell Sherman

      Panama Flo   HELEN TWELVETREES
      RKO-PATHE   Ralph Murphy

      Scarlet Dawn   NANCY CARROLL
      WB   William Dieterle

1933 *Christopher Bean*   MARIE DRESSLER
      MGM   Sam Wood

      Her Splendid Folly   BERYL MERCER
      RKO   William O'Conner

      Jennie Gerhardt   SYLVIA SIDNEY
      PARA   Marion Gering

      Meet The Baron   ZASU PITTS
      MGM   Walter Lang

	My Weakness TCF	David Butler	LILIAN HARVEY
	They Just Had To Get Married UNIV	Edward Ludwig	ZASU PITTS
1934	*Among The Missing* COL	Al Rogell	HENRIETTA CROSMAN
	Bright Eyes TCF	David Butler	LOIS WILSON
	By Candlelight UNIV	James Whale	ELISSA LANDI
	The Man With Two Faces FN	Archie Mayo	EMILY FITZROY
	Sadie Mckee MGM	Clarence Brown	JOAN CRAWFORD
	Servant's Entrance TCF	Frank Lloyd	JANET GAYNOR
1935	*The Farmer Takes A Wife* TCF	Victor Fleming	JANET GAYNOR
	If You Could Only Cook COL	William Seiter	JEAN ARTHUR
	Lady Tubbs UNIV	Alan Crosland	ALICE BRADY
	Page Miss Glory WB	Mervyn LeRoy	MARION DAVIES
	Personal Maid's Secret WB	Arthur G. Collins	RUTH DONNELLY
	Spring Tonic TCF	Clyde Bruckman	ZASU PITTS
1936	*Private Number* TCF	Roy Del Ruth	LORETTA YOUNG
	Sons O'Guns WB	Lloyd Bacon	JOAN BLONDELL

1937	*That Man's Here Again* WB Louis King	MARY MAGUIRE
1938	*Affairs of Annabel* RKO Ben Stoloff	LUCILLE BALL
	The Cowboy and the Lady UA H. C. Potter	MERLE OBERON
	Everybody Sing MGM Edwin L. Marin	FANNY BRICE
	Female Fugitive MONO William Nigh	EVELYN VENABLE
	The Girl Downstairs MGM Norman Taurog	FRANCISKA GAAL
	In Old Chicago TCF Henry King	ALICE BRADY
	Just Around The Corner TCF Irving Cummings	JOAN DAVIS
	Paradise For Three MGM Edward Buzzell	EDNA MAY OLIVER
	Romance in the Dark PARA H. C. Potter	GLADYS SWARTHOUT
	Say It In French PARA Andrew L. Stone	OLYMPE BRADNA
	White Banners WB Edmund Goulding	FAY BAINTER
1939	*Hotel Imperial* PARA Robert Florey	ISA MIRANDA
	The Housekeeper's Daughter UA Hal Roach	PEGGY WOOD
	Mickey, The Kid REP Arthur Lubin	ZASU PITTS
	Miracles For Sale MGM Tod Browning	FLORENCE RICE
	Panama Lady RKO Jack Hively	LUCILLE BALL

Romance Of The Redwoods COL Charles Vidor	JEAN PARKER
Too Busy To Work TCF Otto Brower	JOAN DAVIS
1940	*Free, Blonde And 21* TCF Ricardo Cortez	JOAN DAVIS
	Maisie Was A Lady MGM Edwin L. Marin	ANN SOTHERN
1941	*Ladies In Retirement* COL Charles Vidor	IDA LUPINO
	Small Town Deb TCF Harold Schuster	JANE DARWELL
1942	*Girl Trouble* TCF Harold Schuster	JOAN BENNETT
	Highways By Night RKO Peter Godfrey	JANE RANDOLPH
	Once Upon A Thursday MGM Jules Dassin	MARSHA HUNT
	Tish MGM S. Sylvan Simon	MARJORIE MAIN
1943	*Five Graves To Cairo* PARA Billy Wilder	ANNE BAXTER
	Forever And A Day RKO Rene Clair	IDA LUPINO
	Higher and Higher RKO Tim Whelan	MICHELE MORGAN
	Women In Bondage MONO Steve Sekely	NANCY KELLY
1944	*Mademoiselle Fifi* RKO Robert Wise	SIMONE SIMON
	Passport To Adventure RKO Ray McCarey	ELSA LANCHESTER
	Three Litte Sisters REP Joseph Santley	RUTH TERRY

1945   *Molly And Me*   GRACIE FIELDS
        TCF   Lewis Seiler

An out-of-work actress decides to become a
housekeeper; she puts on a maid costume and acts the
part. She is very efficient and very nurturing to the
master's son. Learning that other staff are cheating
the master, she sacks them; but with a big dinner to
prepare, she enlists her actor friends to provide new
staffing. She also uses actors in a ruse to solve the
master's personal and political problems. All ends
well, but it is difficult to infer whether she will
remain a housekeeper or go back to acting at the first
opportunity.

The Valley Of Decision   GREER GARSON
MGM   Tay Garnett

The daughter of an injured steel mill worker must find
a job, and housework is considered something a
respectable girl can do. Mary becomes a maid in the
home of the Scotts, owners of the mill, and is
considered lucky, because jobs are hard to get,
especially for a girl. Unashamed of her job, she
becomes proficient at serving meals and other duties.
She sews for the daughter of the family and eventually
comes to protect the young woman's virtue as well; and
they become fast friends. The eldest son falls in
love with her (he removes her maid's cap in order to
kiss her), and when she informs her father that she is
going to England, he automatically, and erroneously,
assumes that one of the sons has impregnated her. But
the mill owner wants the two to marry, because she is
of "fine, wholesome stock."

1946   *Cluny Brown*   JENNIFER JONES
        TCF   Ernst Lubitsch

A plumber's niece, Cluny loves plumbing, but she is
shipped off to be a parlor maid at an aristocratic
house in the country because, as her uncle says, "You
are lucky, a girl with no training getting a job in a
respectable home." While her upper class friends and
employers are enchanted with her ability as a plumber,
she loses a potential husband, a chemist, because he
is appalled by her unladylike interest in such things.
She is understandably upset because she does not want
to be a maid all her life and knows a woman's only
chance for "salvation" is through a respectable

marriage. Class issues are predominant in the film,
with Cluny admonished by her fellow servants because
she "was not brought up with the instincts of a second
maid" and is too uppity. To her employers and their
guests she is faceless, with the exception of one
guest, a Czech intellectual who tells her to take off
her silly maid's cap and apron before he kisses her.
He marries her and takes her out of her class by
writing a bestselling novel that can support them both
nicely.

Diary Of A Chambermaid		PAULETTE GODDARD
UA	Jean Renoir	

A nineteenth-century French chambermaid has moved
through twelve jobs in two years. Definitely not
high-class, she has come to a country house looking
for an opportunity to marry well. Claiming she will
marry the first man with money, she wants to have a
house of her own and be its mistress. She does have
her principles, however; she threatens to quit if the
scullery maid who accompanies her is not hired also,
and she cannot bring herself to seduce the crazy old
man next door. But she does flirt with her master.
The film shows her doing chambermaid work: laundry,
scrubbing and polishing floors. Naturally, one wants
out of this drudgery, and marriage is the only
possibility in nineteenth-century France?

Monsieur Beaucaire		JOAN CAULFIELD
PARA	George Marshall	

The Spider Woman Strikes Back		BRENDA JOYCE
UNIV	Arthur Lubin	

The Spiral Staircase		DOROTHY MCGUIRE
RKO	Robert Siodmak	

1947	*The Brasher Doubloon*		NANCY GUILD
	TCF	John Brahm	

Captain From Castile		JEAN PETERS
TCF	Henry King	

The Farmer's Daughter		LORETTA YOUNG
D SELZNICK	H. C. Potter	

This is a double Cinderella story; Young marries the
son of the family, a Congressman, and also gets

elected to Congress herself. A country girl who comes to the city to go to nursing school but is swindled out of her money, she takes the maid job in desperation, but soon proves her effectiveness and wholesome good sense. She's a sincere, smart candidate, and won't give up when the opposition tries to smear her. Her new husband carries her over the threshold, but it happens to be the threshold of the Capitol.

Time Out Of Mind		PHYLLIS CALVERT
UI	Robert Siodmak	
1949	*The Inspector General*	BARBARA BATES
	WB Henry Koster	
1951	*Adventures of Captain Fabian*	MICHELINE PRESLE
	REP William Marshall	
	Bedtime For Bonzo	DIANA LYNN
	UNIV Fred DeCordova	
	Girl On The Bridge	BEVERLY MICHAELS
	TCF Hugo Haas	
	The Lady From Texas	MONA FREEMAN
	UNIV Joseph Pevney	
	The Man With A Cloak	BARBARA STANWYCK
	MGM Fletcher Markle	
	The Tall Target	RUBY DEE
	MGM Anthony Mann	
1952	*The Happy Time*	LINDA CHRISTIAN
	COL Richard Fleischer	
	Les Miserables	ELSA LANCHESTER
	TCF R. Boleslawski	
	Member Of The Wedding	ETHEL WATERS
	COL Fred Zinnemann	

Julie Harris gets top billing here, but the film really belongs to Ethel Waters. She is as much a Mammy as slaves of the previous century, rearing two white children, giving them the love they don't receive from parents, and helping Harris through adolescent trauma. She has family troubles of her

own, but she hardly has time for anything outside the
family she serves. Her function is limited to the
nurturing of other people's children, and in that
sense she knows "her place."

| 1953 | *By The Light Of The Silvery Moon* | MARY WICKES |
| | WB   David Butler | |

| | *The Farmer Takes A Wife* | BETTY GRABLE |
| | TCF   Henry Levin | |

Grable is a household servant here, but the household
is a barge on the Erie Canal, and she serves as cook
for the boatman and his crewman. She is the star
graduate of a local cooking school, considered the
best cook on the Canal, and proud of her
accomplishments. This musical is half over before she
is shown cooking, and she also does the laundry,
washes dishes, and cleans vegetables on deck, all the
while wearing charming gingham dresses with numerous
petticoats.

| | *The Girls Of Pleasure Island* | ELSA LANCHESTER |
| | PARA   F. Hugh Herbert | |

| 1954 | *Ricochet Romance* | MARJORIE MAIN |
| | UNIV   Charles Lamont | |

| 1955 | *Blood Alley* | JOY KIM |
| | WB   William Wellman | |

| | *Footsteps in the Fog* | JEAN SIMMONS |
| | COL   Arthur Lubin | |

| | *The Glass Slipper* | LESLIE CARON |
| | MGM   Charles Walters | |

| | *The Kentuckian* | DIANNE FOSTER |
| | UA   Burt Lancaster | |

| | *Lay That Rifle Down* | JUDY CANOVA |
| | REP   Charles Lamont | |

| 1956 | *Canyon River* | MARCIA HENDERSON |
| | AA   Harmon Jones | |

| 1958 | *China Doll* | LILI HUA |
| | UA   Frank Borzage | |

Houseboat PARA Melville Shavelson		SOPHIA LOREN
Take A Giant Step UA Philip Leacock		RUBY DEE

1959   *The Horse Soldiers*   ALTHEA GIBSON
       UA   John Ford

       Imitation Of Life   JUANITA MOORE
       UNIV   Douglas Sirk

       The Sound And The Fury   ETHEL WATERS
       TCF   Martin Ritt

       The Womaneater   VERA DAY
       COL   Charles Saunders

1960   *The Sundowners*   DEBORAH KERR
       WB   Fred Zimmerman

       Thirteen Ghosts   MARGARET HAMILTON
       COL   William Castle

1962   *Big Red*   JANETTE BERTRAND
       BV   Norman Tokar

       Saintly Sinners   ELLEN CORBY
       UA   Jean Yarbrough

       Satan Never Sleeps   FRANCE NUYEN
       TCF   Leo McCarey

1963   *Hud*   PATRICIA NEAL
       PARA   Martin Ritt

Neal won an Academy Award for her portrayal of Alma, the Banner family's maid. To kindly Mr. Banner she is cook, relegated to the kitchen. To young Lon she is surrogate mother. To Hud's mind she should be relegated to the bedroom. He considers her there to satisfy his sexual desire as well as his demand for clean shirts and a meal at any hour he is hungry. She resists his sexual overtures, refusing to be seduced, coerced, or bought. His brutal sexual assault leaves her ashamed because she realizes she had found him attractive. She is used and abused, left with nothing but a bus ticket.

	Under The Yum Yum Tree COL David Swift	IMOGENE COCA
1964	*A Shot In The Dark* UA Blake Edwards	ELKE SOMMER
	Voice Of The Hurricane SELECT George Fraser	MURIEL SMITH
1965	*Boeing-Boeing* PARA John Rich	THELMA RITTER
	That Funny Feeling UI Richard Thorpe	SANDRA DEE
1966	*Stop The World I Want to Get Off* WB Philip Saville	MILLICENT MARTIN
1967	*Eight On The Lam* UA George Marshall	PHYLLIS DILLER
	Rosie UNIV David Lowell	MARGARET HAMILTON
1968	*For Love of Ivy* CINERAMA Daniel Mann	ABBY LINCOLN
	The Heart Is A Lonely Hunter WB Robert E. Miller	CICELY TYSON
1969	*The Mad Room* COL Bernard Girard	STELLA STEVENS
	Salesman MAYSELES A. & D. Mayseles	MARGARET MCCARRON
1970	*Darker Than Amber* CINC Richard Clouse	JANET MACLACHLAN
	The Hawaiians UA Tom Gries	TINA CHEN
	House Of Dark Shadows MGM Dan Curtis	GRAYSON HALL
1972	*Man Of La Mancha* UA Arthur Hiller	SOPHIA LOREN

1973   *Claudine*   DIAHANN CARROLL
        TCF   John Berry

        Claudine (Carroll) is an unmarried mother of six
        children in Harlem who works as a maid in the suburbs.
        She is shown twice on the bus going to work, and she
        is shown very briefly on the job, where her employer
        does not even speak to her, but complains under her
        breath that the maid is always late. Claudine is not
        supposed to be working, as she is on welfare; but
        somehow she is always home when the social worker
        comes to check up. By far, the majority of the film
        is taken up with romance with a garbage man. Carroll
        was nominated for an Academy Award for this
        performance.

        Some Call It Loving   VERONICA ANDERSON
        PP   James B. Harris

1974   *Benji*   PATSY GARETT
        Mulberry   Joe Camp

        Young Frankenstein   CLORIS LEACHMAN
        TCF   Mel Brooks

ENTERTAINER

Women are overly-represented as stars and aspiring stars in the many branches of the entertainment industry. Outside of biographical films, however, few of the roles show women choosing a career as a lifetime commitment. Rather, they depict the stint as entertainer as a pause along the path to the ultimate goal of wife and mother. Even the biographical films, which often focus on the struggle for a career, usually give equal time to the struggle for a man.

The great number of films featuring entertainers also reflects America's obsession with the movies themselves. Movies and stars have epitomized the "American Dream," the chance for glamour, fame and fortune. While the country struggled through the dark years of the 1920s and '30s, the silver screen presented a happier discovery of talent. Present troubles could be forgotten while moviegoers hummed along and tapped their feet to the inevitable happy ending.

During the war years, an array of patriotic musicals tried to lift the country's morale. The stars in these were often real-life entertainers acting as entertainers for "our boys." Women entertainers often owed their popularity less to their talent than to their fame as "pin-ups."

With the advent of musicals in which music and dance are integrated into the plot and ordinary people sing dialogue to each other, the role of professional entertainer is featured less frequently and, by the 1970s, is seldom found.

1930	*Anybody's Woman*		RUTH CHATTERTON
	PARA	Dorothy Arzner	Chorus Girl
	The Bad One		DOLORES DEL RIO
	UA	George Fitzmaurice	Dancehall Girl
	The Big Party		DIXIE LEE
	TCF	John Blystone	

Bride of the Regiment FN John F. Dillon	MYRNA LOY Dancer
Call of the Flesh MGM Charles Brabin	RENEE ADOREE Dancer
Call of the West SU Albert Ray	DOROTHY REVIER
Chasing Rainbows MGM Charles F. Riesner	BESSIE LOVE Singer/Dancer
Cheer Up and Smile TCF Sidney Lanfield	DIXIE LEE Singer
The Climax UNIV Renaud Hoffman	KATHRYN CRAWFORD Opera Singer
The Dancers TCF Chandler Sprague	MAE CLARKE Dancer
Dancing Sweeties FN Ray Enright	SUE CAROL Dancehall Girl
Dangerous Dan McGrew PARA Malcolm St. Clair	HELEN KANE Medicine Show
The Devil to Pay S GOLDWYN George Fitzmaurice	MYRNA LOY LORETTA YOUNG Actress
Dixiana RKO Luther Reed	BEBE DANIELS Circus
Fast and Loose PARA Fred Newmeyer	CAROLE LOMBARD Chorus Girl
The Floradora Girl MGM Harry Beaumont	MARION DAVIES
Follow the Leader PARA Norman Taurog	ETHEL MERMAN
For the Defense COL John Cromwell	KAY FRANCIS Actress
Framed RKO George Archainbaud	EVELYN BRENT

Free and Easy MGM	Edward Sedgwick	ANITA PAGE Actress
Glorifying the American Girl PARA	Millard Webb	MARY EATON Dancer
The Green Moon SU	Sam Jones	JANE BROWN
Happy Days TCU	Benjamin Stoloff	JANET GAYNOR Singer
Hell's Island COL	Edward Sloman	DOROTHY SEBASTIAN Singer
Her Man PATHE	Tay Garnett	HELEN TWELVETREES
Her Wedding Night PARA	Frank Tuttle	CLARA BOW Movie Star
Hit the Deck RKO	Luther Reed	POLLY WALKER Singer/Dancer
Hold Everything WB	Roy Del Ruth	WINNIE LIGHTNER Singer/Dancer
In Gay Madrid MGM	Robert Z. Leonard	DOROTHY JORDAN Singer/Dancer
It's a Great Life MGM	Sam Wood	ROSETTA DUNCAN VIVIAN DUNCAN Singer/Dancer
Jazz Cinderella CHESTERF	Scott Pembroke	NANCY WELFORD Singer
Just Like Heaven TIFFANY	R. William Hill	ANITA LOUISE Ballerina
Ladies in Love TCF	Edgar Lewis	ALICE DAY Singer
The Lady of Scandal MGM	Sidney Franklin	RUTH CHATTERTON Musical Comedy
A Lady's Morals MGM	Sidney Franklin	GRACE MOORE Opera Singer

The Last Dance		VERA REYNOLDS
AUDIBLE	Scott Pembroke	Taxi Dancer
Let's Go Native		JEANETTE MACDONALD
PARA	Leo McCarey	Singer
Let's Go Places		LOLA LANE
TCF	Frank Strayer	Actress
Lilies of the Field		CORINNE GRIFFITH
FN	Alexander Korda	Chorus Girl
Lord Byron of Broadway		ETHELIND TERRY
MGM	W. Nigh/H. Beaumont	Singer/Dancer
Love at First Sight		SUZANNE KEENER
CAPITOL	Edgar Lewis	
Love Comes Along		BEBE DANIELS
RKO	Rupert Julian	Actress
Man Trouble		DOROTHY MACKAILL
TCF	Bertholz Vietel	Singer
Morocco		MARLENE DIETRICH
PARA	Josef Von Sternberg	Singer
The New Movietone Follies of 1930		MIRIAM SEEGAR
TCF	Benjamin Stoloff	Musical Comedy
		MARJORIE WHITE
		Singer/Dancer
New York Nights		NORMA TALMADGE
UA	Lewis Milestone	Actress
No, No, Nanette		BERNICE CLAIRE
FN	Clarence Badger	Singer/Dancer
Oh, For a Man		JEANETTE MACDONALD
TCF	Hamilton McFadden	Opera Singer
On the Border		ARMIDA
FN	William McGann	Singer/Dancer
The Painted Angel		BILLIE DOVE
FN	Millard Webb	Dancer
Paramount on Parade		JEAN ARTHUR
PARA	Dorothy Arzner	

Phantom of the Opera		MARY PHILBIN
UNIV	Rupert Julien	Opera Singer
Pointed Heels		FAY WRAY
PARA	A. E. Sutherland	Actress
Puttin on the Ritz		JOAN BENNETT
UA	E. H. Sloman	Singer/Dancer
Rain or Shine		JOAN PETERS
COL	Frank Capra	Circus
Recaptured Love		DOROTHY BURGESS
WB	John G. Adolfi	Chorus Girl
Roadhouse Nights		HELEN MORGAN
PARA	Hobart Henley	Singer
Romance		GRETA GARBO
MGM	Clarence Brown	Opera Singer
Royal Family of Broadway		INA CLAIR
PARA	George Cukor	Actress
Safety in Numbers		KATHRYN CRAWFORD
PARA	V. Schertzinger	CAROLE LOMBARD
		Showgirls
Sap from Syracuse		GINGER ROGERS
PARA	A. E. Sutherland	
Sarah and Son		RUTH CHATTERTON
PARA	Dorothy Arzner	Singer
Scarlett Pages		MARION NIXON
FN	Ray Enright	Cabaret Girl
She Couldn't Say No		WINNIE LIGHTNER
WB	Lloyd Bacon	Singer/Dancer
Show Girl in Hollywood		ALICE WHITE
FN	Mervyn LeRoy	Singer/Dancer
Side Show		WINNIE LIGHTNER
WB	Roy Del Ruth	
Sunny		MARILYN MILLER
WB	William A. Seiter	Chorus Girl

Sweet Mama FN	Edward Kline	ALICE WHITE
Swing High WB	Joseph Santley	DOROTHY BURGESS HELEN TWELVETREES Circus
The Truth About Youth FN	William A. Seiter	MYRNA LOY Cabaret Dancer
Wild Company TCF	Leo McCarey	SHARON LYNN Singer
Young Desire UNIV	Lew Collins	MARY NOLAN Carny Dancer

1931 *Anybody's Blonde*
ACTION   Frank Strayer   DOROTHY REVIER
                                        Chorus Girl

Beyond Victory
RKO PATHE   E. D. Derr   ZASU PITTS

Bright Lights
WB   Michael Curtiz   DOROTHY MACKAILL
                                        Actress

Children of Dreams
WB   Alan Crosland   MARGARET SCHILLING
                                        Singer

Dude Ranch
PARA   Frank Tuttle   MITZI GREEN
                                        Actress

Everything's Rosie
RKO   Clyde Bruckman   ANITA LOUISE
                                        Carnival

Fanny Foley Herself
RKO   Melville Brown   EDNA MAY OLIVER
                                        Vaudeville

First Aid
SAWW   Stuart Paton   MARJORIE BEEBE
                                        Taxi Dancer

Goldie
TCF   Benjamin Stoloff   JEAN HARLOW
                                        Carnival

The Good Bad Girl
COL   Roy William Neill   MAE CLARKE
                                        Chorus Girl

Great Lover		IRENE DUNNE
MGM	Harry Beaumont	Singer
The Guardsman		LYNN FONTANNE
MGM	Sidney Franklin	Actress
Homicide Squad		MARY BRIAN
UNIV	George Melford	Dancehall Girl
Iron Man		JEAN HARLOW
UNIV	Tod Browning	Chorus Girl
Kiki		MARY PICKFORD
UA	Sam Taylor	Chorus Girl
The Mad Genius		MARIAN MARSH
WB	Michael Curtiz	Dancer
The Magnificent Lie		RUTH CHATTERTON
PARA	Berthold Viertel	Actress/Singer
Men on Call		MAE CLARKE
TCF	John Blystone	Dancer
Mr. Lemon of Orange		FIFI D'ORSAY
TCF	John Blystone	Singer
My Past		BEBE DANIELS
WB	Roy Del Ruth	Stage Performer
My Sin		TALLULAH BANKHEAD
PARA	George Abbott	Cabaret Singer
The Runaround		MARY BRIAN
RKO	William J. Craft	Dancer
The Smiling Lieutenant		CLAUDETTE COLBERT
PARA	Ernst Lubitsch	Beer Garden Entertainer
Svengali		MARIAN MARSH
WB	Archie Mayo	Opera Singer
Ten Cents a Dance		BARBARA STANWYCK
WB	Lionel Barrymore	Dancehall Girl
Tonight or Never		GLORIA SWANSON
S GOLDWYN	Mervyn LeRoy	Opera Singer

Transatlantic		GRETA NISSEN
TCF	William K. Howard	Dancer
Twenty-four Hours		MIRIAM HOPKINS
PARA	Marion Gering	Singer
Young as You Feel		FIFI D'ORSAY
TCF	Frank Borzage	Singer

1932

Arm of the Law		DOROTHY REVIER
MONO	Louis King	Singer
As You Desire Me		GRETA GARBO
MGM	George Fitzmaurice	Cabaret Girl
Big City Blues		JOAN BLONDELL
WB	Mervyn LeRoy	Chorus Girl
Blonde Venus		MARLENE DIETRICH
PARA	Josef Von Sternberg	Cafe Singer
Blonde of the Follies		MARION DAVIES
MGM	Edmund Goulding	Chorus Girl
Cock of the Air		BILLIE DOVE
UA	Tom Buckingham	Actress
Cohens and Kellys in Hollywood		JUNE CLYDE
UNIV	John F. Dillon	Actress
Dance Team		SALLY EILERS
TCF	Sidney Lanfield	Dancer
Dancers in the Dark		MIRIAM HOPKINS
PARA	David Burton	Taxi Dancer
Dr. Jekyll and Mr. Hyde		MIRIAM HOPKINS
PARA	Roubin Mamoulian	Cabaret Dancer
Flesh		KAREN MORLEY
MGM	John Ford	Dancer
Forgotten Women		MARION SCHILLING
MONO	Richard Thorpe	Actress
Freaks		LEILA HYAMS
MGM	Tod Browning	Trapeze Artist

Girl from Calgary MONO P. Whitman/ D'Usseau	FIFI D'ORSAY Singer
Girl of the Rio RKO Herbert Brenon	DOLORES DEL RIO Dancer
Grand Hotel MGM Edmund Goulding	GRETA GARBO
Hollywood Speaks COL Edward Buzzell	GENEVIEVE TOBIN Actress
The Kid From Spain S GOLDWYN Leo McCarey	LYDA ROBERTI
The Lost Squadron RKO George Archainbaud	MARY ASTOR Actress
Madame Butterfly PARA Marion Gering	SYLVIA SIDNEY Geisha
Make Me a Star PARA William Beaudine	JOAN BLONDELL Actress
Man Against Woman COL Irving Cummings	LILLIAN MILES Torch Singer
The Match King FN Howard Bretherton	LILI DAMITA Movie Star
Midnight Morals MAYFAIR E. Mason Hopper	ALBERTA VAUGHN Taxi Dancer
Movie Crazy PARA Clyde Bruckman	CONSTANCE CUMMINGS Actress
Night Club Hostess COL Irving Cummings	MAYO METHOT Night Club Hostess
The Night Mayor COL Ben Stoloff	EVALYN KNAPP Actress
Night World UNIV Hobart Henley	MAE CLARKE
Once in a Lifetime UNIV Russell Mack	ALINE MACMAHON Actress

Polly of the Circus MGM	Alfred Santell	MARION DAVIES Circus
The Purchase Price WB	William A. Wellman	BARBARA STANWYCK Torch Singer
Rockabye RKO	George Cukor	CONSTANCE BENNETT Actress
Speak Easily MGM	Edward Sedgwick	HEDDA HOPPER Actress
Stepping Sisters TCF	Seymour Felix	JOBYNA HOWLAND Actress
They Never Come Back SU	Fred Newmeyer	DOROTHY SEBASTIAN Night Club Dancer
Three on a Match WB	Mervyn LeRoy	JOAN BLONDELL Chorus Girl
Tomorrow and Tomorrow PARA	Richard Wallace	RUTH CHATTERTON Actress
The Trial of Vivienne Ware TCF	William K. Howard	LILIAN BOND Cabaret Girl
Two Seconds WB	Mervyn LeRoy	VIVIENNE OSBORNE Dancehall Girl
Union Depot WB	Alfred E. Green	JOAN BLONDELL Chorus Girl
Vanity Street COL	Nicholas Grinde	HELEN CHANDLER Showgirl
Wayward PARA	Edward Sloman	NANCY CARROLL Dancer/Singer
What Price Hollywood? RKO	George Cukor	CONSTANCE BENNETT Actress
A Woman Commands RKO	Paul L. Stein	POLA NEGRI Cabaret Girl
The World and the Flesh PARA	John Cromwell	MIRIAM HOPKINS Dancer

1933   *42nd Street*   BEBE DANIELS
        WB   Lloyd Bacon

The star here is really the Busby Berkeley production
numbers, but along the way Ruby Keeler plays the
Broadway understudy who gets her big break and becomes
a star. There is minimal character involvement but
the film epitomizes the cheerful optimism that
Hollywood promoted during this era.

The Big Cage   ANITA PAGE
UNIV   Kurt Neuman   Circus

Bombshell   JEAN HARLOW
MGM   Victor Fleming   Movie Star

Brief Moment   CAROLE LOMBARD
COL   David Burton   Torch Singer

Broadway Bad   JOAN BLONDELL
TCF   Sidney Lanfield   Chorus Girl

Broadway Through a Keyhole   CONSTANCE CUMMINGS
TCF   Lowell Sherman   Chorus Girl

Broadway to Hollywood   ALICE BRADY
MGM   Willard Mack   Vaudeville

Carnival Lady   BOOTS MALLORY
HOLLYWOOD   Howard Higgin   Carnival

Central Airport   SALLY EILERS
WB   William A. Wellman   Air Show Performer

Child of Manhattan   NANCY CARROLL
COL   Eddie Buzzell   Night Club Hostess

The Circus Queen Murder   GRETA NISSEN
COL   Roy William Neill   Trapeze Artist

Dance, Girl, Dance   EVALYN KNAPP
CHESTERF   Frank Strayer   Musical Comedy

Dancing Lady   JOAN CRAWFORD
MGM   Robert Z. Leonard   Dancer

Flying Devils   ARLINE JUDGE
RKO   Russell Budwell   Chorus

Flying Down to Rio		GINGER ROGERS
RKO	Thornton Freeland	Dancer
Footlight Parade		JOAN BLONDELL
WB	Lloyd Bacon	Dancer
Girl Missing		GLENDA FARRELL
WB	Robert Florey	Showgirl
Going Hollywood		MARION DAVIES
MGM	Raoul Walsh	Singer/Dancer
Golddiggers of 1933		JOAN BLONDELL
WB	Mervyn LeRoy	Chorus Girl
Goldie Get Along		LILI DAMITA
RKO	Malcolm St. Clair	
The Half Naked Truth		LUPE VELEZ
RKO	Gregory LaCava	Actress
Hallelujah, I'm a Bum!		MADGE EVANS
UA	Lewis Milestone	
Havana Widows		JOAN BLONDELL
FN	Ray Enright	Chorus Girl
Hello Everybody		KATE SMITH
PARA	William A. Seiter	Radio
Her Bodyguard		WYNNE GIBSON
PARA	William Beaumont	
Hoopla		CLARA BOW
TCF	Frank Lloyd	Carnival Dancer
Hot Pepper		LUPE VELEZ
TCF	John Blystone	Singer/Dancer
Hotel Variety		OLIVE BORDEN
CAPITOL	Raymond Cannon	Singer
I Have Lived		ANITA PAGE
CHESTERF	Richard Thorpe	Actress
I Loved You Wednesday		ELISSA LANDI
TCF	Henry King	Dancer

I Loved a Woman FN	Alfred E. Green	KAY FRANCIS Opera Singer
I'm No Angel PARA	Wesley Ruggles	MAE WEST Circus
King for a Night UNIV	Kurt Neumann	ALICE WHITE Chorus Girl
Lilly Turner WB	William A. Wellman	RUTH CHATTERTON Medicine Show
Luxury Liner PARA	Lothar Mendes	VERREE TEASDALE Opera Singer
Men Are Such Fools RKO	William Nigh	VIVIENNE OSBORNE Singer
Moonlight and Pretzels UNIV	Karl Freund	MARY BRIAN Actress
Morning Glory RKO	Lowell Sherman	KATHARINE HEPBURN Actress
Mr. Skitch TCF	James Cruze	FLORENCE DESMOND Actress
The Past of Mary Holmes RKO	H. Thompson/S. Vorkapich	HELEN MACKELLAR Opera Singer
Sailor Be Good RKO	James Cruze	VIVIENNE OSBORNE Night Club Hostess
Secret Sinners MAYFAIR	Wesley Ford	SUE CAROL
Sin of Norma Moran, The MAJESTIC	Phil Goldstein	ZITA JOHANN Circus
Sing, Sinner, Sing MAJESTIC	Howard Christy	LEILA HYAMS Singer
Take a Chance PARA	L. Schwab/M. Brice	JUNE KNIGHT LILLIAN ROTH Singer
Too Much Harmony PARA	Eddie Sutherland	JUDITH ALLEN

Torch Singer		CLAUDETTE COLBERT
PARA	Alexander Hall	Torch Singer
The Way to Love		ANN DVORAK
PARA	Norman Taurog	Carnival

1934 *Belle of the Nineties*   MAE WEST
PARA   Leo McCarey

Big Time or Bust   GLORIA SHEA
TOWER   Sam Newfield   Circus

Bolero   CAROLE LOMBARD
PARA   Wesley Ruggles   Dancer

Bottoms Up   PAT PATERSON
TCF   David Butler   Actress

The Cat and the Fiddle   JEANETTE MACDONALD
MGM   William K. Howard   Singer

The Circus Clown   PATRICIA ELLIS
FN   Ray Enright   Circus

Countess of Monte Christo   FAY WRAY
UNIV   Karl Freund   Actress

Crime Without Passion   MARGO
PARA   B. Hecht/ C. MacArthur   Dancer

Desirable   VERREE TEASDALE
WB   Archie Mayo   Actress

Enter Madame   ELISSA LANDI
PARA   Elliott Nugent   Opera Singer

The Gay Bride   CAROLE LOMBARD
MGM   Jack Conway   Chorus Girl

George White's Scandals   ALICE FAYE
TCF   George White   Singer

Glamour   CONSTANCE CUMMINGS
UNIV   William Wyler   Actress

Good Dame   SYLVIA SIDNEY
PARA   Marion Gering   Carny Showgirl

The Great Flirtation		ELISSA LANDI
PARA	Ralph Murphy	Actress
Hell Bent for Love		LILIAN BOND
COL	D. Ross Lederman	Night Club Singer
The Human Side		BETTY LAWFORD
UNIV	Edward Buzzell	Actress
I Am Suzanne		LILIAN HARVEY
TCF	Rowland V. Lee	Dancer
I Like It That Way		GLORIA STUART
UNIV	Harry Lachman	Night Club Singer
Journal of a Crime		CLAIRE DODD
WB	William Keighley	Actress
Kid Millions		ETHEL MERMAN
UA	Seymour Felix	Singer
Lady by Choice		CAROLE LOMBARD
COL	Davis Burton	Fan Dancer
Lady Killer		MARGARET LINDSAY
WB	Roy Del Ruth	Movie Star
Let's Fall in Love		ANN SOTHERN
COL	David Burton	Actress/Singer
Little Miss Marker		DOROTHY DELL
PARA	Alexander Hall	Torch Singer
Long Lost Father		HELEN CHANDLER
RKO	Ernest Schoedsack	Singer
Marie Galante		KETTI GALLIAN
TCF	Harry King	Dancehall Girl
The Mighty Barnum		VIRGINIA BRUCE
TCF	Walter Lang	Singer
Miss Fane's Baby Is Stolen		DOROTHEA WIECK
PARA	Alexander Hall	Movie Star
Moulin Rouge		CONSTANCE BENNETT
UA	Sidney Lanfield	Music Hall

Murder at the Vanities	KITTY CARLISLE
PARA Mitchell Leisen	Singer
Music in the Air	GLORIA SWANSON
TCF Joe May	Actress
Myrt and Marge	MYRTLE VAIL
UNIV Al Boasberg	Singer/Dancer
Nana	ANNA STEN
S GOLDWYN Dorothy Arzner	Actress
The Night Is Young	EVELYN LAYE
MGM Dudley Murphy	Ballerina
The Notorious Sophie Lang	GERTRUDE MICHAEL
PARA Ralph Murphy	Actress
The Old-Fashioned Way	JAN DUGGAN
PARA William Beaudine	Actress
One Night of Love	GRACE MOORE
COL V. Schertzinger	Opera Singer
Orient Express	HEATHER ANGEL
TCF Paul Martin	Dancer
Scandals	ALICE FAYE
TCF George White	Singer
Sensation Hunters	ARLINE JUDGE
MONO Charles Vidor	Singer
She Learned about Sailors	ALICE FAYE
TCF George Marshall	Cabaret Singer
She Loves Me Not	MIRIAM HOPKINS
PARA Elliott Nugent	Night Club Dancer
Sing and Like It	ZASU PITTS
RKO William Seiter	Actress
Sisters under the Skin	ELISSA LANDI
COL David Burton	Actress
Social Register	COLLEEN MOORE
COL Marshall Neilan	Chorus Girl

Stingaree		IRENE DUNNE
RKO	William A. Wellman	Opera Singer
Strictly Dynamite		LUPE VELEZ
RKO	Elliott Nugent	Singer/Dancer
Sweet Adeline		IRENE DUNNE
WB	Mervyn LeRoy	Singer/Dancer
Thirty Day Princess		SYLVIA SIDNEY
PARA	Marion Gering	Actress
Transatlantic Merry-Go-Round		NANCY CARROLL
UA	Benjamin Stoloff	Singer
The Trumpet Blows		FRANCES DRAKE
PARA	Stephen Roberts	Dancer
Twentieth Century		CAROLE LOMBARD
COL	Howard Hawks	Actress
Twenty Million Sweethearts		GINGER ROGERS
WB	Ray Enright	Dancer
Upperworld		GINGER ROGERS
WB	Roy Del Ruth	Dancer
Wild Gold		CLAIRE TREVOR
TCF	George Marshall	Night Club Singer
Wine, Women, and Song		MARJORIE MOORE
STATERIGHT	Herbert Brenon	Singer
Wonder Bar		DOLORES DEL RIO
WB	Lloyd Bacon	Dancer
You Belong to Me		HELEN MACK
PARA	Alfred Werker	
Young and Beautiful		JUDITH ALLEN
MASCOT	Joseph Santley	Actress
1935 *After the Dance*		NANCY CARROLL
COL	Leo Bulgakov	Dancer
Annie Oakley		BARBARA STANWYCK
RKO	George Stevens	Wild West Show

Bright Lights		ANN DVORAK
WB	Busby Berkeley	Singer/Dancer
Broadway Hostess		WINIFRED SHAW
WB	Frank McDonald	Torch Singer
Broadway Melody of 1936		ELEANOR POWELL
MGM	Roy Del Ruth	Dancer
Carnival		SALLY EILERS
COL	Walter Lang	Carnival
Coronado		BETTY BURGESS
PARA	Norman McLeod	
The Curtain Falls		HENRIETTA CROSMAN
CHESTERF	Charles Lamont	Actress
Dames		JOAN BLONDELL
WB	Ray Enright	
Dangerous		BETTE DAVIS
WB	Alfred E. Green	Actress
Diamond Jim		BINNIE BARNES
UNIV	Edward Sutherland	Singer
Don't Bet on Blondes		CLAIRE DODD
WB	Robert Florey	Actress
Every Night at Eight		ALICE FAYE
PARA	Raoul Walsh	Singer
Folies Bergere		ANN SOTHERN
TCF	Roy Del Ruth	
George White's 1935 Scandals		ELEANOR POWELL
TCF	George White	Dancer
Go into Your Dance		RUBY KEELER
WB	Archie L. Mayo	Night Club Dancer
Gold Diggers of 1935		GLORIA STUART
FN	Busby Berkeley	
Here's to Romance		ANITA LOUISE
TCF	Alfred E. Green	Singer

Hooray for Love		ANN SOTHERN
RKO	Walter Lang	
I Found Stella Parish		KAY FRANCIS
FN	Mervyn LeRoy	Actress
I Live for Love		DOLORES DEL RIO
WB	Busby Berkeley	
In Caliente		DOLORES DEL RIO
WB	Lloyd Bacon	Dancer
In Person		GINGER ROGERS
RKO	William A. Seiter	Movie Star
It Happened in New York		GERTRUDE MICHAEL
UNIV	Alan Crosland	Movie Star
King Solomon of Broadway		DOROTHY PAGE
UNIV	Alan Crosland	Singer
Lottery Lover		PAT PATERSON
TCF	William Thiele	Chorus Girl
Love in Bloom		GRACIE ALLEN
PARA	Elliott Nugent	Carnival
Love Me Forever		GRACE MOORE
COL	V. Schertzinger	Singer
Mad Love		FRANCES DRAKE
MGM	Karl Freund	Actress
The Man Who Broke the Bank at Monte Carlo		JOAN BENNETT
TCF	Stephen Roberts	Actress
The Melody Lingers On		JOSEPHINE HUTCHINSON
UA	David Burton	Singer
Metropolitan		ALICE BRADY
TCF	Richard Boleslawski	Opera Singer
Music Is Magic		ALICE FAYE
TCF	George Marshall	Singer
One More Spring		JANET GAYNOR
TCF	Henry King	Actress

The Perfect Gentleman		CICELY COURTNEIDGE
MGM	Tim Whelan	Night Club Singer
Reckless		JEAN HARLOW
MGM	Victor Fleming	Musical Comedy
Roberta		GINGER ROGERS
RKO	William A. Seiter	Dancer
Romance in Manhattan		GINGER ROGERS
RKO	Stephen Roberts	Chorus Girl
Rumba		CAROLE LOMBARD
PARA	Marion Gering	Dancer
Shadow of Doubt		VIRGINIA BRUCE
MGM	George B. Seitz	Actress
Ship's Cafe		ARLINE JUDGE
PARA	Robert Florey	Singer
Stars over Broadway		JANE FROMAN
WB	William Keighley	Singer
Stolen Harmony		GRACE BRADLEY
PARA	Alfred Werker	Dancer
Streamline Express		EVELYN VENABLE
REP	Leonard Fields	Actress
Sweet Music		ANN DVORAK
WB	Alfred E. Green	Radio Singer
This Is the Life		JANE WITHERS
TCF	Marshall Neilan	Singer
Thunder Mountain		FRANCES GRANT
TCF	David Howard	Dancehall Singer
Top Hat		GINGER ROGERS
RKO	Mark Sandrich	Dancer
Two for Tonight		THELMA TODD
PARA	Frank Tuttle	Actress
Under the Pampas Moon		KETTI GALLIAN
TCF	James Tinling	Singer

The World Accuses CHESTERF	Charles Lamont	VIVIAN TOBIN Actress
1936	*Adventure in Manhattan* COL Edward Ludwig	JEAN ARTHUR Actress
	Anything Goes PARA Lewis Milestone	ETHEL MERMAN Night Club Hostess
	Banjo on My Knee TCF John Cromwell	BARBARA STANWYCK Singer/Dancer
	Born to Dance MGM Roy Del Ruth	ELEANOR POWELL
	Boulder Dam WB Frank McDonald	PATRICIA ELLIS Night Club Hostess
	Cain and Mabel WB Lloyd Bacon	MARION DAVIES Showgirl
	Charlie Chan at the Opera TCF H. B. Humberstone	CHARLOTTE HENRY Opera Singer
	Come and Get It UA H. Hawks/W. Wyler	FRANCES FARMER Cabaret Singer
	Dancing Feet REP Joseph Santley	JOAN MARSH Taxi Dancer
	Fatal Lady PARA Edward Ludwig	MARY ELLIS Opera Singer
	Follow the Fleet RKO Mark Sandrich	GINGER ROGERS Dancer
	Follow Your Heart REP Aubrey Scott	VIVIENNE OSBORNE Singer
	Forgotten Faces PARA E. A. Dupont	GERTRUDE MICHAEL
	Frankie and Johnny REP Chester Erskin	HELEN MORGAN Singer
	Girl from Mandalay REP Howard Bretherton	KAY LINAKER Singer/Dancer

Give Us This Night PARA Alexander Hall	GLADYS SWARTHOUT Opera Singer
Go West, Young Man PARA Henry Hathaway	MAE WEST
The Great Ziegfield MGM Robert Z. Leonard	MYRNA LOY
King of Burlesque TCF Sidney Lanfield	ALICE FAYE Singer
Klondike Annie PARA Raoul Walsh	MAE WEST Dancehall Singer
The Moon's Our Home PARA William A. Seiter	MARGARET SULLAVAN Movie Star
Next Time We Love UNIV Edward H. Griffith	MARGARET SULLAVAN Singer
Palm Springs PARA Aubrey Scotta	FRANCES LANGFORD Singer
Postal Inspector UNIV Otto Brower	PATRICIA ELLIS Singer
Rose Marie MGM W. S. Van Dyke II	JEANETTE MACDONALD Opera Singer
San Francisco MGM W. S. Van Dyke II	JEANETTE MACDONALD Singer
Show Boat UNIV James Whale	IRENE DUNNE Singer
Sing, Baby, Sing TCF Sidney Lanfield	ALICE FAYE Night Club Singer
Sitting on the Moon REP Ralph Staub	GRACE BRADLEY Singer
Song and Dance Man TCF Allan Dwan	CLAIRE TREVOR
Stage Struck WB Tay Garnett	JOAN BLONDELL Chorus Girl

Suzy		JEAN HARLOW
MGM	George Fitzmaurice	Chorus Girl
Tango		MARION NIXON
CHESTERF	Phil Rosen	Chorus Girl
Times Square Playboy		JUNE TRAVIS
WB	William McGann	Night Club Singer
Trailin' West		PAULA STONE
WB	Noel Smith	Dancehall Girl
Two in the Dark		MARGOT GRAHAME
RKO	Ben Stoloff	Actress
Under Two Flags		CLAUDETTE COLBERT
TCF	Frank Lloyd	Showgirl
Yellow Dust		LEILA HYAMS
RKO	Wallace Fox	Singer
You May Be Next		ANN SOTHERN
COL	Albert S. Rogell	Night Club

1937

Big Town Girl		CLAIRE TREVOR
TCF	Alfred Werker	Radio
Blondes Are Dangerous		DOROTHEA KENT
UNIV	Milton Carruth	Chorus Girl
Border Cafe		ARMIDA
RKO	Lew Landers	
Boy of the Streets		MAUREEN O'CONNER
MONO	William Nigh	
The Bride Wore Red		JOAN CRAWFORD
PARA	Dorothy Arzner	
Broadway Melody of 1938		ELEANOR POWELL
MGM	Roy Del Ruth	Dancer
Carnival Queen		DOROTHEA KENT
UNIV	Nate Watt	Circus
Confession		KAY FRANCIS
FN	Joe May	Singer

Dangerous Number	ANN SOTHERN
MGM Richard Thorpe	Showgirl
Dark Manhattan	CLEO HERNDON
RENALDO Harry Fraser	Night Club Singer
Devil's Playground	DOLORES DEL RIO
COL Erle C. Kenton	Taxi Dancer
Double or Nothing	MARTHA RAYE
PARA Theodore Reed	
Every Day's A Holiday	MAE WEST
PARA A. E. Sutherland	Actress
Fight for Your Lady	IDA LUPINO
RKO Ben Stoloff	Singer
Forty Naughty Girls	ZASU PITTS
RKO Edward Cline	
The Girl Said No	IRENE HERVEY
GN Andrew L. Stone	Dancehall Hostess
The Good Old Soak	JUDITH BARRETT
MGM J. Walter Ruben	Showgirl
High, Wide and Handsome	IRENE DUNNE
PARA Rouben Mamoulian	Singer
The Hit Parade	FRANCES LANGFORD
REP Gus Meins	Singer
Hitting a New High	LILY PONS
RKO Raoul Walsh	Singer
Hollywood Hotel	LOLA LANE
WB Busby Berkeley	Singer
I'll Take Romance	GRACE MOORE
COL Edward H. Griffith	Opera Singer
It Happened in Hollywood	FAY WRAY
COL Harry Lachman	Actress
It's Love I'm After	BETTE DAVIS
WB Archie L. Mayo	Actress

Kid Galahad		BETTE DAVIS
WB	Michael Curtiz	Night Club Singer
The King and the Chorus Girl		JOAN BLONDELL
WB	Mervyn LeRoy	Chorus Girl
King of Gamblers		CLAIRE TREVOR
PARA	Robert Florey	Night Club Singer
Love and Kisses		SIMONE SIMON
TCF	Sidney Lanfield	Singer
Luck of Roaring Camp		JOAN WOODBURY
MONO	I. V. Willet	Singer
Manhattan Merry-Go-Round		TAMARA GEVA
REP	Charles F. Riesner	Singer
Marked Woman		BETTE DAVIS
WB	Lloyd Bacon	
Maytime		JEANETTE MACDONALD
MGM	Robert Z. Leonard	Singer
Melody for Two		PATRICIA ELLIS
WB	Louis King	Singer
Midnight Madonna		MADY CORRELL
PARA	James Flood	Night Club Singer
New Faces of 1937		HARRIET HILLIARD
RKO	Leigh Jason	
Nobody's Baby		LYDA ROBERTI
MGM	Gus Meins	Dancer
On the Avenue		ALICE FAYE
TCF	Roy Del Ruth	Singer
Paid to Dance		JACQUELINE WELLS
COL	C. C. Coleman	Taxi Dancer
Public Wedding		JANE WYMAN
WB	Nick Grinde	Carnival
Ready, Willing, and Able		RUBY KEELER
WB	Ray Enright	Singer/Dancer

San Quentin		ANN SHERIDAN
WB	Lloyd Bacon	Night Club Singer
Shall We Dance		GINGER ROGERS
RKO	Mark Sandrich	Dancer
Something to Sing About		EVELYN DOW
GN	V. Schertzinger	
Stage Door 1937		KATHARINE HEPBURN
RKO	Gregory LaCava	GINGER ROGERS
		Actress
Stand-In		JOAN BLONDELL
WORLDWIDE	Tay Garnett	Actress
A Star Is Born		JANET GAYNOR
D SELZNICK	William Wellman	Movie Star

Gaynor is an actress whose happiness is sacrificed to the Hollywood star system. With her fame, that of her actor-husband-mentor declines and, unable to cope with the role-reversal, he reverts to alcoholism and finally escapes by suicide. The actress pays tribute to her dead husband but also acknowledges what should have been her real role in the final scene when, accepting an award, she calls herself "Mrs. Norman Main."

Sweetheart of the Navy		CECILIA PARKER
GN	Duncan Mansfield	Singer
Swing High, Swing Low		CAROLE LOMBARD
PARA	Mitchell Leisen	
Talent Scout		JEANNE MADDEN
WB	William Clemens	Actress
That Girl from Paris		LILY PONS
RKO	Leigh Jason	Singer
This Is My Affair		BARBARA STANWYCK
TCF	William A. Seiter	Night Club Singer
The Toast of New York		FRANCES FARMER
RKO	Rowland V. Lee	
Tough to Handle		PHYLLIS FRASER
SYNDICATE	Roy Lubey	Night Club Singer

When Love Is Young UNIV Hal Mohr	VIRGINIA BRUCE Singer
When You're in Love COL Robert Raskin	GRACE MOORE Singer
With Love and Kisses TELEVISION Les Goodwins	TOBY WING Singer
Women of Glamour COL Gordon Wiles	VIRGINIA BRUCE Actress
You're a Sweetheart UNIV David Butler	ALICE FAYE Singer

1938   *Alexander's Ragtime Band*
       TCF   Henry King   ALICE FAYE
                                      Singer

Annabel Takes a Tour
RKO   Lew Landers   LUCILLE BALL
                                      Actress

Battle of Broadway
TCF   George Marshall   LOUISE HOVICK
                                      Chorus Girl

Carefree
RKO   Mark Sandrich   GINGER ROGERS
                                    Singer/Dancer

Comet over Broadway
WB   Busby Berkeley   KAY FRANCIS
                                      Actress

Convicted
COL   Leon Barsha   RITA HAYWORTH
                                      Singer/Dancer

Convicts at Large
PRINCIPAL   S. Beald Friedman   PAULA STONE

Crime Ring
RKO   Leslie Goodwins   FRANCES MERCER
                                      Singer

The Duke is Tops
MILDOLLAR   William Nolte   LENA HORNE
                                      Singer

Expensive Husbands
WB   Bobby Connally   BEVERLY ROBERTS
                                      Actress

Fools for Scandal
WB   Mervyn LeRoy   CAROLE LOMBARD
                                      Movie Star

The Great Waltz MGM Julien Duvivier	LUISE RAINER
High Hat IMPERIAL Clifford Sanforth	DOROTHY DARE Singer
Hollywood Round-up COL Ewing Scott	HELEN TWELVETREES Actress
In Old Chicago TCF Henry King	ALICE FAYE Singer
Josette TCF Allan Dwan	SIMONE SIMON Singer
Joy of Living RKO Tay Garnett	IRENE DUNNE Musical Comedy
Love Is a Headache MGM Richard Thorpe	GLADYS GEORGE Actress
Meet the Girls TCF Eugene Forde	LYNN BARI JUNE LANG Singer/Dancer
Night Spot RKO Christy Cabanne	JOAN WOODBURY Singer
Passport Husband TCF James Tinling	PAULINE MOORE Dancer
The Port of Missing Girls MONO Karl Brown	JUDITH ALLEN Cabaret Singer
Secrets of an Actress WB William Keighley	KAY FRANCIS Actress
The Shining Hour MGM Frank Borzage	JOAN CRAWFORD Showgirl
Shopworn Angel MGM H. C. Potter	MARGARET SULLAVAN Chorus Girl
Smiling Along TCF Monty Bank	GRACIE FIELDS Singer

Sweethearts		JEANETTE MACDONALD
MGM	W. S. Van Dyke II	
Swing It, Professor		PAULA STONE
AMBASSADOR	Marshall Neilan	Showgirl
Swing, Sister, Swing		KATHERINE KANE
UNIV	Joseph Santley	Dancer
Vivacious Lady		GINGER ROGERS
RKO	George Stevens	
Walking Down Broadway		CLAIRE TREVOR
TCF	Norman Foster	Chorus Girl
Who Killed Gail Preston?		RITA HAYWORTH
COL	Leon Barsh	Night Club Singer

1939

Balalaika		ILONA MASSEY
MGM	Reinhold Shunzel	Singer
Barricade		ALICE FAYE
MGM	Gregory Ratoff	Singer
Broadway Serenade		JEANETTE MACDONALD
MGM	Robert Z. Leonard	Singer
Destry Rides Again		MARLENE DIETRICH
UNIV	Joseph Pasternak	Dancehall Singer
Dodge City		ANN SHERIDAN
WB	Michael Curtiz	Dancehall Girl
Forged Passport		JUNE LANG
REP	John H. Auer	
Frontier Marshall		BINNIE BARNES
TCF	Allan Dwan	Dancehall Girl
The Girl and the Gambler		STEFFI DUNA
RKO	Lew Landers	Cabaret Girl
The Girl from Mexico, Mexico Spitfire		LUPE VELEZ
RKO	Leslie Goodwins	Singer
Girl from Rio		MOVITA
MONO	Lambert Hillyer	Dancer

The Great Victor Herbert	MARY MARTIN
PARA Andrew L. Stone	Singer
The Hardys Ride High	VIRGINIA GREY
MGM George B. Seitz	Showgirl
Hollywood Cavalcade	ALICE FAYE
TCF Irving Cummings	Actress
Honolulu	ELEANOR POWELL
MGM Edward Bozzell	Singer/Dancer
Ice Follies of 1939	JOAN CRAWFORD
MGM Reinhold Schunzel	Actress
Idiot's Delight	NORMA SHEARER
MGM Clarence Brown	Actress
The Kid from Kokomo	JOAN BLONDELL
WB Lewis Seiler	Dancer
Man about Town	DOROTHY LAMOUR
PARA Mark Sandrich	Singer/Dancer
Midnight	CLAUDETTE COLBERT
REP Joeseph Kane	Showgirl
Naughty but Nice	ANN SHERIDAN
WB Ray Enright	Singer
On Your Toes	ZORINA
WB Ray Enright	Ballerina
Only Angels Have Wings	JEAN ARTHUR
COL Howard Hawks	Showgirl
Roaring Twenties	PRISCILLA LANE
WB Raoul Walsh	Chorus Girl
Rose of Washington Square	ALICE FAYE
TCF Gregory B. Ratoff	Singer
St. Louis Blues	DOROTHY LAMOUR
PARA Raoul Walsh	Singer
Stagecoach	CLAIRE TREVOR
UA John Ford	Dancehall Girl

	The Story of Vernon and Irene Castle	GINGER ROGERS
	RKO H. Potter/G. Haight	Dancer
	Television Spy	JUDITH BARRETT
	PARA Edward Dmytryk	
	These Glamour Girls	LANA TURNER
	MGM S. Sylvan Simon	Dancehall Girl
	Unexpected Father	SHIRLEY ROSS
	UNIV Charles Lamont	Chorus Girl
	We Are Not Alone	JANE BRYAN
	WB Edmund Goulding	Dancer
	Wife, Husband, and Friend	BINNIE BARNES
	TCF Gregory Ratoff	Opera Singer
	Zaza	CLAUDETTE COLBERT
	PARA George Cukor	Music Hall Singer
	The Zero Hour	FRIEDA INESCOURT
	REP Sidney Salkow	Actress
1940	*An Angel from Texas*	ROSEMARY LANE
	WB Ray Enright	Actress
	Argentine Nights	ANDREWS SISTERS
	UNIV Albert S. Rogell	Singers
	Broadway Melody of 1940	ELEANOR POWELL
	MGM Norman Taurog	Dancer
	Chad Hanna	DOROTHY LAMOUR
	TCF Henry King	Circus
	City for Conquest	ANN SHERIDAN
	WB Anatole Litvak	Dancer
	Congo Maisie	ANN SOTHERN
	GM Jenry C. Potter	Showgirl
	Dance, Girl, Dance	MAUREEN O'HARA
	RKO Dorothy Arzner	Dancer
	Dancing on a Dime	GRACE MCDONALD
	PARA Joseph A. Santley	Singer/Dancer

The Farmer's Daughter	MARTHA RAYE
PARA James Hogan	Singer/Dancer
Frontier Crusader	DOROTHY SHORT
PD Peter Stewart	Dancer
Gold Rush Maisie	ANN SOTHERN
MGM Edwin L. Marin	Showgirl
Hit Parade of 1941	MARY BOLAND
REP John H. Auer	Radio
	FRANCES LANGFORD
	Singer
The House across the Bay	JOAN BENNETT
UA Archie Mayo	Singer
I'm Nobody's Sweetheart Now	CONSTANCE MOORE
UNIV Arthur Lubin	Singer
I'm Still Alive	LINDA HAYES
RKO Irving Reis	Movie Star
It All Came True	ANN SHERIDAN
WB Lewis Seiler	
Johnny Apollo	DOROTHY LAMOUR
TCF Henry Hathaway	Singer
LaConga Nights	CONSTANCE MOORE
UNIV Lew Landers	Singer
Ladies Must Live	ROSEMARY LANE
WB Noel Smith	Showgirl
Lady with Red Hair	MIRIAM HOPKINS
WB Kurt Bernhardt	Actress
Lillian Russell	ALICE FAYE
TCF Irving Cummings	Singer
A Little Bit of Heaven	GLORIA JEAN
UNIV Andrew Marton	Radio Singer
Love Thy Neighbor	MARY MARTIN
PARA Mark Sandrich	Singer
Lucky Cisco Kid	MARY BETH HUGHES
TCF H. B. Humberstone	Dancehall Girl

Moon over Burma		DOROTHY LAMOUR
PARA	Louis Kine	Night Club Singer
My Little Chickadee		MAE WEST
UNIV	Edward Cline	
No Time for Comedy		ROSALIND RUSSELL
WB	William Keighley	Actress
Road to Singapore		DOROTHY LAMOUR
PARA	V. Schertzinger	Dancer
Scatterbrain		JUDY CANOVA
REP	Gus Meins	Musical Comedy
Seven Sinners		MARLENE DIETRICH
UNIV	Tay Garnett	
Star Dust		LINDA DARNELL
TCF	Walter Lang	Actress
Strange Cargo		JOAN CRAWFORD
MGM	Frank Borzage	
Tin Pan Alley		ALICE FAYE
TCF	Walter Lang	Singer/Dancer
Torrid Zone		ANN SHERIDAN
WB	William Keighley	Showgirl
Two Girls on Broadway		LANA TURNER
MGM	S. Sylvan Simon	Singer/Dancer
Virginia City		MIRIAM HOPKINS
WB	Michael Curtiz	Singer
Wagons Westward		ANITA LOUISE
REP	Lew Landers	
Waterloo Bridge		VIVIEN LEIGH
MGM	Mervyn LeRoy	Ballerina
Young People		CHARLOTTE GREENWOOD
TCF	Allan Dwan	Vaudeville
1941 *Ball of Fire*		BARBARA STANWYCK
RKO	Howard Hawks	Stripper

Bedtime Story COL	Alexander Hall	LORETTA YOUNG Actress
The Birth of the Blues PARA	V. Schertzinger	MARY MARTIN Singer
Blues in the Night WB	Anatole Litvak	PRISCILLA LANE Singer
Broadway Limited UA	Gordon Douglas	MARJORIE WOODWORTH Actress
Cadet Girl TCF	Ray McCarey	CAROLE LANDIS Singer
Chocolate Soldier MGM	Roy Del Ruth	RISE STEVENS Opera Singer
Cowboy and the Blonde TCF	Ray McCarey	MARY BETH HUGHES Actress
Dance Hall TCF	Irving Pichel	CAROLE LANDIS Singer
Desperate Cargo PRC	William Beaudine	CAROL HUGHES
Father Takes a Wife RKO	Jack Hively	GLORIA SWANSON Actress
Go West, Young Lady COL	Frank R. Strayer	ANN MILLER Dancehall Girl
Hard-Boiled Canary PARA	Andrew L. Stone	SUSANNA FOSTER Singer
High Sierra WB	Raoul Walsh	IDA LUPINO Showgirl
Kiss the Boys Goodbye PARA	V. Schertzinger	MARY MARTIN Chorus Girl
Law of the Tropics WB	Ray Enright	CONSTANCE BENNETT MONA MARIS Singers
Manpower WB	Raoul Walsh	MARLENE DIETRICH Night Club Hostess

The Men in Her Life		LORETTA YOUNG
COL	Gregory Ratoff	Dancer
Moonlight in Hawaii		JANE FRAZEE
UNIV	Charles Lamont	
North from the Lone Star		DOROTHY FAY
COL	Lambert Hillyer	Dancehall Girl
The Parson of Panamint		ELLEN DREW
PARA	William McGann	Dancehall Girl
Rags to Riches		MARY CARLISLE
REP	Joseph Kane	Singer
Road Show		CAROLE LANDIS
UA	Hal Roach	
Road to Zanzibar		DOROTHY LAMOUR
PARA	V. Schertzinger	Singer
Sailors on Leave		SHIRLEY ROSS
REP	Albert S. Rogell	Singer
San Antonio Rose		JANE FRAZEE
UNIV	Charles Lamont	Singer
Sheriff of Tombstone		ELYSE KNOX
REP	Joseph Kane	Singer
A Shot in the Dark		NAN WYNN
WB	William C. McGann	Singer
Sullivan's Travels		VERONICA LAKE
PARA	Preston Sturges	Actress
Sun Valley Serenade		SONJA HENIE
TCF	Bruce Humberstone	
Sunny		ANNA NEAGLE
RKO	Herbert Wilcox	Circus
Sunset Murder Case		SALLY RAND
G.HERLIMAN	Louis Glasnier	Dancer
Swamp Woman		ANN CORIO
PRC	Elmer Clifton	

That Night in Rio TCF Irving Cummings		CARMEN MIRANDA
This Woman Is Mine UNIV Frank Lloyd		CAROL BRUCE Singer
Tight Shoes UNIV Albert S. Rogell		BINNIE BARNES Showgirl
Time Out for Rhythm COL Sidney Salkow		ANN MILLER Dancer
Unfinished Business UNIV Gregory LaCava		IRENE DUNNE Singer
Virginia PARA Edward H. Griffith		MADELEINE CARROLL Showgirl
The Wagons Roll at Night WB Ray Enright		SYLVIA SIDNEY Carnival
Where Did You Get That Girl? UNIV Arthur Lubin		HELEN PARRISH Singer
A Yank in the RAF TCF Henry King		BETTY GRABLE Showgirl
You'll Never Get Rich COL Sidney Lanfield		RITA HAYWORTH Dancer
You're The One PARA Ralph Murphy		BONNIE BAKER Singer
Ziegfield Girl MGM Robert Z. Leonard		JUDY GARLAND Singer
1942	*Almost Married* UNIV Charles Lamont	JANE FRAZEE Night Club Singer
	Arabian Nights UNIV John Rawlins	MARIA MONTEZ Dancer
	Babes on Broadway MGM Busby Berkeley	JUDY GARLAND
	Behind the Eight Ball UNIV Edward F. Cline	CAROL BRUCE Actress

Between Us Girls		DIANA BARRYMORE
UNIV	Henry Koster	Actress
The Big Street		LUCILLE BALL
RKO	Irving Reis	Singer
Broadway		JANET BLAIR
UNIV	William A. Seiter	Singer/Dancer
Crossroads		CLAIRE TREVOR
MGM	Jack Conway	Singer
The Fleet's In		DOROTHY LAMOUR
PARA	Paul Jones	Singer
Footlight Serenade		BETTY GRABLE
TCF	Gregory Ratoff	Singer/Dancer
For Me and My Gal		JUDY GARLAND
MGM	Busby Berkeley	Vaudeville
Foreign Agent		GALE STORM
MONO	William Beaudine	Actress
Get Help to Love		GLORIA JEAN
UNIV	Charles Lamont	Singer
Give Out, Sisters		ANDREWS SISTERS
UNIV	Edward F. Cline	Singers
Grand Central Murder		PATRICIA DONE
MGM	S. Sylvan Simon	Singer
Holiday Inn		MARJORIE REYNOLDS
PARA	Mark Sandrich	Singer
I Wake Up Screaming		BETTY GRABLE
TCF	H. B. Humberstone	Singer
In Old California		BINNIE BARNES
REP	William McGann	Night Club Singer
Journey into Fear		DOLORES DEL RIO
RKO	Norman Foster	Dancer
Jukebox Jenny		HARRIET HILLIARD
UNIV	Harold Young	Singer

The Lady Is Willing COL Mitchell Leisen	MARLENE DIETRICH Actress
Maisie Gets Her Man MGM Roy Del Ruth	ANN SOTHERN Showgirl
The Man in the Trunk TCF Malcolm St. Clair	LYNNE ROBERTS Dancehall Girl
Manila Calling TCF Herbert I. Leeds	CAROLE LANDIS Dancehall Girl
Moonlight in Havana UNIV Anthony Mann	JANE FRAZEE Singer
My Gal Sal TCF Irving Cummings	RITA HAYWORTH Singer/Dancer
My Heart Belongs to Daddy PARA Robert Siodmak	MARTHA O'DRISCOLL Stripper
The Mystery of Marie Roget UNIV Phil Rosen	MARIA MONTEZ Musical Star
Northwest Rangers MGM Joe Newman	PATRICIA DANE Singer
Panama Hattie MGM Norman Z. McLeod	ANN SOTHERN Dancer
Powder Town RKO Rowland V. Lee	JUNE HAVOC Dancer
Private Buckaroo UNIV Edward Cline	ANDREWS SISTERS Singers
Random Harvest MGM Mervyn LeRoy	GREER GARSON Showgirl
Roxie Hart TCF William Wellman	GINGER ROGERS
Ship Ahoy MGM Edward N. Buzzell	ELEANOR POWELL Singer
Sing Your Worries Away RKO Edward Sutherland	JUNE HAVOC Stripper

Springtime in the Rockies		BETTY GRABLE
TCF	Irving Cummings	Singer/Dancer
Sunday Punch		JEAN ROGERS
MGM	David Miller	Chorus Girl
To Be or Not to Be		CAROLE LOMBARD
UA	Ernest Lubitsch	Actress
True to the Army		JUDY CANOVA
PARA	Albert S. Rogell	Circus
Two Yanks in Trinidad		JANET BLAIR
COL	Gregory Ratoff	Singer/Dancer
Unseen Enemy		IRENE HERVEY
UNIV	John Rawlins	Singer
When Johnny Comes Marching Home		JANE FRAZEE
UNIV	Charles Lamont	Singer
Yankee Doodle Dandy		JOAN LESLIE
WB	Michael Curtiz	
The Yanks Are Coming		MARY HEALY
PRC	Alexis Thurn-Taxis	Singer

1943

All By Myself		ROSEMARY LANE
UNIV	Felix E. Feist	Singer
Around the World		JOAN DAVIS
RKO	Allan Dwan	Actress
Best Foot Forward		LUCILLE BALL
MGM	Edward Buzzell	Actress
Campus Rhythm		GALE STORM
MONO	Arthur Dreifuss	Singer
Cinderella Swings It		GLORIA WAREEN
RKO	Christy Cabanne	Singer
Coney Island		BETTY GRABLE
TCF	Walter Lang	Singer/Dancer
Cowboy in Manhattan		FRANCES LANGFORD
UNIV	Frank Woodruff	Singer

The Desert Song	IRENE MANNING
WB Robert Florey	Singer
Doughboys in Ireland	LYNN MERRICK
COL Lew Landers	Singer
DuBarry Was a Lady	LUCILLE BALL
MGM Roy Del Ruth	Singer
Follow the Band	MARY BETH HUGHES
UNIV Jean Yarbrough	Singer
Gals, Incorporated	HARRIET HILLIARD
UNIV Leslie Goodwins	GRACE MACDONALD
	Singers
The Gang's All Here	ALICE FAYE
TCF Busby Berkely	Singer
He's My Guy	JOAN DAVIS
UNIV Edward F. Cline	Comedy
The Heat's On	MAE WEST
COL Gregory Ratoff	Actress
Hello, Frisco, Hello	ALICE FAYE
TCF Bruce Humberstone	Singer
His Butler's Sister	DEANNA DURBIN
UNIV Frank Borsage	Singer
I Dood It	ELEANOR POWELL
MGM Vincente Minnelli	Singer/Dancer
Lady of Burlesque	BARBARA STANWYCK
UA William Wellman	Stripper
Larceny with Music	KITTY CARLISLE
UNIV Edward Lilley	Singer
Let's Face It	BETTY HUTTON
PARA Sidney Lanfield	Singer/Dancer
The Mad Ghoul	EVELYN ANKERS
UNIV James Hogan	Singer
Never a Dull Moment	FRANCES LANGFORD
UNIV Edward Lilley	Singer

Phantom of the Opera UNIV Arthur Lubin	SUSANNA FOSTER Opera Singer
Presenting Lily Mars MGM Norman Taurog	JUDY GARLAND Singer/Dancer
Redhead from Manhatten COL Lew Landers	LUPE VELEZ Singer/Dancer
Rhythm Parade MONO Howard Bretherton	GALE STORM Singer/Dancer
Riding High PARA George Marshall	DOROTHY LAMOUR Burlesque
Salute to Three PARA Ralph Murphy	BETTY RHODES
Sarong Girl MONO Arthur Dreifuss	ANN CORIO Singer
She Has What It Takes COL Charles Barton	JINX FALKENBERG Singer
She's for Me UNIV Reginald DeBorg	GRACE MCDONALD Singer/Dancer
Stage Door Canteen UA Frank Borzage	CHERYL WALKER Singer

This is a generic war film in which an all-star cast of entertainers contributes to the war effort by boosting the morale of servicemen about to go to war. For our boys in uniform, women entertainers are particularly successful at this.

Stormy Weather TCF Andrew Stone	LENA HORNE Singer
Sweet Rosey O'Grady TCF Irving Cummings	BETTY GRABLE Musical Comedy
Tahiti Honey REP John H. Auer	SIMONE SIMON Singer
Tarzan's Desert Mystery RKO William Thiele	NANCY KELLY Magician

Taxi, Mister   GRACE BRADLEY
UA   Harold Young   Burlesque

Thumbs Up   BRENDA JOYCE
REP   Joseph Santley   Singer

Tornado   NANCY KELLY
PARA   William Berke   Showgirl

Two Tickets to London   MICHELE MORGAN
UNIV   Edward L. Marin   Night Club Entertainer

The Woman of the Town   CLAIRE TREVOR
UA   George Archainbaud   Singer

1944   *And the Angels Sing*   DOROTHY LAMOUR
PARA   George Marshall   Singer

Belle of the Yukon   GYPSY ROSE LEE
RKO   William A. Seiter   Saloon Singer

Between Two Women   GLORIA DE HAVEN
MGM   Willis Goldbeck   Singer

Bowery to Broadway   SUSANNA FOSTER
UNIV   Charles Lamont   Singer

The Bridge of San Luis Rey   LYNN BARI
UA   Rowland V. Lee   Singer

Broadway Rhythm   GINNY SIMMS
MGM   Roy Del Ruth   Singer/Dancer

Career Girl   FRANCES LANGFORD
PRC   Wallace F. Fox   Singer

Casanova in Burlesque   JUNE HAVOC
REP   Leslie Goodwins   Burlesque

Christmas Holiday   DEANNA DURBIN
UNIV   Robert Siodmark   Singer

The Climax   SUSANNA FOSTER
UNIV   George Waggner   Singer

Cover Girl   RITA HAYWORTH
COL   Charles Vidor   Dancer

Enemy of Women	CLAUDIA DRAKE
MONO Alfred Zeisler	Actress
Four Jills in a Jeep	KAY FRANCIS
TCF William A. Seiter	
Gambler's Choice	NANCY KELLY
PARA Frank McDonald	Singer
Girl Rush	FRANCES LANGFORD
RKO Gordan Douglas	Singer
Going My Way	RISE STEVENS
PARA Leo McCarey	Opera Singer
Greenwich Village	VIVIAN BLAINE
TCF Walter Lang	Night Club Singer
Hey, Rookie	ANN MILLER
COL Charles Barton	Singer/Dancer
Hi Good-Lookin!	HARRIET HILLIARD
UNIV Edward Lilley	Singer
Hot Rhythm	DONNA DRAKE
MONO William Beaudine	Singer
Irish Eyes Are Smiling	JUNE HAVER
TCF Gregory Ratoff	Singer
Jam Session	ANN MILLER
COL Charles Burton	Dancer
Kismet	MARLENE DIETRICH
MGM William Dieterle	Dancer
Lady, Let's Dance	BELITA
MONO Frank Woodruff	Dancer
The Lodger	MERLE OBERON
TCF John Brahm	Dancer
Lost Angel	MARSHA HUNT
MGM Roy Rowland	Night Club Singer
Lost in a Harem	MARILYN MAXWELL
MGM Charles Riesner	

Maisie Goes to Reno MGM　　　Harry Beaumont		ANN SOTHERN Showgirl
Men on Her Mind PRC　　　Wallace Fox		MARY BETH HUGHES Singer
The Merry Monohans UNIV　　　Charles Lamont		PEGGY RYAN Vaudeville
Music in Manhattan RKO　　　John A. Auer		ANNE SHIRLEY Showgirl
My Gal Loves Music UNIV　　　Edward Lilley		GRACE MCDONALD Singer
Shine on Harvest Moon WB　　　David Butler		ANN SHERIDAN Singer
Show Business RKO　　　Edwin L. Marin		JOAN DAVIS Musical Comedy
Slightly Terrific UNIV　　　Edward F. Cline		ANNE ROONEY Singer/Dancer
Song of the Open Road UA　　　S. Sylvan Simon		JANE POWELL Singer
Step Lively RKO　　　Tim Whelan		GLORIA DE HAVEN
Storm over Lisbon REP　　　George Sherman		VERA RALSTON Singer/Dancer
Swing Fever MGM　　　Tim Whelan		MARILYN MAXWELL Singer
Take It Big PARA　　　Frank McDonald		HARRIET HILLIARD Singer
Two Girls and a Sailor MGM　　　Richard Thorpe		JUNE ALLYSON

1945　*The Affairs of Susan*
　　　　PARA　　　William A. Seiter　　　　　　　　　　JOAN FONTAINE
　　　　　　　　　　　　　　　　　　　　　　　　　　　　Actress

　　　　An Angel Comes to Brooklyn
　　　　REP　　　Leslie Goodwins　　　　　　　　　　　　KAYE DOWD
　　　　　　　　　　　　　　　　　　　　　　　　　　　Singer/Dancer

The Big Show-Off		DALE EVANS
REP	Howard Bretherton	Singer
Blonde from Brooklyn		LYNN MERRICK
COL	Del Lord	Singer
Dangerous Intruder		VEDA ANN BORG
PRC	Vernon Keays	Showgirl
Delightfully Dangerous		CONSTANCE MOORE
UA	Arthur Lubin	Burlesque
Diamond Horseshoe		BETTY GRABLE
TCF	George Seaton	Night Club Singer
Dixie Jamboree		FRANCES LANGFORD
PRC	Christy Cabanne	Singer
Doll Face		VIVIAN BLAINE
TCF	Lewis Seiler	Singer/Dancer
The Dolly Sisters		BETTY GRABLE
TCF	Irving Cummings	JUNE HAVOC
		Singer/Dancer
Duffy's Tavern		BETTY HUTTON
PARA	Hal Walker	Singer/Dancer
Eadie Was a Lady		ANN MILLER
COL	Arthur Dreifuss	Singer/Dancer
Earl Carroll Vanities		CONSTANCE MOORE
REP	Joseph Santley	Singer
Eve Knew Her Apples		ANN MILLER
COL	Will Jason	Singer
Flame of the Barberry Coast		ANN DVORAK
REP	Joseph Kane	Singer
Frisco Sal		SUSANNA FOSTER
UNIV	George Waggner	Singer
George White's Scandals		JOAN DAVIS
RKO	Felix E. Feist	MARTHA HOLLIDAY
		Singer/Dancer

The Great Flamarion REP Anthony Mann	MARY BETH HUGHES Magician's Assistant
Hangover Square TCF John Brahm	LINDA DARNELL Night Club Singer
Hitchhike to Happiness REP Joseph Santley	DALE EVANS Singer
Hotel Berlin WB Peter Godfrey	ANDREA KING Actress
Incendiary Blonde PARA George Marshall	BETTY HUTTON Hostess
Masquerade in Mexico PARA Mitchell Leisen	DOROTHY LAMOUR Night Club
Mexicana REP Alfred Santell	CONSTANCE MOORE Singer
Nob Hill TCF Henry Hathaway	VIVIAN BLAINE Night Club Singer
On Stage Everybody UNIV Jean Yarbrough	PEGGY RYAN Singer
Patrick the Great UNIV Frank Ryan	PEGGY RYAN Dancer
Phantom of 42nd Street PRC Albert Herman	KAY ELDRIDGE Actress
The Picture of Dorian Gray MGM Albert Lewin	ANGELA LANSBURY Singer
Pursuit to Algiers UNIV Roy William Neill	MARJORIE RIORDAN Singer
Radio Stars on Parade RKO Leslie Woodwins	FRANCES LANGFORD Singer
Rhapsody in Blue WB Irving Rapper	JOAN LESLIE Singer
San Antonio WB David Butler	ALEXIS SMITH Singer

Senorita from the West		BONITA GRANVILLE
UNIV	Frank Strayer	Singer
Shady Lady		GINNY SIMMS
UNIV	George Waggner	Singer
A Song for Miss Julie		SHIRLEY ROSS
REP	William Rowland	Singer
The Spider		FAYE MARLOW
TCF	Robert Webb	Magic Show
State Fair		VIVIAN BLAINE
TCF	Walter Lang	Singer
Sunbonnet Sue		GALE STORM
MONO	Ralph Murphy	Singer
Ten Cents a Dance		JANE FRAZEE
COL	Will Jason	Taxi Dancer
That Night with You		SUSANNA FOSTER
UNIV	William A. Seiter	Singer
There Goes Kelly		WANDA MCKAY
MONO	Phil Kartslein	Singer
The Tiger Woman		ADELE MARA
REP	Philip Ford	Dancer
Tonight and Every Night		RITA HAYWORTH
COL	Victor Saville	Showgirl
Weekend at the Waldorf		GINGER ROGERS
MGM	Robert Z. Leonard	Movie Star
What a Blonde		VEDA ANN BORG
RKO	Leslie Goodwins	Showgirl
Why Girls Leave Home		PAMELA BLAKE
PRC	William Berke	Singer
The Wonder Man		VERA ELLEN
RKO	Bruce Humberstone	Dancer
Ziegfield Follies		JUDY GARLAND
MGM	Vincente Minnelli	Singer

1946	*Abie's Irish Rose*		JOANNE DRU
	UA	A. E. Sutherland	Singer/Dancer
	Abilene Town		ANN DVORAK
	UA	Edwin L. Marin	Saloon Singer
	The Bamboo Blonde		FRANCES LANGFORD
	RKO	Anthony Mann	Singer
	Bedlam		ANNA LEE
	RKO	Mark Robson	Actress
	Blue Skies		JOAN CAULFIELD
	PARA	Stuart Heisler	Singer/Dancer
	Cinderella Jones		JOAN LESLIE
	WB	Busby Berkeley	Singer
	Criminal Court		MARTHA O'DRISCOLL
	RKO	Robert Wise	Singer
	Deadline at Dawn		SUSAN HAYWARD
	RKO	Harold Clurman	Dancehall Girl
	Down Missouri Way		MARTHA O'DRISCOLL
	PRC	Josef Berne	Singer
	Earl Carroll Sketchbook		CONSTANCE MOORE
	REP	Albert S. Rogell	Singer
	The Falcon's Alibi		JANE GREER
	RKO	Ray McCarey	Singer
	Gun Town		CLAIRE CARLTON
	UNIV	Wallace W. Fox	Singer
	Her Kind of Man		JANIS PAIGE
	WB	Fred DeCordova	Singer
	If You Knew Susie		JOAN DAVIS
	RKO	Gordon M. Douglas	
	In Old Sacramento		CONSTANCE MOORE
	REP	Joseph Kane	Cabaret Singer
	The Jolson Story		EVELYN KEYES
	COL	Alfred E. Greene	Singer

The Last Crooked Mile REP Philip Ford	ANN SAVAGE Singer
The Man I Love WB Raoul Walsh	IDA LUPINO Singer
Murder in The Music Hall REP John English	VERA RALSTON Dancer
My Darling Clementine TCF John Ford	LINDA DARNELL Singer/Dancer
Night and Day WB Michael Curtiz	JANE WYMAN Showgirl
No Leave, No Love MGM Charles Martin	PAT KIRKWOOD Radio Singer
Nora Prentiss WB Vincent Sherman	ANN SHERIDAN Night Club Singer
Queen of Burlesque PRC Sam Newfield	EVELYN ANKERS Stripper
Rendezvous with Annie REP Allan Dwan	GAIL PATRICK Night Club Singer
Sentimental Journey MGM Norman Taurog	MAUREEN O'HARA Actress
Smooth As Silk UNIV Charles Barton	VIRGINIA GREY Actress
Somewhere in the Night TCF Joseph Mankiewicz	NANCY GUILD Singer
The Spector of the Rose REP Ben Hecht	JUDITH ANDERSON Dancer
Suspense MONO Frank Tuttle	BELITA Ice Dancer
Tangier UNIV George Waggner	MARIA MONTEZ Dancer
Til the Clouds Roll By MGM Richard Whorf	JUDY GARLAND Singer/Dancer

The Time, the Place, and the Girl		JANIS PAIGE
WB	David Butler	MARTHA VICKERS
		Showgirl
Two Sisters from Boston		KATHRYN GRAYSON
MGM	Henry Koster	Opera Singer

1947	*Beat the Band*	FRANCES LANGFORD
	RKO John H. Auer	Singer
	Carnival in Costa Rica	CELESTE HOLM
	TCF Gregory Ratoff	Singer
	Copacabana	CARMEN MIRANDA
	UA Alfred E. Green	Singer/Dancer
	Dead Reckoning	LIZABETH SCOTT
	COL John Cromwell	Singer
	A Double Life	SIGNE HASSO
	UNIV George Cukor	Actress
	The Fabulous Dorseys	JANET BLAIR
	UA Alfred E. Green	Singer
	Heaven Only Knows	MARJORIE REYNOLDS
	UA Albert S. Rogell	Dancehall Girl
	Hit Parade of 1947	CONSTANCE MOORE
	REP Frank McDonald	Singer
	I Walk Alone	LIZABETH SCOTT
	PARA Byron Haskin	Torch Singer
	I Wonder Who's Kissing Her Now	JUNE HAVER
	TCF Lloyd Bacon	Singer/Dancer
	The Imperfect Lady	TERESA WRIGHT
	PARA Lewis Allen	Music Hall
	Lured	LUCILLE BALL
	UA Douglas Sirk	
	Merton of the Movies	VIRGINIA O'BRIEN
	MGM Robert Alton	Actress
	Moss Rose	PEGGY CUMMINS
	TCF Gregory Ratoff	Singer

Mother Wore Tights		BETTY GRABLE
TCF	Walter Lang	Dancer
My Wild Irish Rose		ARLENE DAHL
WB	David Butler	Singer/Dancer
New Orleans		DOROTHY PATRICK
UA	Arthur Lubin	Singer
The Perils of Pauline		BETTY HUTTON
PARA	George Marshall	Actress
Repeat Performance		JOAN LESLIE
EL	Alfred Werker	Actress
Riffraff		ANN JEFFREYS
RKO	Ted Tetzlaff	Night Club Singer
Smashup - The Story of a Woman		SUSAN HAYWARD
UI	Stuart Heisler	Night Club Singer
Song of Schecherazade		YVONNE DE CARLO
UI	Walter Reisch	Dancer
That's My Gal		LYNNE ROBERTS
REP	George Blair	Singer/Dancer
Trail Street		ANN JEFFREYS
RKO	Ray Enright	Saloon Singer
The Trespasser		DALE EVANS
REP	George Blair	Singer
The Unfinished Dance		CYD CHARISSE
MGM	Henry Koster	Ballerina
The Vigilantes Return		MARGARET LINDSAY
UNIV	Ray Taylor	Singer
The Voice of the Turtle		ELEANOR PARKER
WB	Irving Rapper	Actress

1948

April Showers		ANN SOTHERN
WB	James V. Kern	Vaudeville
Black Bart		YVONNE DE CARLO
UNIV	George Sherman	Singer

Easter Parade		JUDY GARLAND
MGM	Charles Walters	Singer/Dancer

It's *Pygmalion*. After ambitious Ann Miller breaks up the act to strike out on her own, Fred Astaire molds an unformed Judy Garland into a succssful new partner. Initially, Garland is content to try to duplicate Miller, but ultimately she finds her own inimitable style and the act triumphs. Poor Astaire continues to think he loves Miller, but finally realizes that Garland is the girl for him and all ends happily. Garland gets career and husband and the audience is treated to wonderful singing and dancing.

Julia Misbehaves		GREER GARSON
MGM	Jack Conway	Actress
Jungle Patrol		KRISTINE MILLER
TCF	Joe Newman	
Lulu Belle		DOROTHY LAMOUR
COL	Leslie Fenton	Saloon Singer
Mary Lou		JOAN BARTON
COL	Arthur Dreifuss	Singer
Miracle of the Bells		ALIDA VALLI
RKO	Irving Pichel	Actress
On an Island with You		ESTHER WILLIAMS
MGM	Richard Thorpe	Actress
The Plunderers		ILONA MASSEY
REP	Joseph Kane	Dancehall Girl
Road House		IDA LUPINO
TCF	Jean Negulesco	Singer
Sofia		PATRICIA MORISON
FILMCLASS	John Reinhardt	Singer
A Song Is Born		VIRGINIA MAYO
RKO	Howard Hawks	Singer
The Velvet Touch		ROSALIND RUSSELL
RKO	John Gage	Actress

When My Baby Smiles at Me TCF	Walter Lang	BETTY GRABLE Vaudeville
Whiplash WB	Lew Seiler	ALEXIS SMITH Singer
Woman from Tangier COL	Harold Daniels	ADELE JERGENS Night Club Singer
Words and Music MGM	Norman Taurog	JUNE ALLYSON JUDY GARLAND Singer/Dancer

1949 *Always Leave Them Laughing*   VIRGINIA MAYO
WB   Roy Del Ruth

The Barkleys of Broadway   GINGER ROGERS
MGM   Charles Walters   Singer/Dancer

The Beautiful Blonde from Bashful Bend   BETTY GRABLE
TCF   Preston Sturges   Dancer

The Bribe   AVA GARDNER
MGM   Robert Z. Leonard   Singer

Colorado Territory   VIRGINIA MAYO
WB   Raoul Walsh   Dancehall Singer

Dancing in the Dark   BETSY DRAKE
TCF   Irving Reis   Actress

Everybody Does It   LINDA DARNELL
TCF   Edmund Goulding   Opera Singer

Flamingo Road   JOAN CRAWFORD
WB   Michael Curtiz   Carny Dancer

The Gal Who Took the West   YVONNE DE CARLO
UNIV   Fred De Cordova   Singer

The Gay Intruders   TAMARA GEVA
TCF   Ray McCarey   Actress

Grand Canyon   MARY BETH HUGHES
SCREENGUIL   Paul Landres   Actress

Holiday in Havana   MARY HATCHER
COL   Joe Newman   Dancer

Jigsaw		JEAN WALLACE
UA	Fletcher Markle	Night Club Singer
The Last Bandit		ADRIAN BOOTH
REP	Joseph Kane	Saloon Singer
Look for the Silver Lining		JUNE HAVER
WB	Davis Butler	Singer/Dancer
Love Happy		VERA ELLEN
UA	David Miller	Dancer
The Lucky Stiff		DOROTHY LAMOUR
UA	Lewis R. Foster	Singer
Malaya		VALENTINA CORTESA
MGM	Richard Thorpe	Singer
My Dream Is Yours		DORIS DAY
WB	Michael Curtiz	Singer
Oh, You Beautiful Doll		JUNE HAVOC
TCF	John M. Stahl	Singer/Dancer
On the Town		VERA ELLEN
MGM	G. Kelly/S. Donen	Dancer
One Last Fling		ALEXIS SMITH
WB	Peter Godfrey	Vaudeville
Red, Hot, And Blue		BETTY HUTTON
PARA	John Farrow	Singer/Dancer
Rose of the Yukon		MYRNA DELL
REP	George Blair	Singer
Roughshod		GLORIA GRAHAME
RKO	Mark Robson	Night Club
Rustlers		LOIS ANDREWS
RKO	Lesley Selander	Singer
Scene of the Crime		GLORIA DE HAVEN
MGM	Roy Rowland	Night Club
Slightly French		DOROTHY LAMOUR
COL	Douglas Sirk	Carny Dancer

Sorrowful Jones MGM Sidney Lanfield	LUCILLE BALL Chorus Girl
The Sun Comes Up MGM Richard Thorpe	JEANETTE MACDONALD Singer
That Midnight Kiss MGM Norman Taurog	KATHRYN GRAYSON Opera Singer
Wild West EUREKA Sherman Scott	LILA LEEDS Chorus Girl
A Woman's Secret RKO Nicholas Ray	MAUREEN O'HARA Singer
You're My Everything TCF Walter Lang	ANNE BAXTER Dancer

1950 | *All about Eve*
TCF   Jos. L. Mankiewicz | BETTE DAVIS
Actress |

It's the old story: ruthless aging actress challenged by ruthless ingenue. When Margo Channing (Davis) says, "Fasten your seatbelts; it's going to be a bumpy night!", the battle is joined. Eve (Anne Baxter) threatens the career and marriage of the older actress, but Channing uses her experience and cunning to hold on to both. Both women are utterly immersed in their careers and will stop at nothing. No quarter is given or requested. Both actresses were nominated for Academy Awards.

Annie Get Your Gun MGM George Sidney	BETTY HUTTON Wild West Show
Blues Buster MONO William Beaudine	ADELE JERGENS Singer
Born Yesterday COL George Cukor	JUDY HOLLIDAY Chorus Girl
Buccaneer's Girl UNIV Fred De Cordova	YVONNE DE CARLO
Bunco Squad RKO Herbert L. Leeds	JOAN DIXON
Conspiracy in Teheran UA William Freshman	MARTA LABARR Ballerina

Cry Murder		CAROL MATHEWS
FILMCLASS	Jack Glenn	Actress
Curtain Call at Cactus Creek		EVE ARDEN
UNIV	Charles Lamont	GALE STORM
		Actress
Dark City		LIZABETH SCOTT
PARA	William Dieterle	Singer
The Daughter of Rosie O'Grady		JUNE HAVER
WB	David Butler	Vaudeville
The Duchess of Idaho		ESTHER WILLIAMS
MGM	Robert Z. Leonard	Swimming Star
For Heaven's Sake		JOAN BENNETT
TCF	George Seaton	
Grounds for Marriage		KATHRYN GRAYSON
MGM	Robert Z. Leonard	Opera Singer
Her Wonderful Lie		JAN KLEPURA
COL	Carmine Gallone	Opera Singer
Hit Parade of 1951		MARIE MCDONALD
REP	John H. Auer	Singer
I'll Get By		JUNE HAVER
TCF	Richard Sale	Singer/Dancer
Key to the City		MARILYN MAXWELL
MGM	George Sidney	Bubble Dancer
Let's Dance		BETTY HUTTON
PARA	Norman Z. McLeod	Singer/Dancer
Molly		GERTRUDE BERG
PARA	Walter Hart	
My Blue Heaven		BETTY GRABLE
TCF	Henry Koster	Singer/Dancer
Nancy Goes to Rio		JANE POWELL
MGM	Robert Z. Leonard	Singer/Dancer
Never Fear		SALLY FORREST
EL	Ida Lupino	Dancer

The Red Danube		JANET LEIGH
MGM	George Sidney	Ballerina
Rio Grande Patrol		JANE NIGH
RKO	Lesley Selander	Dancehall Girl
Sarumba		DORIS DOWLING
EL	Marion Gering	Dancer
Sideshow		TRACEY ROBERTS
MONO	Jean Yarbrough	Carny Dancer
Sierra Passage		LOLA ALBRIGHT
MONO	Frank McDonald	Singer
South Sea Sinner		SHELLEY WINTERS
UNIV	Bruce Humberstone	
Stage Fright		MARLENE DIETRICH
WB	Alfred Hitchcock	Musical Star
Storm over Wyoming		BETTY UNDERWOOD
RKO	Lesley Selander	Dancehall Girl
Sunset Boulevard		GLORIA SWANSON
PARA	Billy Wilder	Movie Star
Tea for Two		DORIS DAY
WB	David Butler	
Three Little Words		VERA ELLEN
MGM	Richard Thorpe	Singer/Dancer
Toast of New Orleans		KATHRYN GRAYSON
MGM	Norman Taurog	Opera Singer
Under the Gun		AUDREY TOTTER
UNIV	Ted Tetzlaff	Singer
Wabash Avenue		BETTY GRABLE
TCF	Henry Koster	Singer/Dancer
West Point Story		VIRGINIA MAYO
WB	Roy Del Ruth	Director
Winchester 73		SHELLEY WINTERS
UI	Anthony Mann	Dancehall Girl

Wyoming Mail		ALEXIS SMITH
UI	Reginald LeBorg	Saloon Singer
Young Man with a Horn		DORIS DAY
WB	Michael Curtiz	Singer

1951 *An American in Paris*   LESLIE CARON
       MGM   Vincente Minnelli   Dancer

Apache Drums   COLEEN GRAY
UNIV   Hugo Fregonese   Dancer

Call Me Mister   BETTY GRABLE
TCF   Lloyd Bacon

Disc Jockey   GINNY SIMMS
AA   Will Jason   Singer

Flame of Stamboul   LISA FERRADAY
COL   Ray Nazarro   Dancer

Fugitive Lady   JANIS PAIGE
REP   Sidney Salkow

Golden Girl   MITZI GAYNOR
TCF   Lloyd Bacon

I'll See You in My Dreams   DORIS DAY
WB   Michael Curtiz   Singer

Kentucky Jubilee   JEAN PORTER
LIPPERT   Ron Ormond

The Lemon Drop Kid   MARILYN MAXWELL
PARA   Sidney Lanfield   Showgirl

Lightning Strikes Twice   RUTH ROMAN
WB   King Vidor   Actress

The Little Ballerina   MARGOT FONTEYN
UI   Lewis Gilbert   Ballerina

Little Egypt   RHONDA FLEMING
UNIV   Fred De Cordova   Dancer

Lullaby of Broadway   DORIS DAY
WB   David Butler

Meet Me after the Show		BETTY GRABLE
TCF	Richard Sale	
Million Dollar Pursuit		PENNY EDWARDS
REP	R. G. Springsteen	Singer
Mr. Imperium		LANA TURNER
MGM	Don Hartman	Singer
New Mexico		MARILYN MAXWELL
UA	Irving Reis	
Oh! Susanna		ADRIAN BOOTH
REP	Joseph Kane	Saloon Singer
Painting the Clouds with Sunshine		VIRGINIA MAYO
WB	David Butler	Singer
Purple Heart Diary		FRANCES LANGFORD
COL	Richard Quine	USO
The Racket		LIZABETH SCOTT
RKO	John Cromwell	Singer
Rawhide		SUSAN HAYWARD
TCF	Henry Hathaway	
Rhythm Inn		JANE FRAZEE
MONO	Paul Landres	Singer
Rich, Young, and Pretty		DANIELLE DARRIEUX
MGM	Norman Taurog	Actress
Royal Wedding		JANE POWELL
MGM	Stanley Donen	Dancer
The Sellout		AUDREY TOTTER
MGM	Gerald Mayer	Singer
Showboat		AVA GARDNER
MGM	George Sidney	Singer
Starlift		JANICE RULE
WB	Roy Del Ruth	

The Strip		SALLY FORREST
MGM	Leslie Kardos	Dancer
Sugarfoot		ADELE JERGENS
WB	Edwin L. Marin	Saloon Singer
Texas Carnival		ESTHER WILLIAMS
MGM	Charles Walters	
Tomahawk		YVONNE DE CARLO
UNIV	George Sherman	Singer
Tomorrow Is Another Day		RUTH ROMAN
WB	Felix Feist	Dancehall Girl
Two Gals and a Guy		JANIS PAIGE
UA	Alfred E. Green	
Valentino		ELEANOR POWELL
COL	Lewis Allen	Actress

1952	*Actor's Blood*		MARSHA HUNT
	UA	Ben Hecht	Actress
	Affair in Trinidad		RITA HAYWORTH
	COL	Vincent Sherman	Dancer
	April in Paris		DORIS DAY
	WB	David Butler	Chorus Girl
	The Bad and the Beautiful		LANA TURNER
	MGM	Vincente Minnelli	Actress
	Because You're Mine		PAULA CORDAY
	MGM	Alexander Hall	Opera Singer
	Bloodhounds of Broadway		MITZI GAYNOR
	TCF	Harmon Jones	
	Carrie		JENNIFER JONES
	PARA	William Wyler	Actress
	Dreamboat		GINGER ROGERS
	TCF	Claude Binyon	Movie Star
	Everything I Have Is Yours		MARGE CHAMPION
	MGM	Robert Z. Leonard	Dancer

Fearless Fagan	JANET LEIGH
MGM Stanley Donen	Singer
The Greatest Show on Earth	BETTY HUTTON
PARA Cecil B. DeMille	Trapeze Artist
Hans Christian Andersen	ZIZIE JEANMARIE
S GOLDWYN Charles Vidor	Ballerina
The I Don't Care Girl	MITZI GAYNOR
TCF Lloyd Bacon	
The Jazz Singer	PEGGY LEE
WB Michael Curtiz	Singer
Just For You	JANE WYMAN
PARA Elliott Nugent	
Limelight	CLAIRE BLOOM
UA Charlie Chaplin	Dancer
Lost in Alaska	MITZI GREEN
UNIV Jean Yarbrough	Singer
Macao	JANE RUSSELL
RKO Josef Von Sternberg	Singer
Meet Danny Wilson	SHELLEY WINTERS
UNIV Joseph Pevney	
Night Without Sleep	LINDA DARNELL
TCF Roy Baker	Movie Star
Phone Call from a Stranger	SHELLEY WINTERS
TCF Jean Negulesco	Night Club
Rainbow 'Round My Shoulder	CHARLOTTE AUSTIN
COL Richard Quine	
Sailor Beware	CORINNE CALVET
PARA Hal Walker	Singer
Scaramouche	ELEANOR PARKER
MGM George Sidney	Actress
Scarlet Angel	YVONNE DE CARLO
UNIV Sidney Salkow	Saloon Girl

She's Working Her Way Through College WB Bruce Humberstone	VIRGINIA MAYO Burlesque
Singing in the Rain MGM Gene Kelly	DEBBIE REYNOLDS Singer/Dancer
The Sniper COL Edward Dmytryk	MARIE WINDSOR Saloon Singer
Somebody Loves Me PARA Irving Brecher	BETTY HUTTON Singer
Something to Live For PARA George Stevens	JOAN FONTAINE Actress
The Star TCF Stuart Heisler	BETTE DAVIS Movie Star
Stars and Stripes Forever TCF Henry Koster	DEBRA PAGET Singer
Stop, You're Killing Me WB Roy Del Ruth	CLAIRE TREVOR Ex-Showgirl
Three for Bedroom C WB Milton H. Bren	GLORIA SWANSON Movie Star
Tropical Heat Wave REP R. G. Springsteen	ESTRALITA Singer
Wall of Death REALART Lewis Gilbert	SUSAN SHAW Carnival
With a Song in My Heart TCF Walter Lang	SUSAN HAYWARD Singer

Jan Froman (Hayward) is a singer who, out of gratitude, marries the manager who has helped her to build a successful career. On an overseas trip to entertain the troops, she is crippled in a plane crash and, during her convalescence, falls in love with the pilot of the plane. She resumes her career but is torn between loyalty to her husband and her true love. While Froman is depicted as a professional entertainer, the anguish of her personal life does not allow her true happiness.

Young Man with Ideas MGM Mitchell Leisen	DENISE DARCEL

1953	*The Actress* MGM	George Cukor	JEAN SIMMONS Actress
	All I Desire UI	Douglas Sirk	BARBARA STANWYCK Actress
	Band Wagon MGM	Vincente Minnelli	CYD CHARISSE
	City That Never Sleeps REP	John H. Auer	MALA POWERS Dancer
	Easy to Love MGM	Charles Walters	ESTHER WILLIAMS Aqua Show
	Fair Wind to Java REP	Joe Kane	VERA RALSTON Dancer
	Forever Female PARA	Irving Rapper	GINGER ROGERS Actress
	Gentlemen Prefer Blondes TCF	Howard Hawks	MARILYN MONROE JANE RUSSELL Singers

Monroe and her roommate are temporarily singers while searching for rich husbands. The film provides showcases for the actresses to perform such memorable numbers as "Diamonds are a Girl's Best Friend" and "Two Little Girls from Little Rock." For Loreli (Monroe) and Dorothy (Russell), however, careers are clearly secondary to their manhunt and Loreli especially is the quintessential golddigger.

	The Girl Next Door TCF	Richard Sale	JUNE HAVER Musical
	Give a Girl a Break MGM	Stanley Donen	DEBBIE REYNOLDS Actress
	The Glass Web UNIV	Jack Arnold	KATHLEEN HUGHES Actress
	Here Come the Girls PARA	Claude Binyon	ARLENE DAHL Music Hall
	Houdini PARA	Goerge Marshall	JANET LEIGH Magician's Assistant

I Love Melvin		DEBBIE REYNOLDS
MGM	Don Weiss	Chorus Girl
Kiss Me Kate		KATHRYN GRAYSON
MGM	George Sidney	Singer
Let's Do It Again		JANE WYMAN
COL	Alexander Hall	Singer/Dancer
Lili		LESLIE CARON
MGM	Charles Walters	Puppeteer
Little Boy Lost		NICOLE MAUREY
PARA	George Seaton	
Main Street to Broadway		TALLULAH BANKHEAD
MGM	Tay Garnett	MARY MURPHY
		Actress
Man in the Attic		CONSTANCE SMITH
TCF	Hugo Fregonese	Actress
Melba		PATRICE MUNSEL
UA	Lewis Milestone	Opera Singer
Never Let Me Go		GENE TIERNEY
MGM	Delmar Daves	Ballerina
Ninety-Nine River Street		EVELYN KEYES
UA	Phil Karlson	Actress
Remains to Be Seen		JUNE ALLYSON
MGM	Don Weis	Singer
She's Back on Broadway		VIRGINIA MAYO
WB	Gordon Douglas	Singer/Dancer
So This Is Love		KATHRYN GRAYSON
WB	Gordon Douglas	Opera Singer
Split Second		JAN STERLING
RKO	Dick Powell	Night Club
The Stars Are Singing		ROSEMARY CLOONEY
PARA	Norman Taurog	Singer
The Story Of Three Loves		MOIRA SHEARER
MGM	Vincente Minnelli	Ballerina

Take Me to Town		ANN SHERIDAN
UNIV	Douglas Sirk	Saloon Singer
Three Sailors and a Girl		JANE POWELL
WB	Roy Del Ruth	
Tonight We Sing		ROBERTA PETERS
TCF	Mitchell Leisen	Singer
Torch Song		JOAN CRAWFORD
MGM	Charles Walters	Singer/Dancer
Violated!		LILI DAWN
PALACE	Walter Strate	Stripper

1954

The Barefoot Contessa		AVA GARDNER
UA	Jos. L. Mankiewicz	Night Club Singer
Black Widow		GINGER ROGERS
TCF	Nunnally Johnson	Actress
Carnival Story		ANNE BAXTER
RKO	Kurt Neumann	Circus
Dawn at Socorro		PIPER LAURIE
UNIV	George Sherman	Dancehall Girl
Deep in My Heart		HELEN TRAUBEL
MGM	Stanley Donen	Singer
Destry		MARI BLANCHARD
UNIV	George Marshall	Singer
Gorilla at Large		ANNE BANCROFT
TCF	Hermon Jones	Trapeze Artist
Jesse James' Woman		PEGGY CASTLE
UA	Donald Berry	Singer
Jubilee Trail		VERA RALSTON
REP	Joseph Inman Kane	Singer
Laughing Anne		MARGARET LOCKWOOD
REP	Herbert Wilcox	Singer
Lucky Me		DORIS DAY
WB	Jack Donohue	Singer/Dancer

The Mad Magician		MARY MURPHY
COL	John Brahm	Magician's Assistant
Monte Carlo Baby		AUDREY HEPBURN
FAVORITE	Jean Boyer	Movie Star
Naked Alibi		GLORIA GRAHAME
UI	Jerry Hopper	Night Club Singer
New Faces		EARTHA KITT
TCF	Harry Horner	Singer
The Other Woman		CLEO MOORE
TCF	Hugo Haas	Actress
Overland Pacific		ADELE JERGENS
UA	Fred F. Sears	Singer
Playgirl		SHELLEY WINTERS
UNIV	Joseph Pevney	Singer
Private Hell 36		IDA LUPINO
FM	Don Siegel	Singer
Red Garters		ROSEMARY CLOONEY
PARA	George Marshall	Dancehall Singer
Ride Clear of Diablo		ABBE LANE
UNIV	Jesse Hibbs	Singer
Ring of Fear		MARIAN CARR
WB	James Edward Grant	Circus
River of No Return		MARILYN MONROE
TCF	Otto Preminger	Singer
So This Is Paris		GLORIA DE HAVEN
UNIV	Richard Quine	Singer
A Star Is Born		JUDY GARLAND
WB	George Cukor	Actress/Singer
There's No Business Like Show Business		ETHEL MERMAN
TCF	Walter Lang	MARILYN MONROE
		Singers
Top Banana		ROSE MARIE
UA	Alfred E. Green	Musical Comedy

Untamed Heiress		JUDY CANOVA
REP	Charles Lamont	Comedy/Singer
Walking My Baby Back Home		JANET LEIGH
UI	Lloyd Bacon	Singer
White Christmas		VERA ELLEN
PARA	Michael Curtiz	ROSEMARY CLOONEY
		Singer/Dancers
White Fire		MARY CASTLE
LIPPERT	John Gilling	Singer

1955   *Ain't Misbehavin'*   PIPER LAURIE
        UNIV   Edward Buzzell   Chorus Girl

        The Bar Sinister   JARMA LEWIS
        MGM   Herman Hoffman

        Bedevilled   ANNE BAXTER
        MGM   Mitchell Reisen   Singer

        Chicago Syndicate   ABBE LANE
        COL   Fred F. Sears   Singer

        Five Against the House   KIM NOVAK
        COL   Phil Karlson   Singer

        Gentlemen Marry Brunettes   JEANNE CRAIN
        UA   Richard Sale   Night Club Entertainer
                                                  JANE RUSSELL
                                                  Singer

        The Girl in the Red Velvet Swing   JOAN COLLINS
        TCF   Richard Fleischer   Chorus Girl

        Guys and Dolls   VIVIAN BLAINE
        S GOLDWYN   Joseph Mankiewicz   Chorus Girl

        Hit the Deck   ANN MILLER
        MGM   Roy Rowland   Dancer

        How To Be Very, Very Popular   BETTY GRABLE
        TCF   Nunnally Johnson   SHEREE NORTH
                                                  Belly Dancers

        I Died a Thousand Times   SHELLEY WINTERS
        WB   Stuart Heisler   Taxi Dancer

I'll Cry Tomorrow MGM Daniel Mann		SUSAN HAYWARD Singer
Interrupted Melody MGM Curtis Bernhardt		ELEANOR PARKER Singer
Killer's Kiss UA Stanley Kubrick		IRENE KANE Taxi Dancer
A Lawless Street COL Joseph H. Lewis		ANGELA LANSBURY Actress
Love Me or Leave Me MGM Charles Vidor		DORIS DAY Singer
Man with the Golden Arm UA Otto Preminger		KIM NOVAK Night Club Singer
My Sister Eileen COL Richard Quine		JANET LEIGH Actress
Paris Follies of 1956 AA Leslie Goodwins		MARGARET WHITING Singer
Pete Kelly's Blues WB Jack Webb		PEGGY LEE Singer
Prince of Players TCF Philip Dunne		MAGGIE MCNAMARA Actress
The Racers TCF Henry Hathaway		BELLA DARVI Dancer
Running Wild UI Abner Biberman		MAMIE VAN DOREN Rock n' Roll
The Seven Little Foys PARA Melville Snavelson		MILLY VITALE Ballerina
The Seven Year Itch TCF Billy Wilder		MARILYN MONROE Actress
Svengali WB Noel Langley		HILDEGARDE NEFF Opera Singer
Three for the Show COL H. C. Potter		BETTY GRABLE Dancer

The Twinkle in God's Eye		COLEEN GRAY
REP	George Blair	Dancer
1956 *Anything Goes*		MITZI GAYNOR
PARA	Robert Lewis	Singer/Dancer
The Best Things in Life Are Free		SHEREE NORTH
TCF	Michael Curtiz	Singer/Dancer
The Broken Star		LITA BARON
UA	Lesley Selander	Saloon Singer
Bus Stop		MARILYN MONROE
TCF	Joshua Logan	Singer
Dakota Incident		LINDA DARNELL
REP	Lewis Foster	Dancehall Girl
The Deadly Companions		MAUREEN O'HARA
UNIV	Jerry Hopper	Dancehall Hostess
Death of a Scoundrel		NANCY GATES
RKO	Charles Martin	Actress
Four Girls in Town		JULIE ADAMS
UNIV	Jack Sher	Singer/Dancer
Gaby		LESLIE CARON
MGM	Curtis Bernhardt	Ballerina
The Girl Can't Help It		JAYNE MANSFIELD
TCF	Frank Tashlin	
The Great Man		JULIE LONDON
UNIV	Jose Ferrer	Singer
Gun Brothers		ANN ROBINSON
UA	Sidney Salkow	Singer
He Laughed Last		LUCY MARLOW
COL	Blake Edwards	Chorus Girl
Hollywood or Bust		ANITA EKBERG
PARA	Frank Tashlin	Actress
The Houston Story		BARBARA HALE
COL	William Castle	Singer

Manfish UA	W. Lee Wilder	BARBARA NICHOLS Chorus Girl
Meet Me in Las Vegas MGM	Ray Rowland	CYD CHARISSE Dancer
The Opposite Sex MGM	David Miller	JOAN COLLINS Chorus Girl
The Rawhide Years UNIV	Rudolph Matepe	COLLEEN MILLER
The She-Creature AIP	Edward L. Cahn	MARLA ENGLISH Magician's Assistant
Teahouse of the August Moon MGM	Daniel Mann	MACHIKO KYO Geisha
Trapeze UA	Carol Reed	GINA LOLLOBRIGIDA Circus
The Vagabond Kind PARA	Michael Curtiz	RITA MORENO Magician's Assistant

1957	*Accused of Murder* REP	Joe Kane	VERA RALSTON Singer
	An Affair to Remember TCF	Leo McCarey	DEBORAH KERR Singer
	Beau James PARA	Melville Shavelson	VERA MILES Singer
	The Big Land WB	Gordon Douglas	VIRGINIA MAYO Saloon Singer
	Bop Girl Goes Calypso UA	Howard W. Koch	JUDY TYLER Singer
	Boy on a Dolphin TCF	Jean Negulesco	SOPHIA LOREN Night Club Entertainer
	The Buster Keaton Story PARA	Sidney Sheldon	RHONDA FLEMING Actress
	Carnival Rock HOWCO	Roger Corman	SUSAN CABOT Singer

Dragon Wells Massacre		KATY JURADO
AA	Harold Schuster	Dancer
The Fuzzy Pink Nightgown		JANE RUSSELL
UA	Norman Taurog	Actress
The Helen Morgan Story		ANN BLYTH
WB	Michael Curtiz	Singer
Hidden Fear		ANNE NEYLAND
UA	Andre DeToth	Singer
Hit and Run		CLEO MOORE
AA	Hugo Haas	
Jeanne Eagels		KIM NOVAK
COL	George Sidney	Actress
The Joker Is Wild		MITZI GAYNOR
PARA	Charles Vidor	Dancer
Kelly and Me		MARTHA HYER
UNIV	Robert Z. Leonard	Actress
Les Girls		MITZI GAYNOR
MGM	George Cukor	Showgirl
Man of a Thousand Faces		JANE GREER
UI	Joseph Pevney	Dancer
		DOROTHY MALONE
		Singer
Monkey on My Back		DIANNE FOSTER
UA	Andre DeToth	Actress
Pal Joey		KIM NOVAK
COL	George Sidney	Singer/Dancer
Panama Sal		ELENA VERDUGO
REP	William Witney	Singer
Prince and the Showgirl		MARILYN MONROE
WB	Laurence Olivier	
Public Pigeon Number 1		VIVIAN BLAINE
RKO	Norman Z. McLeod	Singer
Ride a Violent Mile		PENNY EDWARDS
TCF	Charles M. Warren	Dancehall Girl

Sayonara		MIIKO TAKA
GOETZ	Joshua Logan	Geisha
Sweet Smell of Success		BARBARA NICHOLS
UA	Alex MacKendrick	Night Club Entertainer
The Tarnished Angels		DOROTHY MALONE
UNIV	Douglas Sirk	Air Show
The Wayward Bus		JAYNE MANSFIELD
TCF	Victor Vicus	
Will Success Spoil Rock Hunter?		JAYNE MANSFIELD
TCF	Frank Tashlin	Movie Star

1958	*The Barbarian and the Geisha*		EIKO ANDO
	TCF	John Huston	Geisha
	The Female Animal		HEDY LAMARR
	UNIV	Harry Keller	Actress
	The Geisha Boy		MARIE MCDONALD
	PARA	Frank Tashlin	Chorus Girl
	The Goddess		KIM STANLEY
	COL	John Cromwell	
	Guns, Girls, and Gangsters		MAMIE VAN DOREN
	UA	Edward L. Cahn	Singer
	Gunsmoke in Tuscon		GALE ROBBINS
	AA	Thomas Carr	
	Indiscreet		INGRID BERGMAN
	WB	Stanley Donen	Actress
	Man from God's Country		RANDY STUART
	AA	Paul Landres	Dancehall Girl
	Mardi Gras		CHRISTINE CARERE
	TCF	Edmund Goulding	Movie Star
	Marjorie Morningstar		NATALIE WOOD
	WB	Irving Rapper	Actress
	Merry Andrew		PIER ANGELI
	MGM	Michael Kidd	Acrobat

Party Girl		CYD CHARISSE
MGM	Nicholas Ray	Dancer
Rock-a-Bye-Baby		MARILYN MAXWELL
PARA	Frank Tashlin	Actress
Saddle the Wind		JULIE LONDON
MGM	Robert Parrish	Singer
Saga of Hemp Brown		BEVERLY GARLAND
UNIV	Richard Carlson	Medicine Show
Screaming Mimi		ANITA EKBERG
COL	Gerd Oswald	Stripper
St. Louis Blues		EARTHA KITT
PARA	Allan Reisner	Singer
Stage Struck		SUSAN STRASBERG
BV	Sidney Lumet	Actress
Too Much, Too Soon		DOROTHY MALONE
WB	Art Napoleon	
Villa!!		MARGIA DEAN
TCF	James B. Clark	Singer

1959

Alias Jesse James		RHONDA FLEMING
HOPE	Norman Z. McLeod	Saloon Girl
The Blue Angel		MAY BRITT
TCF	Edward Dmytryk	Singer
The Flying Fontaines		EVY NORLUND
COL	George Sherman	Circus
The Gazebo		DEBBIE REYNOLDS
MGM	George Marshall	Actress
Imitation of Life		LANA TURNER
UNIV	Douglas Sirk	Actress

Turner plays an actress so driven by ambition that she
neglects both daughter and lover. By the time she
realizes her own need for love and marries her
long-suffering suitor, she has alienated her daughter,
who has fallen into unrequited love with her mother's
now-husband. Thus the actress learns the harsh lesson
of her single-minded involvement in her career and,
with her new insight, is reconciled with her daughter.

It Started with a Kiss MGM George Marshall	DEBBIE REYNOLDS Dancer	
The Man Who Understood Women TCF Nunnally Johnson	LESLIE CARON Actress	
Operation Dames AIP Louis Steumen	EVE MEYER	
Say One for Me TCF Frank Tashlin	DEBBIE REYNOLDS Singer/Dancer	
Some Like It Hot UA Billy Wilder	MARILYN MONROE Singer	
These Thousand Hills TCF Richard Fleischer	LEE REMICK Gambling Hall Hostess	
Tokyo after Dark PARA Norman T. Herman	MICHI KOBI	
The Wild and the Innocent UNIV Jack Sher	JOANNE DRU Dancehall Girl	

1960 *Can-Can*
TCF   Walter Lang

SHIRLEY MACLAINE
Dancer

G. I. Blues
PARA   Norman Taurog

JULIET PROWSE
Dancer

Heller in Pink Tights
PARA   George Cukor

SOPHIA LOREN
Actress

The Hypnotic Eye
AA   George Blair

ALLISON HAYS
Magician's Assistant

It Started in Naples
PARA   Melville Shavelson

SOPHIA LOREN
Stripper

Let's Make Love
TCF   George Cukor

MARILYN MONROE
Actress

Murder, Inc.
TCF   Stuart Rosenberg

MAY BRITT
Dancer

North to Alaska
TCF   Henry Hathaway

CAPUCINE
Dancehall Girl

Pepe		ZSA ZSA GABOR
COL	George Sidney	Actress
The Rat Race		DEBBIE REYNOLDS
PARA	Robert Mulligan	Taxi Dancer
1961 *The Big Show*		ESTHER WILLIAMS
TCF	James B. Clark	Circus
A Cold Night in August		LOLA ALBRIGHT
AA	Alexander Singer	Stripper
Cry for Happy		MIIKO TAKA
COL	George Marshall	Geisha
Flower Drum Song		NANCY KWAN
UNIV	Henry Koster	Singer/Dancer
The George Raft Story		JULIE LONDON
AA	Joseph M. Newman	Singer
Mad Dog Call		KAY DOUBLEDAY
COL	Burt Balaban	Stripper
Night Tide		LINDA LAWSON
VIRGO	Curtis Harrington	Carnival
Too Late Blues		STELLA STEVENS
PARA	John Cassavetes	Singer
Walk the Angry Beach		RUE MCCLANAHAN
J.P. HAYES	John P. Hayes	Stripper
1962 *Belle Summers*		POLLY BERGEN
COL	E. Silverstein	Singer
Don't Knock the Twist		LINDA SCOTT
COL	Oscar Rudolph	Singer
Forty Pounds of Trouble		SUZANNE PLESHETTE
UNIV	Norman Jewison	Singer
Girls, Girls, Girls!		STELLA STEVENS
PARA	Norman Taurog	Singer
Gypsy		NATALIE WOOD
WB	Mervyn LeRoy	Stripper

While the title role (Wood) is the professional entertainer in this film, her stagedoor mother Rose (Rosalind Russell) is crucial for her career. A frustrated entertainer herself, she pushed her two daughters into a vaudeville act. When sister June fled Rose's domination, dowdy Louise carried on and eventually found her calling as a classy stripper, Gypsy Rose Lee. After a brief rebellion, Gypsy Rose is reconciled with her mother and all ends happily. Even good girls can be strippers.

It Happened in Athens TCF	Andrew Marton	JAYNE MANSFIELD Actress
Jumbo MGM	Charles Walters	DORIS DAY Singer/Circus
My Geisha PARA	Jack Cardiff	SHIRLEY MACLAINE Actress
Satan in High Heels COSMIC	Jerald Intrator	MEG MYLES Carnival
State Fair TCF	Jose Ferrer	ANN-MARGRET Singer/Dancer
Sweet Bird of Youth MGM	Richard Brooks	GERALDINE PAGE Actress
Two Tickets to Paris COL	Greg Garrison	LISA JAMES Dancer
1963 *Bye Bye Birdie* COL	George Sidney	JANET LEIGH ANN-MARGRET Singer/Dancer
Dime with a Halo MGM	Boris Sagal	BARBARA LUNA Stripper
Follow the Boys MGM	Richard Thorpe	CONNIE FRANCIS
Greenwich Village Story SHAWN	Jack O'Connell	MELINDA PLANK Ballerina
How the West Was Won MGM	John Ford	DEBBIE REYNOLDS Dancehall Singer

I Could Go On Singing UA Ronald Neame		JUDY GARLAND Singer
Island of Love WB Morton Dacosta		BETTY BRUCE Stripper
My Six Loves PARA Gower Champion		DEBBIE REYNOLDS Actress
Shock Corridor AA Samuel Fuller		CONSTANCE TOWERS Stripper
The Stripper TCF Franklin Schaffner		JOANNE WOODWARD
1964	*Adorable Julia* SEVENARTS Alfred Weidenmann	LILLI PALMER Actress
	Bedtime Story UI Ralph Levy	SHIRLEY JONES TV Actress
	The Carpetbaggers PARA Edward Dmytryk	CARROLL BAKER Movie Star
	Circus World PARA Henry Hathaway	CLAUDIA CARDINALE RITA HAYWORTH Circus
	The Pleasure Seekers TCF Jean Negulesco	ANN-MARGRET Singer/Dancer
1965	*Dear Brigitte* TCF Henry Koster	BRIGITTE BARDOT Movie Star
	Harlow PARA Gordon Douglas	CARROLL BAKER Actress
	Harlow MAGNA Alex Segal	CAROL LYNLEY Actress
	The Hot Bed TAP Harry Epstein	JOSETTE Exotic Dancer
	Inside Daisy Clover WB Robert Mulligan	NATALIE WOOD Actress

Once a Thief		ANN-MARGRET
MGM	Ralph Nelson	Night Club Singer
The Rounders		SUE ANN LANGDON
MGM	Burt Kennedy	Stripper
Three Weeks of Love		TAMIKO AYA
POLIMER	William E. Brusseau	Actress

1966

Blindfold		CLAUDIA CARDINALE
UNIV	Philip Dunne	Chorus Girl
Boy, Did I Get a Wrong Number		ELKE SOMMER
UA	George Marshall	Actress
The Drifter		SADJA MARR
FM	Alex Matter	Cafe Singer
Gunpoint		JOAN STALEY
UNIV	Earl Bellamy	Dancehall Girl
Harper		SHELLEY WINTERS
WB	Jack Smight	Actress
Lord Love a Duck		TUESDAY WELD
UA	George Axelrod	Actress
Mister Buddwing		SUZANNE PLESHETTE
MGM	Delbert Mann	Actress
Mozambique		VIVI BACH
SEVENARTS	Robert Lynn	Night Club Singer
Plastic Dome of Norma Jean		SHARON HENESY
J.COMPTON	Juleen Compton	Psychic

1967

The Cool Ones		DEBBIE WATSON
WB	Gene Nelson	Singer
Enter Laughing		ELAINE MAY
COL	Carl Reiner	Actress
Frank's Great Adventure		MONIQUE VON VOOREN
JERICHO	Phil Kaufman	Singer
Good Times		CHER BONO
COL	Charles Lamont	Singer

Gunn		LAURA DEVON
PARA	Blake Edwards	Singer
Hostile Guns		YVONNE DE CARLO
PARA	R. G. Springsteen	Dancehall Hostess
Jack of Diamonds		ZSA ZSA GABOR
MGM	Don Taylor	Actress
The Ride to Hangman's Tree		MELODIE JOHNSON
UNIV	Al Rafkin	Singer/Dancer
Tell Me in the Sunlight		SHARY MARSHALL
MOVIERAMA	Steve Cochran	Stripper
What Am I Bid?		KRISTIN NELSON
EMERSON	Gene Lash	Singer
Woman Times Seven		SHIRLEY MACLAINE
TCF	Vittorio DeSica	Actress

1968

Dayton's Devils		LAINIE KAZAN
CUE	Jack Shea	Singer
Flesh		GERI MILLER
ANDYWARHOL	Paul Morrissey	Topless Dancer
Funny Girl		BARBRA STREISAND
COL	William Wyler	Vaudeville

Fanny Brice (Streisand) has always dreamed of being a proper married lady but discovers her gift for entertaining. Initially it seems she can have it all - fame, wealth and a beautiful if unsuccessful gambler husband. As so often, however, he is unable to cope with her success and his failure and, in the end, she finds the strength to continue her career alone. It lasts; the husband doesn't.

The Killing of Sister George		BERYL REID
CINERAMA	Robert Aldrich	SUSANNAH YORK
		Actresses
The Legend of Lylah Clare		KIM NOVAK
MGM	Robert Aldrich	Actress
Money Jungle		LOLA ALBRIGHT
CUE	Francis D. Lyon	Singer

| *The Night They Raided Minskys* | | BRITT EKLAND |
| UA | William Friedkin | Stripper |

| *Star* | | JULIE ANDREWS |
| TCF | Robert Wise | Singer/Dancer |

| *Sweet Ride* | | JACQUELINE BISSET |
| TCF | Harvey Hart | |

| *Where Were You When The Lights Went Out?* | | DORIS DAY |
| MGM | Hy Averback | Actress |

| 1969 | *Charro* | | INA BALIN |
| | NG | Charles M. Warren | Dancehall Hostess |

| | *Cockeyed Cowboys of Calico County* | | NANETTE FABRAY |
| | UNIV | Tony Leader | Singer/Dancer |

| | *Finney* | | JOAN SUNDSTROM |
| | GOLD COAST | Bill Hare | Singer |

| | *Flareup* | | RAQUEL WELCH |
| | MGM | James Nielson | Actress |

| | *Marlowe* | | GAYLE HUNNICUT |
| | MGM | Paul Bogart | Actress |

| | *Me, Natalie* | | PATTY DUKE |
| | CINC | Fred Coe | Singer |

| | *The Monitors* | | SUSAN OLIVER |
| | CUE | Jack Shea | Actress |

| | *Myra Breckinridge* | | RAQUEL WELCH |
| | TCF | Michael Sarne | Actress |

| | *Sweet Charity* | | SHIRLEY MACLAINE |
| | UNIV | Bob Fosse | Dancehall Hostess |

| | *The Trouble with Girls* | | MARILYN MASON |
| | MGM | Peter Tewksbury | Actress |

| | *Young Billy Young* | | ANGIE DICKINSON |
| | UA | Burt Kennedy | Dancehall Girl |

| 1970 | *Beyond the Valley of the Dolls* | | DOLLY REED |
| | TCF | Russ Meyer | Singer |

Darling Lily

Man From O. R. G. Y.		LOUISE MORITZ
CINEMATION	James A. Hill	Comedienne

The Only Game in Town		ELIZABETH TAYLOR
TCF	George Stevens	Chorus Girl

Trash		GERI MILLER
CINEMA V	Paul Morrissey	Go-Go Dancer

1971   *Made for Each Other*   RENEE TAYLOR
       TCF   Robert B. Bean   Actress

       Star-Spangled Girl   SANDY DUNCAN
       PARA   Jerry Paris   Actress

       Sweet Savior   RENAY GRANVILLE
       TWA   Bob Roberts   Actress

1972   *Black Girl*   LESLIE UGGAMS
       CINERAMA   Ossie Davis   Dancer

       Bluebeard   JOEY HEATHERTON
       CINERAMA   Edward Dmytryk   Singer

       Butterflies Are Free   GOLDIE HAWN
       COL   Milton Katselas   Actress

       Cabaret   LIZA MINNELLI
       AA   Bob Fosse   Singer

       Hickey and Boggs   ROSALIND CASH
       UA   Robert Culp   Go-Go Dancer

       Hit Man   PAM GRIER
       MGM   George Armitage   Actress

       Play It As It Lays   TUESDAY WELD
       UNIV   Frank Perry   Actress

       The Poseidon Adventure   CAROL LYNLEY
       TCF   Ronald Neame   Singer

       Slaughterhouse Five   VALERIE PERRINE
       UNIV   George Roy Hill   Starlet

       Trouble Man   PAULA KELLY
       TCF   Ivan Dixon   Singer

Women in Revolt		CANDY DARLING
ANDYWARHOL	Andy Warhol	Actress
1973	*Black Caesar*	GLORIA HENDRY
	AIP Larry Cohen	Singer
	The Don Is Dead	ANGEL TOMPKINS
	UNIV Richard Fleischer	Singer
	The Exorcist	ELLEN BURSTYN
	WB William Friedkin	Actress
	The Great Waltz	MARY COSTA
	MGM Andrew L. Stone	Singer
	Heat	SYLVIA MILES
	ANDYWARHOL Paul Morrissey	Actress
	Hurry Up, or I'll Be 30	LINDA DE COFF
	AE Joseph Jacoby	Actress
	Lady Sings the Blues	DIANA ROSS
	PARA Sidney J. Furie	Singer
	Paper Moon	MADELINE KAHN
	PARA Peter Bogdanovich	Carnival
	Serpico	CORNELIA SHARPE
	PARA Sidney Lumet	Dancer
1974	*Black Samson*	CONNIE STRICKLAND
	WB Charles Brill	Dancer
	Blazing Saddles	MADELINE KAHN
	WB Mel Brooks	Dancehall
	The Girl from Petrovka	GOLDIE HAWN
	UNIV Robert E. Miller	Singer
	Lenny	JAN MINER
	UA Bob Fosse	Comedienne
		VALERIE PERRINE
		Dancer
	Phantom of the Paradise	JESSICA HARPER
	TCF Brian DePalma	Singer

1975	*The Adventures of Sherlock Holmes'* *Smarter Brother*	MADELINE KAHN
	TCF Gene Wilder	Actress
	At Long Last Love	MADELINE KAHN
	TCF Peter Bogdanovich	Showgirl
	The Day of the Locust	KAREN BLACK
	PARA John Schlesinger	Actress

FACTORY WORKER

In 1930, 17.5 percent of American working women were employed in manufacturing and mechanical industries, yet the movies of the '30s do not feature women factory workers. The few films which portray such work indicate that the woman does not view it as a career, that she cannot wait to be rescued from the drudgery by a man who will support her. As the nation geared up for and entered World War II, Hollywood capitalized on the need for women workers in defense plants and made a number of films for the specific purpose of encouraging women to make this contribution to the war effort. However, these films did not take seriously the participation of women in the labor force and had no real understanding of the contribution women were making at the time. Perhaps this accounts for the frequency with which factory workers break into song and dance. The films viewed women working in defense plants as a purely temporary phenomenon, expecting that they would leave the factories to return home after the war. Post-war films about women factory workers are almost non-existent, although women continued to play an important role in manufacturing.

1931   *An American Tragedy*   SYLVIA SIDNEY
       PARA   Josef Von Sternberg

> In this adaptation of Theodore Dreiser's novel,
> Sidney's Roberta is a pathetic, sympathetic factory
> worker, seduced, impregnated, victimized and allowed
> to drown.

       Possessed   JOAN CRAWFORD
       MGM   Clarence Brown

> Crawford is never shown working in the paper box
> factory; in the first scene she is walking out of the
> factory, complaining about the hard work, determined
> to do something better with her life. Despite her
> protestations of independence, her major effort is
> directed toward finding a man to support her. Then
> her job becomes that of mistress, and she is viewed as

a commodity, an investment. She sacrifices her lover for his career, claiming, "I am just a factory girl, smelling of sweat and glue;" but the nobility of her love guarantees that she will attain the goal of marriage.

1933   *Iron Master*   LILA LEE
        AA   Chester M. Franklin

        Three-cornered Moon   CLAUDETTE COLBERT
        PARA   Elliott Nugent

1936   *Riff-Raff*   JEAN HARLOW
        MGM   J. Walter Ruben

1938   *Dramatic School*   LUISE RAINER
        MGM   Robert B. Sinclair

1942   *Priorities On Parade*   ANN MILLER
        PARA   Albert A. Rogell   BETTY RHODES

In one of the first Hollywood films to encourage women to take jobs in defense plants, a welding instructor has to assert her authority over male students but must also prove she is a woman. Rhodes convinces the members of a band to remain at work in the factory and is favorably contrasted with a singer-dancer (Ann Miller) who would not dream of doing such work. In a night club Rhodes makes a patriotic speech lauding the women who have interrupted other careers, as well as left their homes, to make their contributions to the war effort.

        The Traitor Within   JEAN PARKER
        REP   Frank McDonald

1943   *Gangway For Tomorrow*   MARGO
        RKO   John H. Auer

        Good Luck, Mr. Yates   CLAIRE TREVOR
        COL   Ray Enright

        Hers To Hold   DEANNA DURBIN
        UNIV   Frank Ryan

A rich young woman takes a job in a war plant to be near the man she loves.

        He's My Guy   IRENE HERVEY
        UNIV   Edward F. Cline

A vaudeville troupe goes to work in a defense plant, but the plot revolves around a contretemps between a husband-wife team.

Swing Shift Maisie   ANN SOTHERN
MGM   N. Z. McLeod

Swingtime Johnny   ANDREWS SISTERS
UNIV   Edward F. Cline

Tender Comrade   GINGER ROGERS
RKO   Edward Dmytryk

Four "war wives" set up house together for the duration of the war. At the beginning there is a scene at Douglas Aircraft, where they work as welders and riveters, but the rest of the action takes place in the house they share, and the rest of their conversation concerns their men. Rogers's husband had not allowed her to work before the war, but now it is necessary. However, he has explicitly told her that his job is being held for him and that after the war everything will be like before; she will quit work and "We'll have that kid when it is all over."

1944   *I Love A Soldier*   PAULETTE GODDARD
       PARA   Mark Sandrich

Goddard takes pride in her expertise as a welder. She spends all day working in a shipyard and a good part of the night dancing with servicemen, considering both activities her contribution to the war effort. The film's climax is her decision to marry a soldier.

Meet The People   LUCILLE BALL
MGM   Charles Reisner

A Broadway star comes to a factory to sell war bonds, and stays on to be a riveter. Other workers resent the publicity she receives, until she learns the sincerity and the importance of the effort all the workers are making.

Rosie The Riveter   JANE FRAZEE
REP   Joseph Santley

The plot revolves around the wartime room shortage; Frazee and her sidekick (Vera Vague) work the day

shift at an airplane factory and share one room with
two men who work the night shift, which meets with
Frazee's boyfriend's disapproval. However, she
develops her own independence, learns to rivet, and
puts on musical shows at the factory.

Since You Went Away   CLAUDETTE COLBERT
UA   John Cromwell

In the best of the "home front" films, Colbert, who
was nominated for best actress, is the loyal, loving
wife who writes every night to her soldier husband,
even when he is missing in action. At one point she
writes, "I hope you won't be too shocked when you
learn I am actually training for work in a shipyard.
Yes, tremendous changes are taking place in the
pampered woman, and I am doing nicely. I am training
to be a lady welder." The scene showing her learning
to weld consumes less than ten seconds, and there is
no further mention of her factory work, except for a
reference to a conversation with a foreign-born
co-worker.

Sweethearts of The U.S.A.   UNA MERKEL
MONO   Lew Collins

The Very Thought Of You   ELEANOR PARKER
WB   Delmar Daves

A working-class woman is employed in a parachute
factory, and there is one brief scene in which she and
a co-worker (Faye Emerson) are shown folding
parachutes. Otherwise the focal points of the film
are romance, marriage to a soldier, and pregnancy.
Child care is easily found, and the worker eagerly
awaits the return of her husband and the end of the
factory work.

1945   *Sensation Hunters*   DORIS MERRICK
        MONO   Christy Cabanne

1951   *A Place In The Sun*   SHELLEY WINTERS
        PARA   George Stevens

In this remake of *An American Tragedy*, Winters gets
second billing after Elizabeth Taylor but she was
nominated for the Best Actress Oscar. Her role is
important as an example of naive, uneducated young
women who left the farm to come to town and for whom

factory work is the only respectable employment
opportunity. She hopes for marriage to rescue her
from the monotony of work and from loneliness.
Looking drab, sad and distracted on the production
line, she also goes to the movies alone and is easy
prey for seduction. She still dresses like a
schoolgirl, wearing loafers and bobby sox and is
jealous of women who are richer and prettier than she.
Always meek, mousy and subservient when trying to get
and keep her man, she is led by the desperation of
pregnancy to threaten to expose their affair and ruin
her lover's career if he does not marry her. She
meets the tragic fate of victims whom society thinks
can be tossed aside.

He Ran All The Way   SHELLEY WINTERS
UA   John Berry

1952   *Jet Job*   ELENA VERDUGO
       MONO   William Beaudine

1954   *Carmen Jones*   DOROTHY DANDRIDGE
       TCF   Otto Preminger

After the fight in the parachute factory in the first
scene, Dandridge does not set foot in a factory, but
depends on men to support her.

1956   *Carousel*   SHIRLEY JONES
       TCF   Henry King

Although she is not shown working, there is reference
early in the film to the fact that Jones's character,
Julie, works in a cotton mill. "All Bascom's girls
have to be respectable," so they all live in the
mill-run boarding house, where there is a strict
curfew. She loses her job because she stays out late.
After her marriage to Billy (Gordon MacRae) their
troubles arise because he cannot find work, yet
nothing is said about her returning to work. When
Billy returns from heaven years later and sees that
Julie has "managed all right," there is no indication
of how she has supported herself and her daughter.

1957   *The Pajama Game*   DORIS DAY
       WB   G. Abbott/S. Donen

Day is a union member (chairman of the grievance
committee) and sewing machine operator who takes her

work seriously. When it comes to choosing between her
lover and the union, she sticks with the latter; but
love and an hourly raise both come to fruition. The
implication is she will both marry and continue with
the company, a happy union of labor and management.

1967   *Who's Minding the Mint?*   DOROTHY PROVINE
        COL   Howard Morris

In this case the factory is the U.S. Bureau of
Engraving; the product manufactured is money. Provine
is a dimwit who cuts the money into bills and who
tries to woo a fellow worker by making fudge for him.
She agrees to help him print extra money to pay back
some he accidentally destroyed, because she would do
anything to win his heart and get a husband. She has
dreamed of their working side by side, planning for
the future. But she balks when she learns money will
be stolen, and she proves to be the one with
principles, and one who will get her man after all.

FASHION INDUSTRY/MODEL

The fashion industry might seem to be an area where women could make it big in the movies, as some have done in reality, but roles as designers or heads of fashion houses are rare.

Model is considered as glamorous an occupation as actress, with the model often struggling at the beginning, impecunious, waiting for a big break. Or sometimes she is an aspiring actress, just taking modeling jobs until she gets a break in the theatre.

1930	*On Your Back*		IRENE RICH
	TCF	Guthrie McClintic	
1931	*Bought*		CONSTANCE BENNETT
	WB	Archie Mayo	
	The Common Law		CONSTANCE BENNETT
	RKO	Paul L. Stein	
	Inspiration		GRETA GARBO
	MGM	Clarence Brown	
	Kiss Me Again		BERNICE CLAIRE
	FN	William A. Seiter	
	The Reckless Hour		DOROTHY MACKAILL
	FN	John F. Dillon	
	The Woman Between		LILI DAMITA
	RKO	V. Schertzinger	
1932	*Forbidden Company*		SALLY BLANE
	CHESTERF	Richard Thorpe	
	Pleasure		FRANCES DADE
	ARTCLASS	Otto Brower	

Sinners in the Sun PARA Alexander Hall		CAROLE LOMBARD
Strange Case Of Clara Deane PARA Louis Gasnier		WYNNE GIBSON
1933	*Employee's Entrance* WB Roy Del Ruth	LORETTA YOUNG
	Her Resale Value MAYFAIR Breezy Eason	JUNE CLYDE
	She Had To Say Yes FN Busby Berkeley	LORETTA YOUNG
1934	*The Affairs of Cellini* UA Gregory LaCava	FAY WRAY
	Blind Date COL Roy Willian Neill	ANN SOTHERN
	Fashions Of 1934 WB William Dieterle	BETTE DAVIS
	Red Head MONO Melville Brown	GRACE BRADLEY
1935	*Dressed To Thrill* TCF Harry Lachman	TUTTA ROLF
	Feather in Her Hat COL Alfred Santell	PAULINE LORD
	Roberta RKO William A. Seiter	IRENE DUNNE HELEN WESTLEY

In this film Ginger Rogers palms herself off as European nobility, but Irene Dunne gets top billing as real nobility, an aristocratic Russian exile reduced to working as the assistant to Madame Roberta, the famous Paris couturiere. However, the princess does not bemoan her reduced circumstances; she is an able assistant and good businesswoman and has been designing all the clothes under Roberta's label. Worldly and sophisticated, she takes Roberta's naive nephew John in hand when he inherits the business, and, although they become partners, she runs everything. She leaves the firm after quarreling with John over a dress for his girlfriend; however, she returns to save the reputation of the company.

1936	*The Bride Walks Out* RKO Leigh Jason	BARBARA STANWYCK
	Don't Gamble With Love COL Dudley Murphy	ANN SOTHERN
	The Golden Arrow WB Alfred E. Green	BETTE DAVIS
	His Brother's Wife MGM W. S. Van Dyke II	BARBARA STANWYCK
	Smartest Girl In Town RKO Joseph Santley	ANN SOTHERN
	They Met In A Taxi COL Alfred E. Green	FAY WRAY
1937	*Artists And Models* PARA Raoul Walsh	IDA LUPINO
	Dangerously Yours TCF Mal St. Clair	PHYLLIS BROOKS
	Double Wedding MGM Richard Thorpe	MYRNA LOY

Loy is the snooty, serious fashion designer and head of a chain of dress shops who runs everyone's life, except that of the wealthy woman who is her backer. She is shown at her desk, receiving reports and fitting the wedding gown she has designed for her sister, but she is not shown designing or waiting on customers. She wears severe, tailored clothes, and in the final scene of knockabout slapstick she wears a "mannish" hat and a four-in-hand tie. Satisfied with her income, she lives well, with a staff, in a comfortable suburban house but is apparently going to give it all up to marry a free-spirited ne'er-do-well.

Girl Overboard UNIV Sidney Salkow	GLORIA STUART
Stolen Holiday WB Michael Curtiz	KAY FRANCIS
Vogues Of 1938 UA Irving Cummings	JOAN BENNETT

1938	*Mannequin* MGM Frank Borzage	JOAN CRAWFORD
	The Rage of Paris UNIV Henry Koster	DANIELLE DARRIEUX
	She Married An Artist COL Marion Gering	LULI DESTE
1939	*Hotel For Women* TCF Gregory Ratoff	LINDA DARNELL
1940	*I Take This Woman* MGM W. S. Van Dyke II	HEDY LAMARR
	Ma, He's Making Eyes At Me UNIV Harold Schuster	CONSTANCE MOORE
	Secrets Of A Model CP Sam Newfield	SHARON LEE
1942	*Careful, Soft Shoulders* TCF Oliver H. P. Garrett	VIRGINIA BRUCE
1943	*Follies Girl* PRC William Rowland	WENDY BARRIE
	Reunion In France MGM Jules Dassin	JOAN CRAWFORD
1944	*Dead Man's Eyes* UNIV Reginald LeBorg	JEAN PARKER
1945	*Bluebeard* PRC Edgar G. Ulmer	JEAN PARKER
	Crime Doctor's Warning COL William Castle	DUSTY ANDERSON
	Easy To Look At UNIV Ford Beebe	GLORIA JEAN
	Fashion Model MONO William Beaudine	MARJORIE WEAVER
1946	*Inside Job* UNIV Jean Yarbrough	ANN RUTHERFORD

	Lover Come Back UNIV William A. Seiter	LUCILLE BALL
1947	*Daisy Kenyon* TCF Otto Preminger	JOAN CRAWFORD
1948	*The Girl From Manhattan* UA Alfred E. Green	DOROTHY LAMOUR
1949	*A Kiss In The Dark* WB Delmar Daves	JANE WYMAN
	Neptune's Daughter MGM Edward Buzzell	ESTHER WILLIAMS
1950	*A Life Of Her Own* MGM George Cukor	LANA TURNER
	Storm Warning WB Stuart Heisler	GINGER ROGERS
	Where The Sidewalk Ends TCF Otto Preminger	GENE TIERNEY
1951	*The Guy Who Came Back* TCF Joseph Newman	JOAN BENNETT
	I Can Get It For You Wholesale TCF Michael Gordon	SUSAN HAYWARD
1952	*Lovely to Look At* MGM Mervyn LeRoy	KATHRYN GRAYSON
	Models Inc. MPC Reginald LeBorg	COLEEN GRAY
1953	*Affair With A Stranger* RKO Roy Rowland	JEAN SIMMONS
	The French Line RKO Lloyd Bacon	JANE RUSSELL
	Hot News AA Edward Bernds	GLORIA HENRY
	How To Marry A Millionaire TCF Jean Negulesco	MARILYN MONROE

Three models rent an elegant apartment as headquarters for trapping wealthy husbands. Bacall, recently divorced, masterminds the plan; she's the smart one; Grable is the dumb one; and Monroe is hilariously nearsighted. Since they are all working steady, they have some money to put into the caper; but after three months they have had no success and are no longer able to afford their lifestyle. They eventually catch their prey--one rich, two poor. At one point they are shown working in a fancy couturier house, so the audience is treated to a fashion show.

1954   *It Could Happen To You*   JUDY HOLLIDAY
        COL   George Cukor

        Rear Window   GRACE KELLY
        PARA   Alfred Hitchcock

Lisa (Kelly) is simply too perfect--too beautiful, too talented, too sophisticated, too high society--for her news photographer boyfriend Jeff. Her main problem is that she wants to get married, and Jeff claims she cannot join him in his rough-traveling life. Throughout the film Lisa must prove herself, prove that life to her is not "just a new dress and a lobster dinner," as Jeff thinks. She has to prove she is brave, even foolhardy, and clever enough to help solve the mystery; prove she can travel light by packing a Mark Cross overnight bag; prove she has feminine talents by making coffee. Modeling is strictly incidental to this Park Avenue debutante who never wears the same dress twice. She describes her day as lunch and cocktails, with only a short time spent modeling. When she buys Jeff a silver cigarette box and orders dinner up from "21," he says, "That's no way to spend your hard-earned money," without a hint of the sarcasm the line deserves. Since all action takes place in Jeff's apartment, she is not seen at work, but she does model her nightgown and peignoir for him. In the end she is wearing blue jeans, presumably ready to take off on a dangerous assignment with Jeff, but she is reading *Vogue*.

1955   *Artists And Models*   SHIRLEY MACLAINE
        PARA   Frank Taslin

        The Looters   JULIE ADAMS
        UNIV   Abner Bibberman

The Seven Year Itch   MARILYN MONROE
TCF   Billy Wilder

Monroe is not seen at work, but her work is shown in a
photograph of her in a revealing two-piece bathing
suit which appears in a slick camera magazine.
However, now she considers herself an actress because
she gets to say lines; she does a toothpaste
commercial regularly on a television program. In a
subsequent segment her trying-to-be-seductive neighbor
imagines this commercial: Monroe with a wonderfully
dazzling smile and sexy costume talking about the
toothpaste and then turning to the television audience
to warn them about what a horrible, lecherous monster
he is. Typically, Monroe is sweet, innocently
seductive and not too bright.

They Were So Young   JOHANNA MATZ
LIPPERT   Kurt Neumann

1956 *Nightfall*   ANNE BANCROFT
COL   Jacques Tourneur

1957 *Designing Woman*   LAUREN BACALL
MGM   Vincente Minnelli

This weak attempt at a take-off on *Woman of the Year*
has the sportswriter with uncouth friends married to a
chic fashion designer with unlikeable show business
friends. Instead of the story depending on his
jealousy of her celebrity, the real problem is her
jealousy of his former girlfriend. In the first scene
Bacall is shown painting a dress design, and when the
sportswriter, who knows she works but does not know at
what, first sees her sketching, their conversation is:
He: "What's that?" She: "Sketch for a dress.
That's what I do." He: "For a living?" When he
describes her to his former girlfriend, it's only a
physical description, with mention of her stylish
clothes, but he does not report that she is a
designer. Viewing her elegant apartment, he is amazed
at "the fact that you live like this just from drawing
those little pictures." Bacall remarks often that she
loves her work, and she is shown in various scenes
designing, selecting fabrics or working with the dress
on a model. She also designs the costumes for a
Broadway show. As in *Woman of the Year*, there is also
an issue with her name, although here it causes less
friction: she informs her maid she is Mrs. Hagen now,

but she continues to use her maiden name professionally. Her husband does not object, but when he tries to reach her on the phone, he first asks for Mrs. Michael Hagen, and then corrects himself, "no, Miss Marilla Brown." When Bacall and the ex-girlfriend make up their differences, the girlfriend refers to her as Mrs. Hagen in order to compliment her.

1957   *Funny Face*   AUDREY HEPBURN
       PARA   Stanley Donen

A fashion photographer turns a plain, mousy, intellectual bookstore clerk into a high fashion model in Paris. Though constantly complaining, "This just isn't me," she comes to love the limelight, and the phony intellectual life of Paris. She gets back down to earth in the photographer's arms. Though she cannot sing or dance, Hepburn lends her usual charm and grace to this musical.

1958   *Raw Wind In Eden*   ESTHER WILLIAMS
       UNIV   Richard Wilson

       The Restless Years   TERESA WRIGHT
       UNIV   Helmut Kautner

1960   *A Dog Of Flanders*   MONIQUE AHRENS
       TCF   James B. Clark

       Weddings And Babies   VIVECA LINDFORS
       M.ENGEL   Morris Engel

1961   *Bachelor Flat*   CELESTE HOLM
       TCF   Frank Tashlin

       Back Street   SUSAN HAYWARD
       UI   David Miller

In this remake Hayward runs a store but expresses her desire to be a fashion designer. The Marine who falls in love with her encourages her to pursue her dream of becoming famous and having her own salon. Missing her opportunity for marriage, she sells her store and gets a job with a designer in New York. Her career is a very important aspect of the film as she moves up in the fashion world, eventually becoming a partner in her famous boss's firm and establishing salons in Rome and Paris. The Marine, now a department store owner, applauds her success; but, despite that success, when she becomes his mistress, she permits him to buy her a house in the country. His wife tries to ruin Hayward's business as well as her reputation, and Hayward is forced to pay a price for behavior which is not approved by society. "You cannot break the rules; you cannot live your own life; you cannot ignore the world," she admits. She feels everyone is laughing at her because the affair has become sordid, and she loses her lover. But her comfort is that his children remain with her after his death.

	No Love For Johnnie		MARY PEACH
	EMBASSY	Ralph Thomas	
1962	*The Interns*		SUZY PARKER
	COL	David Swift	
	If A Man Answers		PAMELA SEARLE
	UNIV	Henry Levin	
1963	*An Affair Of The Skin*		VIVECA LINDFORS
	ZENITH	Ben Maddow	
	A New Kind Of Love		JOANNE WOODWARD
	PARA	Melville Shavelson	
1966	*Made In Paris*		ANN-MARGRET
	MGM	Boris Sagal	
	The Oscar		ELKE SOMMER
	PARA	Russel Rouse	
1967	*Round Trip*		ELLEN FAISON
	CP	Pierre D. Gaisseau	
1968	*The Pink Jungle*		EVA RENZI
	UNIV	Delbert Mann	
1969	*The Appointment*		ANOUK AIMEE
	MGM	Sidney Lumet	
	Goodbye Columbus		ALI MCGRAW
	PARA	Larry Pierce	
	John and Mary		SUNNY GRIFFIN
	TCF	Peter Yates	
	Number One		JESSICA WALTERS
	UA	Tom Gries	

1970	*Whirlpool* CINEMATION J. R. Larrath	VIVIAN NEYES
1971	*The Love Machine* COL Jack Haley, Jr.	JODI WEXLER
	Puzzle Of A Downfall Child UNIV Jerry Schatzberg	FAYE DUNAWAY
1972	*Portnoy's Complaint* WB Ernest Lehman	KAREN BLACK
1973	*Ciao! Manhattan* MARON John Palmer	EDIE SEDGWICK
	L'amour ALTURA Andy Warhol	JANE FORTH
	Two People UNIV Robert Wise	LINDSAY WAGNER
1975	*Friday Foster* AIP Arthur Marks	PAM GRIER
	Mahogany PARA Barry Gordy	DIANA ROSS

An aspiring dress designer works as a secretary in a Chicago department store but is mistaken for a model by a fashion photographer. He brings her to Rome where she becomes the rage as a model, all the while aiming to be a designer. As a design student she was always unconventional and unable to sell her designs in Chicago. In Rome she is a woman with a dream, and she models her own design at a charity auction instead of the gown assigned to her. Although people deride her extravagant design, a rich aristocrat purchases her dress and sets her up in business. Her first show is a smash, but she gives it all up to return to her lover, a Chicago black activist and politician. Although early in their relationship she had complained that he did not think her career was important, she now agrees to work in his campaigns, stick by his side and support him in his beliefs. Evidently success as a model, then designer, in Rome was not her true goal. Success is bad for you, the film says; it is better to work for your people. Ross designed the costumes to this film and sings the theme song, "Do You Know Where You're Going To?"

GAMBLER

The lady gambler is really a businesswoman, who is usually associated with a man for support and respectability. By the end of the film, she has usually given up this independence for love.

1933	*The House On 56th Street* WB Robert Florey	KAY FRANCIS
	Tillie And Gus PARA Francis Martin	ALISON SKIPWORTH
1934	*Gambling* TCF Rowland V. Lee	WYNNE GIBSON
	Gambling Lady WB Archie Mayo	BARBARA STANWYCK
1935	*Barbary Coast* S GOLDWYN Howard Hawks	MIRIAM HOPKINS
	Black Sheep TCF Allan Dwan	CLAIRE TREVOR
1941	*The Lady Eve* PARA Preston Sturges	BARBARA STANWYCK

The credits show a cartoon slobbering snake, so we already know woman equals sin in this film. Stanwyck is a con woman who, with her father as partner, gambles with and cheats passengers on an ocean liner. She is very seductive, and in addition to victims she is also looking for a man for herself. "My ideal is a little short guy with lots of money," she says; "so he will look up to me and I will be his ideal." But she realizes if a woman waits for a man to propose, she will die of "old maidhood;" thus women have to be adventuresses. She falls in love with a rich victim and ends up doing the ethical thing.

1942   *Lady For A Night*   JOAN BLONDELL
        REP   Leigh Jason

This film might better be categorized as businesswoman, since Blondell runs a gambling boat in the
Mississippi but is never shown gambling herself. She
does, however, entertain the customers with song and
dance. Wanting to be respectable, she marries an
impecunious aristocrat but is never accepted by
Memphis society. After she is acquitted of murder in
the case of her husband's accidental death, her former
partner lures her back into the business and she
changes the name of his King's Club to the Queen's
Club.

        Wild Bill Hickok Rides   CONSTANCE BENNETT
        WB   Ray Enright

        Win Town   CONSTANCE BENNETT
        UNIV   Ray Enright

1943   *Silver Queen*   PRISCILLA LANE
        UA   Lloyd Bacon

1946   *California*   BARBARA STANWYCK
        PARA   John Farrow

1949   *The Lady Gambles*   BARBARA STANWYCK
        UNIV   Michael Gordon

1950   *Bandit Queen*   BARBARA BRITTON
        LIPPERT   William Berke

1951   *Belle Le Grand*   VERA RALSTON
        REP   Allan Dwan

        Frenchie   SHELLEY WINTERS
        UNIV   Louis King

        Little Egypt   RHONDA FLEMING
        UNIV   Frederick DeCordova

1952   *Apache War Smoke*   GLENDA FARRELL
        MGM   Harold Kress

1956   *The Birds And The Bees*   MITZI GAYNOR
        PARA   Norman Taurog

1957   *The Buckskin Lady*   PATRICIA MEDINA
       UA   Clark K. Hittleman

1966   *A Big Hand For The Little Lady*   JOANNE WOODWARD
       WB   Fielder Cook

A man, his wife and child happen upon a Texas hotel
where a big annual poker game is in progress. The
husband gets into the game, has lost almost all their
money, but is determined to stay in on a last hand
because he feels it cannot lose. When he has a heart
attack, his wife, who has never before played poker,
must take over the hand. Out of chips, she tries to
borrow money from the bank, using her poker hand as
collateral. She wins the pot, and only later in
another town is it revealed that it was all a scam,
and that she is a professional gambler.

GOVERNESS

Governesses are sometimes merely considered domestic servants. In other films they are truly the teachers of the children in their charge.

1930   *The Man From Blankley's*   LORETTA YOUNG
        WB   Alfred E. Green

1931   *Devotion*   ANN HARDING
        RKO   Robert Milton

1934   *Jane Eyre*   VIRGINIA BRUCE
        MONO   Christy Cabanne

1935   *Two Sinners*   MARTHA SLEEPER
        REP   Arthur Lubin

1936   *13 Hours By Air*   ZASU PITTS
        PARA   Mitchell Leisen

        Professional Soldier   GLORIA STUART
        TCF   Tay Garnett

1940   *All This And Heaven Too*   BETTE DAVIS
        WB   Anatole Litvak

Davis is an Englishwoman who comes to France as the governess in the home of a French Duke; she is to teach music, drawing, and behavior to three girls. She is also in charge of a four-year-old boy. Despite her status as the granddaughter of a Baron, she is treated as a servant by the jealous Duchess. There is some mystery concerning her birth, and for this reason she knows she will never marry. The Duke wonders why she became a governess and she claims it is because she loves children. When the Duke falls in love with her, the Duchess dismisses her and prevents her from receiving the offer of another position. After a prison sentence for complicity in the killing of the Duchess, she goes to America to teach at a girls' school.

1941   *Adam Had Four Sons*   INGRID BERGMAN
        COL   Gregory Ratoff

Bergman is the perfect governess who arrives from Sweden to care for four American boys. Although the family is surprised that the new governess is so young, she proves to be sensible and loving; the entire family comes to love and depend on her, never treating her as an inferior. After the wife dies and the husband suffers financial losses, the boys are sent away to school and Bergman is sent back to Europe. During World War I the husband regains his fortune and sends for Bergman, even though the sons are grown and in the service. But she realizes the family needs her, especially when she sacrifices herself to keep the family together and avoid heartbreak and scandal. Of course, she marries the father.

1941   *Tall Dark And Handsome*   VIRGINIA GILMORE
        TCF   Bruce Humberstone

        A Woman's Face   JOAN CRAWFORD
        MGM   George Cukor

1944   *Jane Eyre*   JOAN FONTAINE
        TCF   Robert Stevenson

        My Pal, Wolf   JILL ESMOND
        RKO   Alfred Werker

1945   *The Unseen*   GAIL RUSSELL
        PARA   Lewis Allen

1946   *Anna And The King Of Siam*   IRENE DUNNE
        TCF   John Cromwell

The printed explanation at the beginning of this biography of Anna Glenowens introduces "a young Englishwoman faced with the then difficult problem of earning her own living who had accepted a post teaching English to the children of the King of Siam." Because she is young, the King says she does not look like a scientific person, but he later decides she is sufficiently knowledgeable to teach the children and also qualified to teach English to his wives. Anna quickly learns that women simply do not exist in Siam, and the King is amazed that sometimes he can be wrong and a woman right. Although she was engaged for teaching school, she also assists the King with his correspondence, and she helps him understand concepts of liberty and justice. She also teaches the wives how to behave when European dignitaries come for dinner. There are many scenes of Anna in her classroom as she develops her relationship with the children.

Dragonwyck		GENE TIERNEY
TCF	Joseph Mankiewicz	

1948	*To The Ends Of The Earth*	SIGNE HASSO
	COL Robert Stevenson	

1950	*Love That Brute*	JEAN PETERS
	TCF Alexander Hall	

1956	*The Eddie Duchin Story*	VICTORIA SHAW
	COL George Sidney	

1964	*Mary Poppins*	JULIE ANDREWS
	BV Robert Stevenson	

This is an anti-feminist film, since the reason the children need a nanny is because their mother is always off trying to get the vote for women. Mary Poppins (Andrews) is shown as the better woman because she does what women are supposed to do: care for and discipline the children. The fact that she is effective more through her quasi-magical powers rather than normal abilities makes it seem that even capable women cannot really do what society expects them to do.

1965	*The Sound Of Music*	JULIE ANDREWS
	TCF Robert Wise	

Maria (Andrews) is a novice nun sent to be governess to the Baron's seven children. Evidently the children go to school when it is not summer, but Maria, although she is not a teacher, is expected to drill them in their studies. At least she teaches them music. Often behaving with the exuberance of a child herself, she is wise and understands what the children are experiencing as they grow up. By mid-picture, she

is their step-mother. Andrews received a Best Actress
nomination for this film.

1972 *Every Little Crook And Nanny*   LYNN REDGRAVE
      MGM   Cy Howard

471-33

GOVERNMENT OFFICIAL

During the 1930-1975 period there were very few women in political office; therefore it is not surprising that it is rare to see women politicians or elected officials in Hollywood movies.

1939   *Ninotchka*   GRETA GARBO
        MGM   Ernst Lubitsch

Garbo shows she can be dead-pan funny as the Envoy Extraordinary from the Soviet Board of Trade who comes to Paris to handle the sale of jewels confiscated from a Russian Duchess. When the other Russian agents who are bungling the job get word that an envoy is coming, they expect a man and are surprised and delighted to find her. If they had known, they would have greeted her with flowers, but she protests, "Don't make an issue of my womanhood. We are here for working." A former sergeant in the cavalry, she insists on carrying her own bags and does not want to stay in a fancy hotel. In her unfashionable masculine suit and low-heeled oxfords, she is a fast stair-climber. Love changes all this, as she buys a fashionable, even silly, hat and puts on lipsticks and gets tipsy on champagne. But she is willing to give up her lover in order to obtain money for bread for the Russian people. Though much of the communist revolution is ridiculed here, Garbo is presented as admirable for not betraying her ideals and for her devotion to duty. But then, that's only until her lover can get her out of Russia again.

1948   *A Foreign Affair*   JEAN ARTHUR
        PARA   Billy Wilder

As a Congresswoman on a fact-finding mission to post-war Berlin to check on the morale of the troops, Arthur is efficient, serious, and businesslike. When the commanding officer comments that it is "delightful

of Congress to send us a lady for a change," she
retorts that he can dispense with the soft soap. With
her severe hairdo and "a face like a scrubbed kitchen
floor," she disapproves of fraternizing with the
Germans. When an officer kisses her, she can only
pull herself together by stating, "I am a Congresswoman. I am here on official business." The other
Congressmen do not believe Cupid has struck; "No,"
they say, "we know Miss Frost. You cannot shoot an
arrow through steel." But of course she gives up her
frosty reserve for love, admitting that before, as a
Congresswoman, she was "just drifting."

1949   *All the King's Men*   MERCEDES MCCAMBRIDGE
        COL   Robert Rossen

As a political operative, McCambridge is highly
influential in the manipulation and election of Willie
Stark. She is tough, opportunistic, and cynical,
obviously an Eastern outsider in the little Southern
towns. She grabs a bottle of liquor like one of the
boys, and her mannish suits are only slightly offset
by her more feminine hats. She has a soft spot for
Willie, regarding him with affection as well as
shrewdness, and her loyalty to him is as fierce as
that of his long-suffering wife. After his election,
she is constantly with him, but her role has become
less assertive; she is always shown slightly behind
him, framed by his other (male) cronies. Relegated to
the title of "secretary," she still calls some of the
shots; but as it becomes clear that she is his
mistress, she talks less, appears to have less power.
She cannot be poised, beautiful, and desirable like
her rival Anne (Joanne Dru) anymore than she can be
good and self-sacrificing like Mrs. Stark. So she
cannot be a woman; she can only operate in a man's
world by acting like a man. This role earned
McCambridge the Best Supporting Actress Oscar,
although hers is really the lead role.

1951   *Goodbye My Fancy*   JOAN CRAWFORD
        WB   Vincent Sherman

1953   *Call Me Madam*   ETHEL MERMAN
        TCF   Walter Lang

Merman is her wonderfully brassy self in this film
based loosely on the appointment of Perle Mesta as
Ambassador to Luxembourg. To ridicule such an

appointment, the Ambassador is depicted as so ignorant she doesn't know where the country to which she is Ambassador is located; upon being presented to the Grand Duke, she falls flat on her rear end. Her idea of being a good Ambassador is to send chicken soup to the Grand Duke when he is indisposed, but she finally gets around to reading the Foreign Service book and starts running the embassy, taking over from the fussy charge d'affaires who disapproves of a woman Ambassador. She wants the President to be proud of her, but she is more concerned about her fancy clothes and knock-your-eyes-out jewels, and wants to look terrific for the Foreign Minister, with whom she has fallen in love. Though she gets fired, all ends well, because she gets her man.

1964   *Kisses for My President*   POLLY BERGEN
        WB   Curtis Bernhardt

This film is very insulting to women, but not because of the way it depicts a woman President of the United States. Leslie Harrison (Bergen) was elected by 40 million women (apparently no man voted for her), and she is shown as a well-qualified and competent President. She is shrewd and has no trouble outsmarting a ludicrous Latin American dictator. She refuses to be intimidated by a powerful Senator, who, despite her professional demeanor, smarmily greets her with "It is a pleasure to see so lovely creature behind that noble desk." The "joke" here is that her husband is the First Lady, and by focussing on his role as an aberration, the film proclaims that a woman President is just as ridiculous a notion. Harrison is so outside her womanly role that her husband never gets a chance to make love to her; they are always interrupted by the telephone, and Harrison must leave the bedroom to solve some crisis. So how do the film makers solve the dilemma of a capable husband with nothing to do as "First Lady"? They get the President pregnant, so she has to resign because the strenuous demands of her office might cause her to lose the baby, and family comes first. This gets everyone back in the role they should have stayed in. As her husband points out: "Chalk it up to the superiority of man. It took 40 million women to get you into the White House;" and she good-humoredly finishes the sentence: "And only one man to get me out."

1964   *The Prize*   **ELKE SOMMER**
        MGM   Mark Robson

INTERIOR DECORATOR

Despite its popularity as a profession for women, interior design occurs rarely as the occupation of the main female character in Hollywood films. And in only one, *Pillow Talk*, is her work a concern of the film and the primary aspect of her life.

1931	*My Sin* PARA	George Abbott	TALLULAH BANKHEAD
1934	*Gallant Lady* UA	Gregory LaCava	ANN HARDING
1947	*Out Of The Blue* EL	Leigh Jason	ANN DVORAK
1954	*Witness To Murder* UA	Roy Rowland	BARBARA STANWYCK
1959	*Pillow Talk* UNIV	Michael Gordon	DORIS DAY

This comedy includes numerous scenes of Day at work, at the shop, at the office of a client, at various dealers selecting items, at the home of a client, at a client's party. There are many other references to her work; she informs the telephone company she cannot tolerate a party line because she must call clients; she refers to someone as a client, and the response is, "Client? You a lawyer or something?" Her boss compliments her work and a client refers to her as the most talented girl he ever met. Because she is a professional and lives alone, her party-line nemesis assumes she is sexually repressed, that she brightens up her drab, empty life by listening in on the party line. When he hires her to decorate his apartment, she wants to refuse but agrees so her boss will not lose the business. "I am a decorator," she tells the client; "you are a client; I am here because you are paying for my professional services." This, of course, leads to romance.

1961 *Goodbye Again*   INGRID BERGMAN
     UA   Anatole Litvak

JOURNALIST

The "sob sister" early became a staple of Hollywood fiction,
with a plethora of women reporters running around getting
scoops in the films of the 30's. The Torchy Blane series of
six films in the 30's was extremely popular, particularly in
small towns, where the average filmgoer for the first time
became aware of journalism as a profession for women. All
too often, however, the attitude toward the newspaper world
is ambiguous; it is shown as an inappropriately cynical and
exploitative world for women, yet reporting is depicted as
glamorous work. Usually the woman's primary problem is a
conflict between the motivation to demonstrate that she is
capable "newspaperman" and the desire for a "normal" life as
a wife.

1930	*The Divorcee*		NORMA SHEARER
	MGM	Robert Z. Leonard	
	King Of Jazz		LAURA LAPLANTE
	UNIV	John Murray	
	Young Man Of Manhattan		CLAUDETTE COLBERT
	PARA	Monta Bell	
1931	*Cimarron*		IRENE DUNNE
	RKO	Wesley Ruggles	
	Dance, Fools, Dance		JOAN CRAWFORD
	MGM	Harry Beaumont	

Crawford is a spoiled devil-may-care rich girl whose
family goes broke, so she takes a job as a newspaper
reporter. Her fellow reporters think she got the job
because she is a "good looker," but she realizes she
has to learn and becomes buddies with a more
experienced male reporter. Her former suitor is
surprised when he hears she is working, and she does
not want her friends to know where she is working; she
does not want to go back to this old crowd. "You

don't know the thrill of trying to make it on your own," she claims. In order to investigate the mob, she masquerades as a moll-cum-dancer and gets a job in a night club. She learns responsibility and ethics, and therefore does not demur in exposing her brother as a member of the mob. She leaves the newspaper after earning respect and marries her suitor.

The Finger Points		FAY WRAY
FN	John F. Dillon	
Five Star Final		ONA MUNSON
WB	Mervyn LeRoy	
Sob Sister		LINDA WATKINS
TCF	Alfred Santell	
Up For Murder		GENEVIEVE TOBIN
UNIV	Monta Bell	
Up Pops The Devil		LILYAN TASHMAN
PARA	A. E. Sutherland	
1932	*The Famous Ferguson Case*	JOAN BLONDELL
WB	Lloyd Bacon	
The Final Edition		MAE CLARKE
COL	Howard Higgins	
Forbidden		BARBARA STANWYCK
COL	Frank Capra	
She Wanted a Millionaire		UNA MERKEL
TCF	John G. Blystone	
1933	*Clear All Wires*	BENITA HUME
MGM	George Hill	
Devil's Mate		PEGGY SHANNON
MONO	Phil Rosen	
Headline Shooters		FRANCES DEE
RKO	Otto Brower	
High Gear		JOAN MARSH
GOLDSMITH	Leigh Jason	
The Mad Game		CLAIRE TREVOR
TCF	Irving Cumming	

	The Mystery Of The Wax Museum WB Michael Curtiz	GLENDA FARRELL
	Picture Snatcher WB Lloyd Bacon	ALICE WHITE
	A Shriek In The Night M.HOFFMAN Albert Ray	GINGER ROGERS
	The Sphinx MONO Phil Rosen	SHEILA TERRY
	Strange Adventure MONO Phil Whitman	JUNE CLYDE
1934	*Hi, Nellie!* WB Mervyn LeRoy	GLENDA FARRELL
	Hold That Girl TCF Hamilton MacFadden	CLAIRE TREVOR
	Last Trail TCF James Tinling	CLAIRE TREVOR
	Name the Woman COL Albert Rogell	ARLINE JUDGE
	Orient Express TCF Paul Martin	DOROTHY BURGESS
	The Quitters FD Richard Thorpe	EMMA DUNN
	Whirlpool COL Roy William Neill	LILA LEE
1935	*After Office Hours* MGM Robert Z. Leonard	CONSTANCE BENNETT
	The Daring Young Man TCF William A. Seiter	MAE CLARKE
	Death From a Distance INVINCIBLE Frank Strayer	LOLA LANE
	Men Without Names PARA Ralph Murphy	MADGE EVANS

Murder Man MGM	Tim Whelan	VIRGINIA BRUCE
Reckless Road MAJESTIC	Burt Lynwood	JUDITH ALLEN
The Payoff WB	Robert Florey	PATRICIA ELLIS
Too Tough To Kill COL	D. Ross Lederman	SALLY O'NEIL
Under Pressure TCF	Raoul Walsh	FLORENCE RICE

1936

Big Brown Eyes PARA	Raoul Walsh	JOAN BENNETT
Brilliant Marriage INVINCIBLE	Phil Rosen	INEZ COURTNEY
Bulldog Edition REP	Charles Lamont	EVALYN KNAPP
Cheers of the Crowd MONO	Vin Moore	IRENE WARE
Front Page Woman WB	Michael Curtiz	BETTE DAVIS

Davis is totally inexperienced and naive but determined to make it as a newspaperman. Her colleagues wonder why she works when she doesn't have to and tell her women make lousy newspapermen. The other woman reporter is fat, ugly, dresses like a man and drinks with the boys. Davis wears a fox stole and looks like a society girl. She is clever, but is never shown as competent as her boyfriend, who wants her to marry him and forget the newspaper business. They get involved in a professional rivalry, and she agrees to give up her career if she proves she is a good newspaperman. The boyfriend asserts, "I'm going to teach her once and for all that a woman's place is in the home," and tricks her mercilessly. She's always a step behind him, but she gets the scoop and is praised: "Now that's being a good newspaperman." With this compliment she is ready to give it all up for marriage.

Human Cargo   CLAIRE TREVOR
TCF   Allan Dwan

Mr. Deeds Goes To Town   JEAN ARTHUR
COL   Frank Capra

This film depicts the metamorphosis of a woman from a reporter with aggressive, traditionally male characteristics to a weak, passive bride-to-be, carried out of the courtroom (i.e. out of the corrupt newsroom of the big, bad city) in the arms of her male rescuer. Arthur uses the oldest trick in the book to get the attention of a country bumpkin with a large inheritance who shuns the press. She is merciless in her exploitation of him, all the while excoriating herself for being so manipulative, claiming she has to get out of this rotten business. His idealism prevails over her cynicism, and it's off to a bucolic life in the country.

Smart Blonde   GLENDA FARRELL
WB   Frank McDonald

Thirty-Six Hours To Live   GLORIA STUART
TCF   Eugene Forde

We're Only Human   JANE WYATT
RKO   James Flood

1937   *The Adventurous Blonde*   GLENDA FARRELL
WB   Frank McDonald

Back In Circulation   JOAN BLONDELL
WB   Ray Enright

Behind the Headlines   DIANA GIBSON
RKO   Richard Rosson

Beware of Ladies   JUDITH ALLEN
REP   Irving Pichel

Conflict   JEAN ROGERS
UNIV   David Howard

Criminals of the Air   ROSALIND KEITH
COL   C. C. Coleman, Jr.

The Devil Is Driving   JOAN PERRY
COL   Harry Lachman

Espionage		MADGE EVANS
MGM	Kurt Neumann	
Exclusive		FRANCES FARMER
PARA	Alexander Hall	
Fly Away Baby		GLENDA FARRELL
WB	Frank McDonald	
It Can't Last Forever		BETTY FURNESS
COL	Hamilton MacFadden	
Laughing At Trouble		JANE DARWELL
TCF	Frank R. Strayer	
Marry The Girl		MARY BOLAND
WB	William McGann	
One Mile From Heaven		CLAIRE TREVOR
TCF	Allan Dwan	
Parole Racket		ROSALIND KEITH
COL	C. C. Coleman, Jr.	
Public Cowboy Number 1		ANN RUTHERFORD
REP	Joseph Kane	
Special Agent K-7		QUEENIE SMITH
SYNDICATE	Raymond K. Johnson	
Step Lively, Jeeves		PATRICIA ELLIS
TCF	Eugene Forde	
That's My Story		CLAUDIA MORGAN
UNIV	Sidney Salkow	
There Goes My Girl		ANN SOTHERN
RKO	Ben Holmes	
Trouble In Morocco		MAE CLARKE
COL	Ernest Schoedsack	
Wild Money		LOUISE CAMPBELL
PARA	Louis King	
Woman in Distress		IRENE HERVEY
COL	Lynn Shores	

Women Men Marry		JOSEPHINE HUTCHINSON
MGM	Errol Taggert	
1938	*Arson Gang Busters*	ROSALIND KEITH
	REP	Joseph Kane	
Blondes at Work		GLENDA FARRELL
WB	Frank McDonald	
Exposed		GLENDA FARRELL
UNIV	Harold Schuster	
Four's A Crowd		ROSALIND RUSSELL
WB	Michael Curtiz	
International Crime		ASTRID ALLWYN
GN	Charles Lamont	
Jury's Secret		FAY WRAY
UNIV	Roy W. Hill	
Mr. Moto's Gamble		LYNN BARI
TCF	James Tinling	
No Time to Marry		MARY ASTOR
COL	Harry Lachman	
One Wild Night		JUNE LANG
TCF	Eugene Forde	
Personal Secretary		JOY HODGES
UNIV	Otis Garrett	
Red Barry		FRANCES ROBINSON
UNIV	Ford Beebe/A. James	
Strange Faces		DOROTHEA KENT
UNIV	Errol Taggert	
Tenth Avenue Kid		BEVERLY ROBERTS
REP	Bernard Vorhaus	
Torchy Blane In Panama		LOLA LANE
WB	William Beaudine	
Torchy Gets Her Man		GLENDA FARRELL
WB	William Beaudine	

1939	*The Adventures Of Jane Arden* WB Terry Morse	ROSELLA TOWNE
	Mr. Wong In Chinatown MONO William Nigh	MARJORIE REYNOLDS
	News Is Made At Night TCF Alfred Werker	LYNN BARI
	Newsboys' Home UNIV Harold Young	WENDY BARRIE
	North Of Shanghai COL D. Ross Nederman	BETTY FURNESS
	Off The Record WB James Flood	JOAN BLONDELL
	Sued For Libel RKO Leslie Goodwins	LINDA HAYES
	They Asked For It UNIV Frank McDonald	JOY HODGES
	Timber Stampede RKO David Howard	MARJORIE REYNOLDS
	Torchy Blane In Chinatown WB William Beaudine	GLENDA FARRELL
	Torchy Plays With Dynamite WB Noel Smith	JANE WYMAN
	Torchy Runs For Mayor WB Ray McCarey	GLENDA FARRELL
	Winner Take All TCF Otto Brower	GLORIA STUART
1940	*Arise My Love* PARA M. Leisen	CLAUDETTE COLBERT
	The Bride Wore Crutches TCF Shepard Traube	LYNNE ROBERTS
	City Of Chance TCF Ricardo Cortez	LYNN BARI

Double Alibi   MARGARET LINDSAY
UNIV   Philip Rosen

Emergency Squad   LOUISE CAMPBELL
PARA   Edward Dymtryk

His Girl Friday   ROSALIND RUSSELL
COL   Howard Hawks

The most famous woman-as-newspaperman comedy of the all features an adrogynous Russell at home in the jailhouse newsroom, wearing man-tailored suits and a hat just like her fellow newshounds. Though she protests she is going to quit this rotten business and settle down with an insurance salesman in Albany, her colleagues laugh at the notion of Hildy "washing out didies." Printer's ink is in her blood, and her editor (and ex-husband) desperately needs her to get a scoop, help free a condemned prisoner and embarrass the local political machine. She accomplishes all this in her own rough-and-tumble way and ends up sending the insurance salesman back to Albany so she can have another honeymoon with the editor, a honeymoon which will simply consist of getting another story.

The Invisible Killer   GRACE BRADLEY
PRODPIC   Sherman Scott

The Leather-Pushers   ASTRID ALLWYN
UNIV   John Rawlins

Meet The Wildcat   MARGARET LINDSAY
UNIV   Arthur Lubin

Outside The Three-Mile Limit   IRENE WARE
COL   Lewis D. Collins

Third Finger Left Hand   MYRNA LOY
MGM   Robert Z. Leonard

1941 *Behind The News*   DORIS DAVENPORT
REP   Joseph Santley

The Big Boss   GLORIA DICKSON
COL   Charles Barton

Borrowed Hero MONO Lewis Collins		FLORENCE RICE
City Of Missing Girls SELECT Elmer Clifton		ASTRID ALLWYN
The Great Mr. Nobody WB Ben Stoloff		JOAN LESLIE
I Wanted Wings PARA Mitchell Leisen		CONSTANCE MOORE
Jesse James At Bay REP Joseph Kane		SALLY PAYNE
Man At Large TCF Eugene Forde		MARJORIE WEAVER
Meet John Doe LIBERTY Frank Capra		BARBARA STANWYCK

A smart reporter who has been writing a "lavendar and old lace" column creates a John Doe to represent idealism and bring hope to a Depression-ridden people. Originally she does it for money, and she cynically accepts the luxuries and limited power the fascist publisher offers her. While she's in charge of the development of the John Doe club she is a good politico as well as a journalist, but eventually Doe's idealism seduces her and she is reduced to a sniveling, lovesick hysteric who begs Doe not to sacrifice himself. She, however, is willing to sacrifice her career to try to build something good with him.

Mr. District Attorney REP William Morgan		FLORENCE RICE
Mystery Ship COL Lew Landers		LOLA LANE
No Greater Sin UNIVERSITY William Nigh		LUANA WALTERS
Phantom Submarine COL Lional Banks		ANITA LOUISE
Sealed Lips UNIV George Waggner		JUNE CLYDE

Sleepers West		LYNN BARI
TCF	Eugene Forde	
The Smiling Ghost		BRENDA MARSHALL
WB	Lewis Seiler	

1942 *Cairo*   JEANETTE MACDONALD
      MGM   W. S. Van Dyke II

The Carter Case		VIRGINIA GILMORE
REP	Bernard Vorhaus	
The Corpse Vanishes		LUANA WALTERS
MON	Wallace Fox	
The Falcon Takes Over		LYNN BARI
RKO	Irving Reis	
The Falcon's Brother		JANE RANDOLPH
RKO	Stanley Logan	
Just Off Broadway		MARJORIE WEAVER
TCF	Herbert L. Leeds	
The Lady Has Plans		PAULETTE GODDARD
PARA	Sidney Lanfield	
Murder In The Big House		FAYE EMERSON
WB	B. Reeves Eason	
Pardon My Stripes		SHEILA RYAN
REP	John H. Auer	
Phantom Killer		JOAN WOODBURY
MONO	William Beaudine	
Somewhere I'll Find You		LANA TURNER
MGM	Wesley Ruggles	
Who Is Hope Schuyler?		SHEILA RYAN
TCF	Thomas Z. Loring	
Woman of the Year		KATHARINE HEPBURN
MGM	George Stevens	

In this first Hepburn-Tracy pairing, sportswriter Tracy claims, "The Woman of the Year" isn't really a woman at all. Why? Because she won't stay home with the child she has adopted without consulting her

husband.   A   famous   international   reporter   and
columnist, "The number two dame in the country after
Mrs. Roosevelt," Hepburn speaks several languages and
is ever so classy compared to slightly uncouth Tracy,
yet she seduces him with her ignorance of baseball.
She barely finds time to fit a wedding into her busy
schedule, and insists that they live in her apartment
because everybody knows her address.   She refuses to
change her name, an act which is symbolic of her
dominant position and which finally forces Tracy to
walk out.   Her attempt at a reconciliation consist of
a hilarious effort at cooking, a scene which implies
that she isn't a real woman because she does not know
how to separate eggs.   To win back her husband she
agrees to compromise, and she will use both her name
and his.

	You Can't Escape Forever	BRENDA MARSHALL
	WB Jo Graham	
1943	*The Apeman*	LOUISE CURRIE
	MONO William Beaudine	
	Night For Crime	GLENDA FARRELL
	PRC Alexis Thurn-Taxis	
	Passport To Suez	ANN SAVAGE
	COL Andre DeToth	
	Power of the Press	GLORIA DICKSON
	COL Lew Landers	
	Secrets of the Underground	VIRGINIA GREY
	REP William Morgan	
	Sundown Kid	LINDA JOHNSON
	REP Elmer Clifton	
	Whistling In Brooklyn	JEAN ROGERS
	MGM S. Sylvan Simon	
1944	*The Contender*	ARLINE JUDGE
	PRC Sam Neufield	
	The Fighting Seabees	SUSAN HAYWARD
	REP Edward Ludwig	
	Lady In The Dark	GINGER ROGERS
	PARA Mitchell Leisen	

Lifeboat   TALLULAH BANKHEAD
TCF   Alfred Hitchcock

Bankhead is a famous reporter who manages to have her
typewriter and movie camera with her on board the
lifeboat; she films the other survivors reaching the
boat and then is accused of callously viewing the
whole disaster as material for her next book. She is
one of the strongest, most capable and sensible people
on board, keeping the ship's log, making decisions,
finally laughing at her distress over losing all her
possessions. She is obviously a survivor, and a
professional who attempts to practice her profession
even drifting in a lifeboat.

Mark Of The Whistler   JANIS CARTER
COL   William Castle

One Mysterious Night   JANIS CARTER
COL   Oscar Boetticher

1945   *Christmas In Connecticut*   BARBARA STANWYCK
       WB   Peter Godfrey

       I Ring Doorbells   ANNE GWYNNE
       PRC   Frank Strayer

       One Exciting Night   ANN SAVAGE
       PARA   William C. Thomas

       Rogues Gallery   ROBIN RAYMOND
       PRC   Albert Herman

1946   *Badman's Territory*   ANN RICHARDS
       RKO   Tim Whelan

       Deadline For Murder   SHEILA RYAN
       TCF   James Tinling

       One More Tomorrow   ANN SHERIDAN
       WB   Peter Godfrey

       Perilous Holiday   RUTH WARRICK
       COL   Edward H. Griffith

       The Searching Wind   SYLVIA SIDNEY
       PARA   William Dieterle

Young Widow UA Edwin L. Marin		JANE RUSSELL

1947   *Big Town After Dark*   HILLARY BROOKE
       PARA   William C. Thomas

       The Corpse Came COD   JOAN BLONDELL
       COL   Henry Levin

       Danger Street   JANE WITHERS
       PARA   Lew Landers

       Dishonored Lady   HEDY LAMARR
       UA   Robert Stevenson

       I Cover Big Town   HILLARY BROOKE
       PARA   William C. Thomas

       Magic Town   JANE WYMAN
       RKO   William A. Wellman

Wyman runs, but does not own, a small-town newspaper;
and while she might be categorized as an executive,
she seems to do everything, including write stories.
Trained by her father, the previous editor, she is
authoritative, and an important citizen of the town,
determined to push through a plan for a new civic
center. A principled person, she will not let the
smooth-talking pollster who comes to town talk her out
of a story which makes her a "bad guy" to the town.
Ever courageous, she and the pollster pull the town
together as they fall in love.

       The Senator Was Indiscrete   ELLA RAINES
       UNIV   George S. Kaufman

       The Trouble With Women   TERESA WRIGHT
       PARA   Sidney Lanfield

1948   *Behind Locked Doors*   LUCILLE BREMER
       EL   Oscar Boetticher

       Big Town Scandle   HILLARY BROOKE
       PARA   William C. Thomas

       Blonde Ice   LESLIE BROOKS
       FILMCLASS   Jack Bernhard

The Fatal Hour MONO William Nigh	MARJORIE REYNOLDS
The Gallant Legion REP Joseph Kane	ADRIAN BOOTH
June Bride WB Bretaigne Windust	BETTE DAVIS
Scandal Sheet COL Nick Grinde	ONA MUNSON
State Of The Union MGM Frank Capra	ANGELA LANSBURY
Two-Fisted Rangers COL Joseph Lewis	IRIS MEREDITH

1949   *Duke of Chicago* — AUDREY LONG
REP   George Blair

Follow Me Quietly — DOROTHY PATRICK
RKO   Richard Fleischer

The Fountainhead — PATRICIA NEAL
WB   King Vidor

In this drama based loosely on the career of Frank Lloyd Wright, Neal is primarily the love interest and her role as a professional woman for a small part of the film practically goes unnoticed. Neal is the daughter of a famous architect who writes a minor architecture column for a daily newspaper but spends most of her time on her father's estate. She quits in protest when the paper condemns the work of an architect she thinks is brilliant. Although she falls in love with the architect, she marries the newspaper publisher. Later when the publisher courageously decides to support the architect against public opinion, she asks for her old job back, saying now she is proud to work for the paper. Since th staff has quit, she, her husband and one loyal employee courageously put out the newspaper.

The House Across The Street — JANIS PAIGE
WB   Richard Bare

Ride, Ryder, Ride! — PEGGY STEWARD
EL   Lewis D. Collins

Tough Assignment   MARJORIE STEELE
LIPPERT   William Beaudine

1950   *Hoedown*   JEFF DONNELL
       COL   Ray Nazarro

       Three Secrets   PATRICIA NEAL
       WB   Robet Wise

       To Please A Lady   BARBARA STANWYCK
       MGM   C. Brown

1951   *Angels In The Outfield*   JANET LEIGH
       MGM   Clarence Brown

       Cave of Outlaws   ALEXIS SMITH
       UNIV   William Castle

       Lone Star   AVA GARDNER
       MGM   Vincent Sherman

       Superman And The Mole Men   PHYLLIS COATES
       LIPPERT   Lee Sholem

       The Texas Rangers   GALE STORM
       COL   Phil Karlson

1952   *Assignment Paris*   MARTA TOREN
       COL   Robert Parrish

       Park Row   MARY WELCH
       UA   Samuel Fuller

       Scandal Sheet   DONNA REED
       COL   Phil Karlson

       Washington Story   PATRICIA NEAL
       MGM   Robert Pirosh

1953   *Down Among The Sheltering Palms*   GLORIA DE HAVEN
       TCF   Edmund Goulding

       Sabre Jet   COLEEN GRAY
       UA   Louis King

       Shadows of Tombstone   JEANNE COOPER
       REP   William Witney

	Sky Commando		FRANCES GIFFORD
	COL	Fred F. Sears	
	A Tale of Five Women		BARBARA KELLY
	UA	Romollo Marcellini	
1954	*Living It Up*		JANET LEIGH
	PARA	Norman Taurog	
	Make Haste To Live		DOROTHY MCGUIRE
	REP	William A. Seiter	
	Playgirl		SHELLEY WINTERS
	UNIV	Joseph Penney	
	The Scarlet Spear		MARTHA HYER
	UA	George Breakston	
1955	*Texas Lady*		CLAUDETTE COLBERT
	RKO	Tim Whelan	
1956	*High Society*		CELESTE HOLM
	MGM	Charles Walters	
	Run For The Sun		JANE GREER
	UA	Roy Boulting	
	Satellite In The Sky		LOIS MAXWELL
	WB	Paul Dickson	
	While The City Sleeps		IDA LUPINO
	RKO	Fritz Lang	
1957	*Beginning Of The End*		PEGGY CASTLE
	REP	Bert I. Gordon	
	Crime Of Passion		BARBARA STANWYCK
	UA	Gerd Oswald	
	The Land Unkown		SHAWN SMITH
	UNIV	Virgil Vogel	
	Top Secret Affair		SUSAN HAYWARD
	WB	H. C. Potter	
	Undersea Girl		MARA CORDAY
	AA	John Peysee	

1958	*Another Time, Another Place* PARA Lewis Allen	LANA TURNER
	Blood of Dracula AIP Herbert L. Strock	LOUISE LEWIS
1959	*Beloved Infidel* TCF Henry King	DEBORAH KERR
	The Best Of Everything TCF Jean Negulesco	HOPE LANGE JOAN CRAWFORD
1960	*College Confidential* UI Albert Zugsmith	JAYNE MEADOWS
1961	*All Hands On Deck* TCF Norman Taurog	BARBARA EDEN
1964	*Flight From Ashiya* UA Michael Anderson	SHIRLEY KNIGHT
	Youngblood Hawke WB Delmer Daves	SUZANNE PLESHETTE
1965	*The Great Race* WB Blake Edwards	NATALIE WOOD

Early in the century a Nellie Bly-like reporter covers an around-the-world automobile race. She is considered an oddity as a woman journalist, but she shares the drivers' crazy adventures and winds up with the winner.

1968	*Interlude* COL Kevin Billington	BARBARA FERRIS
1969	*The Love God?* UNIV Nat Hiken	ANNE FRANCIS
1972	*Stand Up And Be Counted* COL Jackie Cooper	JACQUELINE BISSET
1973	*Lost Horizon* COL Charles Jarrott	SALLY KELLERMAN
	Sisters AIP Brian DePalma	JENNIFER SALT

1974   *The Towering Inferno*   FAYE DUNAWAY
        TCF   John Guillermin

1975   *Friday Foster*   PAM GRIER
        AIP   Arthur Marks

LAW ENFORCEMENT

Women's prison movies, one of the most exploitative genres ever conceived, have their women wardens, but since women police officers are such a recent phenomenon, they are not seen in movies until the 1970s. Even then, their roles are subsidiary, and they are shown doing much less real police work than their counterparts on television.

| 1930 | *Conspiracy* | | BESSIE LOVE |
| | RKO | Christy Cabanne | |

| 1931 | *Enemies of the Law* | | MARY NOLAN |
| | INDEP | Lawrence C. Windom | |

| | *The Vice Squad* | | KAY FRANCIS |
| | PARA | John Cromwell | |

| 1933 | *The Nuisance* | | MADGE EVANS |
| | MGM | Jack Conway | |

| 1934 | *Woman Unafraid* | | LUCILE GLEASON |
| | GOLDSMITH | William J. Cowan | |

| 1935 | *We're In The Money* | | JOAN BLONDELL |
| | WB | Ray Enright | |

| 1936 | *Wanted: Jane Turner* | | GLORIA STUART |
| | RKO | Edward Killy | |

| | *Yellow Cargo* | | ELEANOR HUNT |
| | GN | Crane Wilbur | |

| 1937 | *Bank Alarm* | | ELEANOR HUNT |
| | GN | Louis Gasnier | |

| | *China Passage* | | CONSTANCE WORTH |
| | RKO | Edward Killy | |

Girl From Scotland Yard PARA Robert Vignola	KAREN MORLEY
The Gold Racket GN Louis J. Gasnier	ELEANOR HUNT
Murder Goes To College PARA Charles Riesner	LYNNE OVERMAN
Navy Spy GN Crane Wilbur	ELEANOR HUNT
Condemned Women RKO Lew Landers	ESTHER DALE
Delinquent Parents TIMES Nick Grinde	HELEN MACKELLAR

1938   *Held For Ransom*   BLANCHE MCLAFFEY
       GN   Clarence Buckee

       Women in Prison   SARAH PADDEN
       COL   Lambert Hillyer

1939   *The Amazing Mr. Williams*   JOAN BLONDELL
       COL   Alexander Hall

       Overland Mail   JEAN JOYCE
       MONO   Robert Hill

       Society Smugglers   IRENE HERVEY
       UNIV   Joe May

       A Woman Is The Judge   FRIEDA INESCOURT
       COL   Nick Grinde

1940   *Convicted Woman*   FRIEDA INESCOURT
       COL   Nick Grinde

       Enemy Agent   HELEN VINSON
       UNIV   Lew Landers

1942   *Design For Scandal*   ROSALIND RUSSELL
       MGM   Norman Taurog

       Holt Of The Secret Service   EVELYN BRENT
       COL

1943   *Always A Bridesmaid*   GRACE MCDONALD
        UNIV   Erle C. Kenton

        Good Morning Judge   LOUISE ALLBRITTON
        UNIV   Jean Yarbrough

        Submarine Alert   WENDY BARRIE
        PARA   Frank MacDonald

1945   *Youth On Trial*   MARY CURRIER
        COL   Oscar Boetticher

1946   *Danger Woman*   BRENDA JOYCE
        UNIV   Lewis D. Collins

        It Shouldn't Happen To A Lady   CAROLE LANDIS
        TCF   Herbert I. Leeds

1947   *The Bachelor And The Bobby-Soxer*   MYRNA LOY
        RKO   Irving Reis

        Undercover Maisie   ANN SOTHERN
        MGM   Harry Beaumont

1948   *The Paleface*   JANE RUSSELL
        PARA   Norman Z. McLeod

1949   *Tell It To The Judge*   ROSALIND RUSSELL
        COL   Norman Foster

        Trouble Preferred   PATRICIA KNUDSON
        TCF   James Tinling

1950   *Borderline*   CLAIRE TREVOR
        UI   William A. Seiter

        Caged   HOPE EMERSON
        WB   John Cromwell

        Mule Train   SHEILA RYAN
        COL   John English

        So Young, So Bad   CATHERINE MCLEOD
        UA   Bernard Verhaus

        Undercover Girl   ALEXIS SMITH
        UI   Joseph Pevney

	Woman From Headquarters REP	George Blair	VIRGINIA HUSTON
1951	*The Company She Keeps* RKO	John Cromwell	LIZABETH SCOTT
	FBI Girl LIPPERT	William Berke	AUDREY TOTTER
1952	*The Narrow Margin* RKO	Richard Fleischer	MARIE WINDSOR
	Target RKO	Stuart Gilmore	LINDA DOUGLAS
1953	*I Believe In You* UNIV	M. Ralph/B. Dearned	LELIA JOHNSON
	Trouble Along the Way WB	Michael Curtiz	DONNA REED
1954	*The Weak & The Wicked* AA	J. Lee Thompson	JEAN TAYLOR
1955	*Women's Prison* COL	Lewis Seiler	IDA LUPINO
1956	*Gunslinger* AMER REL	Roger Corman	BEVERLY GARLAND
	Swamp Woman FAVORITE	Roger Corman	CAROL MATTHEWS
	Wetbacks BANNER	Hank McCeune	NANCY GATES
1957	*The Delicate Delinquent* PARA	Don McGuire	MARTHA HYER
	Man On Fire MGM	Ranald MacDougall	INGER STEVENS
1958	*The Mugger* UA	William Berke	NAN MARTIN
1959	*Riot In Juvenile Prison* UA	Edward L. Cahn	MARCIA HENDERSON

| 1961 | *The Second Time Around* | DEBBIE REYNOLDS |
| | TCF   Vincent Sherman | |

| 1968 | *Coogan's Bluff* | SUSAN CLARK |
| | UNIV   Donald Siegel | |

| 1972 | *Fuzz* | RAQUEL WELCH |
| | UA   Richard A. Colla | |

Although she has the title Detective, Welch does no detecting in this film. She appears in four scenes: the first one introduces her to a Boston police station. Though fully covered in an ordinary coat, everyone gives her the eye. She explains that she has been sent as a decoy for rapists, but she worries that fellow officers who don't know her will think she's a hooker. In the second scene, her fellow officers play a little joke on her by sending to her a woman who comes in frequently to complain about an imaginary rapist. The third scene has her rolling around in a sleeping bag with a fellow officer in a park to cover up their stake-out as they try to catch an extortionist. In the last scene she is finally doing her job, competently, as a rapist decoy. Although one officer invites her out for coffee, there is no office romance.

| 1973 | *Cleopatra Jones* | TAMARA DOBSON |
| | WB   Jack Starrett | |

| 1974 | *The Midnight Man* | SUSAN CLARK |
| | UNIV   Roland Kibber | |

| 1975 | *Cleopatra Jones & The Casino* | TAMARA DOBSON |
| | PANAV   Chuck Bail | |

| | *Report To The Commissioner* | SUSAN BLAKELY |
| | UA   Milton Katselas | |

LAWYER

Women lawyers are as scarce in Hollywood films of 1930-1975 as they were in the law firms and courtrooms of America during that period. In 1930 women constituted 2 percent of the legal profession, and by 1970 they still represented only 4.7 percent of lawyers and judges. Most films tend to treat such professional women as smart women but rare birds.

1930	*Scarlet Pages*		ELSIE FERGUSON
	SU	Ray Enright	
1933	*Ann Carver's Profession*		FAY WRAY
	COL	Eddie Buzzell	
1934	*The Defense Rests*		JEAN ARTHUR
	COL	Lambert Hillyer	
	Two Heads on a Pillow		MIRIAM JORDAN
	LIBERTY	William Nigh	
1935	*To Beat The Band*		HELEN BRODERICK
	RKO	Ben Stoloff	
1936	*Career Woman*		CLAIRE TREVOR
	TCF	Lewis Seiler	
	The Law In Her Hands		MARGARET LINDSAY
	FN	William Clemens	
1937	*Portia On Trial*		FRIEDA INESCOURT
	REP	Geroge Nichols, Jr.	
1939	*Disbarred*		GAIL PATRICK
	PARA	Robert Florey	
	A Woman is the Judge		FRIEDA INESCOURT
	COL	Nick Grinde	
1940	*The Man Who Talked Too Much*		VIRGINIA BRUCE
	WB	Vincent Sherman	

1941	*Dangerous Lady* PRC Bernard B. Ray	JUNE STOREY
	She Couldn't Say No WB William Clemens	EVE ARDEN
1942	*Design For Scandal* MGM Norman Taurog	ROSALIND RUSSELL
1943	*Good Morning Judge* UNIV Jean Yarbrough	LOUISE ALLBRITTON
1946	*The Truth About Murder* RKO Lew Anders	BONITA GRANVILLE
1947	*Suddenly It's Spring* PARA Mitchell Leisen	PAULETTE GODDARD
1948	*Eyes Of Texas* REP William Whitney	LYNNE ROBERTS
	I, Jane Doe REP John H. Auer	RUTH HUSSEY
	Smart Woman MONO Edward A. Blatt	CONSTANCE BENNETT
	The Walls Of Jericho TCF Russell Birdwell	ANNE BAXTER
1949	*Adam's Rib* MGM George Cukor	KATHARINE HEPBURN

The issue here is equal treatment for women before the law. In this Tracy-Hepburn pairing as a legal couple, they are on opposite sides as she defends a woman accused of shooting her philandering husband. Although the marriage is based on mutual respect, the difference of opinion in the case, and Hepburn's courtroom tactics, which he considers a circus, drive them to the point of divorce. Hepburn makes her case, that "woman as the equal of man should be equal before the law," in court, but Tracy shows her that no one has the right to twist the law; and he ridicules her with, "You're so cute when you get causy." He maintains that marriage is a contract and that Hepburn has violated its terms, presumably those that oblige the wife not to excel over the husband. "I'm old fashioned," he admits; "I like two sexes. All of a sudden I don't like being married to what is known as a new woman." "Win the case and lose my husband" is Hepburn's lament, and the film's ambiguous attitude is epitomized by Tracy's famous last line "Vive la difference!"

Courtin' Trouble		VIRGINIA BELMONT
MONO	Ford Beebe	

1950	*Devil's Doorway*	PAULA RAYMOND
	MGM Anthony Mann	

	Sierra	WANDA HENDRIX
	UI Alfred E. Green	

1951	*The Groom Wore Spurs*	GINGER ROGERS
	UI Richard Whorf	

1952	*Just This Once*	JANET LEIGH
	MGM Don Weis	

1957	*God Is My Partner*	MARION ROSS
	TCF William F. Claxton	

LIBRARIAN

The librarian is generally shown as the stereotypical spinster, hushing people in the library, repressed among her books.

1937   *Navy Blues*   MARY BRIAN
        REP   Ralph Staub

1946   *Adventure*   GREER GARSON
        MGM   Victor Fleming

When a seaman loses his soul, his buddy takes him into the library to learn how to find it; instead the buddy finds love with the lovely librarian. At first she is too smart and standoffish for him, but eventually she succumbs to his charm. He appreciates her independence, though he doesn't like it when she gives him that "library look." Realizing she had been "living in a morgue," she marries, much to her friend's surprise, and there is no more talk of the library as the sailor goes back to sea. The entire film contains only the one scene of her at work in the library.

1947   *Good News*   JUNE ALLYSON
        MGM   Charles Walters

1956   *Storm Center*   BETTE DAVIS
        COL   Daniel Taradash

Davis is the respected librarian of a small town, the widow of a war hero. With no children of her own, she is like a second mother to the children of the town, but the town turns against her when she refuses to remove from the library books some parents and the Town Council consider communistic. She sticks it out and courageously proves her point concerning the dangers of censorship.

1957   *The Desk Set*   KATHARINE HEPBURN
       TCF   Walter Lang

       Hepburn and her female colleagues staff the
       information and research library of a large
       broadcasting company. They know how to find
       everything quickly and their efficiency is superior to
       the computer, the installation of which they fear will
       mean the end to their jobs. Hepburn's love affair
       with the computer expert moves along smartly too.

1962   *The Music Man*   SHIRLEY JONES
       WB   Morton DaCosta

       There is only one library scene in this film, a
       delightful musical number, "Marian the Librarian,"
       about being quiet in the library. But there are many
       references to Marian's occupation and the fact that
       she is the best-read and most cultured person in the
       small Iowa town. Being a librarian doesn't make her
       stuffy or repressed -- just selective when it comes to
       men.

       Rome Adventure   ANGIE DICKINSON
       WB   Delmer Daves   SUZANNE PLESHETTE

MILITARY

World War II naturally produced a spate of films showing
women in the armed forces. However, by far the majority of
these films are about nurses in the service. These films
are included here rather than under Nurse because emphasis is
placed on the nurses' military duties and their contribution
to the war effort. WACS and WAVES received less attention,
and their love life was generally deemed more important than
their participation in the war.

1939   *Navy Secrets*   FAY WRAY
MONO   Howard Bretherton

Panama Patrol / GN — Charles Lamont — CHARLOTTE WYNTERS

They Made Her A Spy / RKO — Jack Hively — SALLY EILERS

1941 A Yank in the RAF / TCF — Henry King — BETTY GRABLE

International Squadron / WB — Lewis Seiler — OLYMPE BRADNA

1942 Army Surgeon / RKO — A. E. Sutherland — JANE WYATT

Atlantic Convoy / COL — Lew Landers — VIRGINIA FIELD

Flying Tigers / REP — David Miller — ANNA LEE

The Navy Comes Through / RKO — Edward Sutherland — JANE WYATT

Parachute Nurse / COL — Charles Barton — MARGUERITE CHAPMAN

She's In The Army		VEDA ANN BORG
MONO	Jean Yarbrough	
This Above All		JOAN FONTAINE
TCF	Anatole Litvak	
To The Shores Of Tripoli		MAUREEN O'HARA
TCF	Bruce Humberstone	
Wings For the Woman		ANNA NEAGLE
RKO	Hubert Wilcox	

1943 | *A Guy Named Joe* | | IRENE DUNNE |
| MGM | Victor Fleming | |

| *Bomber's Moon* | | ANABELLA |
| TCF | Charles Fuhr | |

| *Cry Havoc* | | MARGARET SULLAVAN |
| MGM | Richard Thorpe | |

| *So Proudly We Hail* | | CLAUDETTE COLBERT |
| PARA | Mark Sandrich | |

1944 | *Here Come The WAVES* | | BETTY HUTTON |
| PARA | Mark Sandrich | |

| *Ladies Courageous* | | LORETTA YOUNG |
| UNIV | John Rawlins | |

| *Marine Raiders* | | RUTH HUSSEY |
| RKO | Harold Schuster | |

| *The Navy Way* | | JEAN PARKER |
| PARA | William Berke | |

| *See Here Private Hargrove* | | DONNA REED |
| MGM | Wesley Ruggles | |

| *Up In Arms* | | DINAH SHORE |
| RKO | Elliot Nugent | |

| *A WAVE, A WAC And A Marine* | | ELYSE KNOX |
| MONO | Phil Karlstein | |

1945 | *Betrayal From The East* | | NANCY KELLY |
| RKO | William Berke | |

	Keep Your Powder Dry	LANA TURNER
	MGM Edward Buzzell	
	Pride Of The Marines	ROSEMARY DECAMP
	WB Delmer Daves	
	They Were Expendable	DONNA REED
	MGM John Ford	
1946	*Homecoming*	LANA TURNER
	MGM Mervin LeRoy	
1947	*Where There's Life*	SIGNE HASSO
	PARA Sidney Lanfield	
1949	*Alaska Patrol*	HELEN WESTCOTT
	FILMCLASS Jack Bernhard	
	I Was A Male War Bride	ANN SHERIDAN
	TCF Howard Hawks	

Sheridan is a WAC officer who marries a French officer during the occupation of Europe, then finds that she cannot bring him back to the United States because the regulations state only wives of servicemen can immigrate. Sheridan is shown as a competent officer, but she is not up to the comic potential of the plot, so the funniest thing about this film is Cary Grant in a WAC uniform.

1950	*The Admiral Was a Lady*	WANDA HENDRIX
	WB Albert S. Rogell	
	Experiment Alcatraz	JOAN DIXON
	RKO Edward Cahn	
	Pygmy Island	ANN SAVAGE
	COL William Berke	
	Twelve O'Clock High	JOYCE MACKENZIE
	TCF Henry King	
1951	*Force Of Arms*	NANCY OLSON
	WB Michael Curtiz	
	G.I. Jane	JEAN PORTER
	LIPPERT Reginald LeBorg	

Leave It To The Marines LIPPERT Samuel Neufield		MARA LYNN
Operation Pacific WB George Waggner		PATRICIA NEAL
U.S.S. Teakettle TCF Henry Hathaway		JANE GREER
The Wild Blue Yonder REP Allan Dwan		VERA RALSTON

1952   *Red Snow*   CAROL MATTHEWS
        COL   B. Petroff/H. S. Franklin

        Skirts Ahoy   ESTHER WILLIAMS
        MGM   Sidney Lanfield

        Sound Off   ANN JAMES
        COL   Richard Quine

        Thunderbirds   MONA FREEMAN
        REP   John H. Auer

        WAC From Walla Walla   JUDY CANOVA
        REP   William Whitney

1953   *Battle Circus*   JUNE ALLYSON
        MGM   Richard Brooks

        Glory At Sea   JOAN RICE
        IFP   Compton Bennett

        Never Wave At A WAC   ROSALIND RUSSELL
        IA   Norman Z. McLeod

A spoiled Washington hostess, Russell joins the Army
at the suggestion of her Senator father. She takes it
as a joke, thinking she can do whatever she likes in
the Army, especially join her officer lover in Paris.
She orders her officer's bars from Tiffany's and can
in no way keep up with the other recruits, who are
shown as serious and competent, even the former
burlesque dancer (Marie Wilson). She wants out,
saying she would not make a good soldier; but then her
loyalty to the WAC and her pride in its
accomplishments well up, and she joins a new batch of
recruits.

1954   *Flight Nurse*   JOAN LESLIE
        REP   Allan Dwan

        Francis Joins The WACS   JULIE ADAMS
        UI   Arthur Lubin

        The mule has a better role in this film than any of
        the women, but the officers and women in this WAC
        battalion prove that women in uniform are serious
        business, good for other things beside kitchen and
        clerical work; and they do not like for men to
        demonstrate any superiority.

1955   *The Crooked Web*   MARI BLANCHARD
        COL   Nathan Juran

        Mister Roberts   BETSY PALMER
        WB   John Ford

1956   *D-Day, The Sixth of June*   DANA WYNTER
        TCF   Henry Koster

        The Lieutenant Wore Skirts   SHEREE NORTH
        TCF   Frank Tashlin

1957   *Battle Hell*   SOPHIE STEWART
        DISTCORP   Michael Anderson

        Jet Pilot   JANET LEIGH
        H.HUGHES   Joseph Von Sternberg

        Operation Mad Ball   KATHRYN GRANT
        COL   Richard Quine

        Three Brave Men   NINA FOCH
        TCF   Philip Dunne

        Time Limit   DOLORES MICHAELS
        UA   Karl Malden

1958   *No Time For Sergeants*   JEAN WILLES
        WB   Mervyn LeRoy

        South Pacific   MITZI GAYNOR
        MAGNA   Joshua Logan

        Tank Battalion   MARJORIE HELLEN
        AIP   Sherman A. Rose

1959	*Battle Flame* AA R. G. Springsteen	ELAINE EDWARDS
	Cuban Rebel Girls J.BRENNER Barry Mahon	MARIE EDMUND
	Don't Give Up The Ship PARA Norman Taurog	DINA MERRILL
	On The Beach UA Stanley Kramer	LOLA BROOKS
	Operation Petticoat UNIV Blake Edwards	JOAN O'BRIEN
	A Private's Affair TCF Raoul Walsh	BARBARA EDEN JESSE ROYCE LANDIS
	Up Periscope WB Gordon Douglas	ANDRA MARTIN
1960	*Wake Me When It's Over* TCF Mervyn LeRoy	MARGO MOORE
1961	*Circle of Deception* TCF Jack Lee	SUZY PARKER
	The Sergeant Was A Lady UNIV Bernard Glasser	VENETIA STEVENSON
1962	*The Horizontal Lieutenant* MGM Richard Thorpe	PAULA PRENTISS
1963	*Captain Newman, M.D.* UNIV David Miller	ANGIE DICKINSON

This Army nurse seems to be running her own ward until
the psychiatrist woos her into moving over to the
psychiatric ward. From then on she is subservient,
simply part of his team, never with any authority or
administrative duties; she makes no decisions. He
even sends her for coffee! His first reference to her
is, "I wouldn't want to call an attractive girl like
that a liar." Until she learns otherwise, she thinks
his "wooing" is romantic; she has checked and learned
that he is not married. Despite her two years at
Barnard, good nurse's training and experience, he
wants her for his ward because, "You are a good
looking woman. It is important to have a good looking

woman around; it gives a man incentive. One look at
your legs and any man in that ward would come through
the mattress for you." And there are many shots of
her legs. She says when the war is over she wants to
get out of the Army and have some babies. "You ought
to be pretty good at that" is his open-ended comment,
with no comment on the future of her career.

1964	*The Americanization Of Emily* MGM Arthur Hiller	JULIE ANDREWS
	Ensign Pulver WB Joshua Logan	MILLIE PERKINS
1965	*In Harm's Way* PARA Otto Preminger	JILL HAWORTH PATRICIA NEAL
	Sergeant Deadhead AIP Norman Taurog	EVE ARDEN
1966	*The Navy Vs. The Night Monsters* REALART Michall Hoey	MAMIE VAN DOREN
	Wounded In Action MYRIAD Irving Sunasky	MAURA MCGIVENEY
1968	*Nobody's Perfect* UNIV Alan Rafkin	NANCY KWAN
	The Private War of Sergeant O'Farrell UA Frank Tashlin	PHYLLIS DILLER
1970	*Catch 22* PARA Mike Nichols	PAULA PRENTISS
	Hornet's Nest UA Phil Karlson	SYLVA KOSCINA
	M.A.S.H. TCF Robert Altman	SALLY KELLERMAN

MISCELLANEOUS

Very often reviews of a motion picture reveal nothing about the occupation of the leading female role. Sometimes she is simply referred to as a "working girl" or a "career girl." Where there is no other information to go on, such roles are listed here. Many "nightclub hostess" roles also fall into the miscellaneous category when it is impossible to tell what such a designation implies, as sometimes this "hostess" is really a prostitute, sometimes a businesswoman, sometimes an entertainer.

1930	*Common Clay* TCF	Victor Fleming	CONSTANCE BENNETT
	A Man From Wyoming PARA	Rowland V. Lee	JUNE COLLYER
	Our Blushing Brides MGM	Harry Beaumont	DOROTHY SEBASTIAN
	Thirteenth Chair MGM	Tod Browning	MARGARET WYCHERLY
	The Woman Racket MGM	R. Obert/A. Kelly	BLANCHE SWEET
1931	*The Mad Parade* PARA	William Beaudine	EVELYN BRENT
	Man To Man WB	Allan Dwan	LUCILLE POWERS
	The Right of Way FN	Frank Lloyd	LORETTA YOUNG
1932	*Back Street* UNIV	John M. Stahl	IRENE DUNNE

Hat Check Girl		SALLY EILERS
TCF	Sidney Lanfield	

Honor of the Press   RITA LEROY
MAYFAIR   Breezy Eason

Madison Square Garden   MARION NIXON
PARA   Harry Joe Brown

Molly Louvain   ANN DVORAK
WB   Michael Curtiz

Three Wise Girls   JEAN HARLOW
COL   William Beaudine

1933   *Arizona To Broadway*   JOAN BENNETT
        TCF   James Tinling

        Ever In My Heart   BARBARA STANWYCK
        WB   Archie Mayo

        My Lips Betray   JEAN PARKER
        TCF   John Blystone

        Out All Night   ZASU PITTS
        UNIV   Sam Taylor

1934   *Blind Date*   ANN SOTHERN
        COL   Roy William Neill

        Coming-out Party   ALISON SKIPWORTH
        TCF   John Blystone

        Have a Heart   JEAN PARKER
        MGM   David Butler

        Lineup   MARION NIXON
        COL   Howard Higgins

1935   *Convention Girl*   ROSE HOBART
        FD   Luther Reed

        Curly Top   JANE DARWELL
        TCF   Irving Cummings

        The Good Fairy   MARGARET SULLAVAN
        UNIV   William Wyler

Rainbow Valley		LUCILLE BROWN
MONO	R. N. Bradbury	
Straight From the Heart		MARY ASTOR
UNIV	Scott R. Beal	
Stranded		KAY FRANCIS
WB	Frank Borzage	
The Woman In Red		BARBARA STANWYCK
FN	Robert Florey	

1936	*The Final Hour*		MARGUERITE CHURCHILL
	COL	D. Ross Lederman	
	Florida Special		SALLY EILERS
	PARA	Ralph Murphy	
	The Man I Marry		DORIS NOLAN
	UNIV	Ralph Murphy	
	Swing Time		GINGER ROGERS
	RKO	George Stevens	
	A Woman Rebels		KATHARINE HEPBURN
	RKO	Mark Sandrich	
1937	*Man In Blue*		NAN GREY
	UNIV	Milton Carruth	
	Midnight Court		ANN DVORAK
	WB	Frank McDonald	
	The Plainsman		JEAN ARTHUR
	PARA	Cecil B. DeMille	
	Racing Lady		ANN DVORAK
	RKO	Wallace Ford	
	The Singing Marine		DORIS WESTON
	WB	Ray Enright	
	The Thirteenth Chair		DAME MAY WHITTY
	MGM	George Seitz	
	This Way Please		BETTY GRABLE
	PARA	Robert Florey	

	Time Out For Romance TCF Malcolm St. Clair	CLAIRE TREVOR
	Westbound Mail COL Folmer Blangsted	ROSALIND KEITH
1938	*Accidents Will Happen* WB Willian Clemens	GLORIA BLONDELL
	Blind Alibi RKO Lew Landers	WHITNEY BOURNE
	The Goldwyn Follies UA George Marshall	ANDREA LEEDS
	Secret of Treasure Island COL Elmer Clifton	GWEN PAGE
	Storm In A Teacup UA Victor Saville	SARA ALLGOOD
	Swing Your Lady WB Ray Enright	LOUISE FAZENDA
	Time Out For Murder TCF Bruce Humberstone	GLORIA STUART
	When Were You Born? WB William McGann	ANNA MAY WONG
1939	*Charlie Chan In Reno* TCF Norman Foster	PHYLLIS BROOKS
	Inside Story TCF Ricardo Cortez	JEAN ROGERS
	Mountain Rhythm REP B. Reaves Eason	JUNE STOREY
	She Married A Cop REP Sidney Salkow	JEAN PARKER
	Union Pacific PARA Cecil B. DeMille	BARBARA STANWYCK
1940	*Cherokee Strip* PARA Lesley Selander	FLORENCE RICE

Comrade X		HEDY LAMARR
MGM	King Vidor	
Frontier Vengeance		BETTY MORAN
REP	Nate Watt	
Glamour For Sale		ANITA LOUISE
COL	D. Ross Lederman	
Men Against The Sky		WENDY BARRIE
RKO	Leslie Goodwins	
Opened By Mistake		JANICE LOGAN
PARA	George Archainbaud	
Saturday's Children		ANNE SHIRLEY
WB	Vincent Sherman	
South Of Pago Pago		FRANCES FARMER
UA	Alfred E. Green	
Wyoming		MARJORIE MAIN
MGM	Richard Thorpe	
Youth Will Be Served		JANE DARWELL
TCF	Otto Brower	
Zanzibar		LOLA LANE
UNIV	Harold Schuster	

1941

Blonde Comet		VIRGINIA VALE
PRC	William Beaudine	
Confirm Or Deny		JOAN BENNETT
TCF	Archie Mayo	
It Started With Eve		DEANNA DURBIN
UNIV	Henry Koster	
New Wine		ILONA MASSEY
UA	Reinhold Schunzel	
A Night At Earl Carroll's		ROSE HOBART
PARA	Kurt Neumann	

1942

Boss Of Hangtown Mesa		HELEN DEVERELL
UNIV	Joseph H. Lewis	

The Hard Way WB	Vincent Sherman	IDA LUPINO
I Married An Angel MGM	W. S. Van Dyke II	JEANETTE MACDONALD
Juke Girl WB	Curtis Bernhardt	ANN SHERIDAN
The Postman Didn't Ring TCF	Harold Schuster	BRENDA JOYCE
Three Girls About Town COL	Leigh Jason	JOAN BLONDELL

1943 *The Crystal Ball*
      UA   Elliot Nugent   PAULETTE GODDARD

      Flesh And Fantasy
      UNIV   Julien Duvivier   BETTY FIELD

      Happy Go Lucky
      PARA   Curtis Bernhardt   MARY MARTIN

      Headin' For God's Country
      REP   William Morgan   VIRGINIA DALE

      Melody Parade
      MONO   Arthur Dreifuss   MARY BETH HUGHES

      Two Senoritas From Chicago
      COL   Frank Woodruff   JOAN DAVIS

1944 *Abbott and Costello*
      UNIV   Jean Yarbrough   MARION HUTTON

      Hat Check Honey
      UNIV   Edward F. Cline   GRACE MCDONALD

      Hi Beautiful
      UNIV   Leslie Goodwins   MARTHA O'DRISCOLL

      In Our Time
      WB   Vincent Sherman   IDA LUPINO

      It Happened Tomorrow
      UA   Rene Clair   LINDA DARNELL

	Rationing MGM	Willis Goldbeck	MARJORIE MAIN
1945	*Bring On The Girls* PARA	Syndey Lanfield	VERONICA LAKE
	Jealousy REP	Gustav Machaty	JANE RANDOLPH
	The Stork Club PARA	Hal Walker	BETTY HUTTON
	This Land Of Ours UNIV	William Dieterle	MERLE OBERON
	Two O'Clock Courage RKO	Anthony Mann	ANN RUTHERFORD
	You Came Along PARA	John Farrow	LIZABETH SCOTT
1946	*Johnny Comes Flying Home* TCF	Benjamin Stoloff	MARTHA STEWART
1947	*Carnegie Hall* UA	Edgar G. Ulmer	MARSHA HUNT
	Glamorous Girl COL	Arthur Dreifuss	VIRGINIA GREY
	I'll Be Yours UI	William A. Seiter	DEANNA DURBIN
	Jungle Flight PARA	Peter Stewart	ANN SAVAGE
	Nightmare Alley TCF	Edmund Goulding	JOAN BLONDELL
1948	*Cafe Hostess* COL	Sidney Salkow	ANN DVORAK
	Enchantment RKO	Irving Reis	TERESA WRIGHT
	Kiss The Blood Off My Hands UNIV	Norman Foster	JOAN FONTAINE

	The Mating Of Millie COL Henry Lewis	EVELYN KEYES
	Sons Of Adventure REP Yakima Canutt	LYNNE ROBERTS
1949	*The Crooked Way* UA , Robert Florey	ELLEN DREW
	Homicide WB Felix Jacoves	HELEN WESTCOTT
	On The Town MGM G. Kelly/S. Donen	BETTY GARRETT
1950	*The Lawless* PARA Joseph Losey	GAIL RUSSELL
	Never A Dull Moment RKO George Marshall	IRENE DUNNE
	Stage To Tuscon COL Ralph Murphy	KAY BUCKLEY
1951	*Bedtime For Bonzo* UNIV Frederick DeCordova	DIANA LYNN
	Double Dynamite RKO Irving Cummings	JANE RUSSELL
	You Can Never Tell UNIV Lou Breslow	PEGGY DOW
1952	*Because Of You* UNIV Joseph Pevney	LORETTA YOUNG
	Don't Bother To Knock TCF Roy Baker	MARILYN MONROE
	The Green Glove UA Rudolph Mate	GERALDINE BROOKS
	Kangaroo TCF Lewis Milestone	MAUREEN O'HARA
	The Model And The Marriage Broker TCF George Cukor	THELMA RITTER

One Minute To Zero		ANN BLYTH
RKO	Tay Garnett	

Sky Full Of Moon		JAN STERLING
MGM	Norman Foster	

1953 *Beneath The Twelve Mile Reef*   TERRY MOORE
      TCF   Robert D. Webb

      Calamity Jane   DORIS DAY
      WB   David Butler

In this musical rough and tough Calamity (Day) seems
to earn her living riding shotgun on the stagecoach.
The plot focuses on her rivalry with an entertainer
with a beautiful figure, "the way a woman should be,"
as Calamity is reminded by her friend, Bill Hickok.
Bill is constantly asking her why she doesn't fix her
hair and otherwise behave like the "lady" everyone
expects a woman to be. Bill complains, "You look like
a man and you dress like a man, but you think like a
female." In the end she is wearing a very traditional
white wedding gown as she weds Bill.

      Murder Without Tears   JOYCE HOLDEN
      AA   William Beaudine

      Slight Case of Larceny   ELAINE STEWART
      MGM   Don Weis

1954 *Hell's Half Acre*   ELSA LANCHESTER
      REP   John H. Auer

      River Beat   PHYLLIS KIRK
      LIPPERT   Guy Green

      Shield For Murder   MARLA ENGLISH
      UA   E. O'Brien/H. Koch

1955 *Angela*   MARA LANE
      TCF   Dennis O'Keefe

      The Cobweb   LAUREN BACALL
      MGM   Vincente Minnelli

      Las Vegas Showdown   COLEEN GRAY
      AA   Sidney Salkow

	The Man From Bitter Ridge	MARA CORDAY
	UNIV Jack Arnold	
	The Phoenix City Story	KATHRYN GRANT
	AA Phil Karlson	
1956	*Magnificent Roughnecks*	NANCY GATES
	AA Sherman A. Rose	
	1984	JAN STERLING
	COL Michael Anderson	
1957	*The Buster Keaton Story*	ANN BLYTH
	PARA Sidney Sheldon	
	Darby's Rangers	VENETIA STEVENSON
	WB William Wellman	
	The Girl In Black Stockings	ANNE BANCROFT
	UA Howard W. Koch	
	Gun Battle At Monterey	MARY BETH HUGHES
	AA Carl Hittleman	
	Interlude	JUNE ALLYSON
	UNIV Douglas Sirk	
	Lizzie	ELEANOR PARKER
	MGM Hugo Haas	
	Silk Stockings	CYD CHARISSE
	MGM Rouben Mamoulian	
1958	*The Matchmaker*	SHIRLEY BOOTH
	PARA Joseph Anthony	
	The Roots Of Heaven	JULIETTE GRECO
	TCF John Huston	
1959	*Born To Be Loved*	CAROL MORRIS
	UNIV Hugo Haas	
1960	*The Apartment*	SHIRLEY MACLAINE
	UA Billy Wilder	

MacLaine operates an elevator, but since this is a
push-button elevator, she is unnecessary; she is
merely decorative and as dispensable as the other
hordes of women who work in the big office building.

Like the other women, she is presumed to exist for the
sexual pleasure of the men.   Portrayed as not too
bright (she is a fast typist, but cannot spell, so
she's in the elevator rather than the typing pool),
she can escape from boring work and sexual
exploitation only in the love of a decent schnook.

The Rat Race		DEBBIE REYNOLDS
PARA	Robert Mulligan	
SOS Pacific		PIER ANGELI
UI	Guy Green	
The Tingler		JUDITH EVELYN
COL	William Castle	

1961	*On The Double*		DIANA DORS
	PARA	Melville Shavelson	
	Parrish		CONNIE STEVENS
	WB	Delmer Daves	
	West Side Story		NATALIE WOOD
	UA	Robert Wise	

Maria (Wood) works in a bridal shop, but it is not
clear what she does, since the scenes in the shop only
show her singing and dancing.   However, her
girlfriends work at sewing machines, not in the front,
so it may be assumed that Maria does the same.

1962	*Experiment In Terror*		LEE REMICK
	COL	Blake Edwards	

Remick plays a bank teller threatened by an
extortionist who will kill her and her 16-year-old
sister, for whom she is responsible, if she does not
steal $100,000 from the bank for him.   She contacts
the FBI and is very sensible in cooperating with them.
She is shown working at the bank, having to act
natural with customers while wondering if one of them
might be the killer.   She is courageous in resisting
the killer's threats, and even bawls him out when he
does not show up for a rendezvous.   One interesting
point about the film is that there is no romance (one
of her male co-workers takes her to lunch and asks her
for a date, but of course she is too preoccupied to
deal with that); she does not get involved with the
FBI man who has saved her life.   In the end she only

shows love for her sister and relief at finding her safe; there is not even a scene of her thanking the FBI. Despite her unusual situation, the scenes of her work are realistic; but the mystery and the way the FBI goes about its business of solving it are the main concern.

1963   *For Love or Money*   MITZI GAYNOR
       UNIV   Michael Gorgon

       Tammy And The Doctor   SANDRA DEE
       UI   Harry Keller

1964   *Black Like Me*   EVA JESSYE
       CP   Carl Lerner

       Honeymoon Hotel   NANCY KWAN
       MGM   Henry Levin

       Seven Days In May   COLETTE JACKSON
       PARA   John Frankenheimer

1965   *Beach Ball*   CHRIS NOEL
       PARA   Lennie Weinrile

       Dear Heart   GERALDINE PAGE
       WB   Delbert Mann

Page introduces herself as a postmaster with, "I suppose I should say postmistress, but that sounds rather racy." In New York for a postmasters' convention, she is a stereotypical spinster except that she is popular with her men colleagues as well as the women, and it is revealed that she had had an affair with one of the men the year before. Otherwise, she is stereotypically lonely, thinks it's a big deal to get a new hairdo, is thrilled when she is paged in the hotel lobby and tips the bellboy to do it again; and she is obviously starved for romance.

       Joy In The Morning   YVETTE MIMIEUX
       MGM   Alex Segal

       The Loved One   ANJANETTE COMER
       MGM   Tony Richardson

       When The Boys Meet The Girls   CONNIE FRANCIS
       MGM   Alvin Ganzer

1966   *The Oscar*   ELEANOR PARKER
       PARA   Russel Rouse

1967   *Caprice*   DORIS DAY
       TCF   Frank Tashlin

       Who's Minding The Mint?   DOROTHY PROVINE
       COL   Howard Morris

1968   *Isabel*   GENEVIEVE BUJOLD
       PARA   Paul Almond

1969   *Hello Dolly*   BARBRA STREISAND
       TCF   Gene Kelly

       Take The Money And Run   JANET MARGOLIN
       PALOMAR   Woody Allen

1970   *The Baby Maker*   BARBARA HERSHEY
       NG   James Bridges

       *Suppose They Gave A War & Nobody Came*SUZANNE PLESHETTE
       ENGEL/AUER   Hy Averback

       The Way We Live Now   LINDA SIMON
       UA   Barry Brown

1971   *Desperate Characters*   SHIRLEY MACLAINE
       ITC/TDJ   Frank D. Gilroy

       Fiddler on the Roof   MOLLY PICON
       UA-MIRISCH   Norman Jewison

       A Gunfight   KAREN BLACK
       PARA   Lamont Johnson

       Minnie And Moscowitz   GENA ROWLANDS
       UNIV   John Cassavetes

       One Is A Lonely Number   TRISH VAN DEVERE
       MGM   Mel Stuart

       P. S. I Love You   MARY LOU MELLACE
       TCF   Steven Hilliard

       The Reckoning   RACHEL ROBERTS
       COL   Jack Gold

	Ruby		RUTH HURD
	SU	Dick Bartlett	
	The Ski Bum		CHARLOTTE RAMPLING
	AE	Bruce Clark	
	T. R. Baskin		CANDICE BERGEN
	PARA	Herbert Ross	
	Who Says I Can't Ride A Rainbow?		NORMA FRENCH
	TRANSVUE	Edward Mann	
1972	*The Carey Treatment*		JENNIFER O'NEILL
	MGM	Blake Edwards	
	Lady Liberty		SOPHIA LOREN
	UA	Mario Monicelli	
	They Only Kill Their Masters		KATHARINE ROSS
	MGM	James Goldstone	
1973	*40 Carats*		LIV ULLMANN
	COL	Milton Katselas	
	Hit!		GWEN WELLES
	PARA	Sidney J. Furie	
	The Legend of Hell House		PAMELA FRANKLIN
	TCF	John Hough	
1974	*Honeybaby, Honeybaby*		DIANA SANDS
	KELLY-JORDAN	Michael Schultz	
1975	*Dog Day Afternoon*		PENNY ALLEN
	WB	Sidney Lumet	
	Smile		BRENDA DI CARLO
	UA	Michael Ritchie	

MUSICIAN

Like artists and writers, women musicians rarely seem as devoted to their art as men do in the movies. Their inability to balance love and career is exacerbated by the dedication that music requires.

1930   *Dangerous Paradise*   NANCY CARROLL
        PARA   William A. Wellman

        Melody Man   ALICE DAY
        COL   William Neill

1932   *They Call It Sin*   LORETTA YOUNG
        FN   Thornton Freeland

        The Woman In Room 13   ELISSA LANDI
        TCF   Henry King

1933   *Rainbow Over Broadway*   JOAN MARSH
        CHESTERF   Richard Thorpe

1934   *The Cat and the Fiddle*   JEANETTE MACDONALD
        MGM   William K. Howard

1935   *Break Of Hearts*   KATHARINE HEPBURN
        RKO   Philip Moeller

        I Dream Too Much   LILY PONS
        RKO   John Cromwell

1937   *Rhythm in the Clouds*   PATRICIA ELLIS
        REP   John H. Auer

1939   *Intermezzo*   INGRID BERGMAN
        UA   Gregory Ratoff

1940   *My Love Came Back*   OLIVIA DE HAVILLAND
        WB   Kurt Bernhardt

Rhythm On The River   MARY MARTIN
PARA   V. Schertzinger

Victory   BETTY FIELD
PARA   John Cromwell

1941   *The Great Lie*   MARY ASTOR
       WB   Edmund Goulding

Astor plays a concert pianist and shares top billing
with Bette Davis, the wife of Astor's lover.

Lady Be Good   ANN SOTHERN
MGM   Norman Z. McLeod

Melody For Three   FAY WRAY
RKO   Erle C. Kenton

1943   *Hit Parade of 1943*   SUSAN HAYWARD
       REP   Albert S. Rogelle

Something To Shout About   JANET BLAIR
COL   Gregory Ratoff

Three Hearts For Julia   ANN SOTHERN
MGM   Richard Thorpe

1944   *Music For Millions*   JUNE ALLYSON
       MGM   Henry Koster

Song Of Russia   SUSAN PETERS
MGM   Gregory Ratoff

1945   *Out Of This World*   DIANA LYNN
       PARA   Hal Walker

Swingin' On A Rainbow   JANE FRAZEE
REP   William Beaudine

1946   *I've Always Loved You*   CATHERINE MCLEOD
       REP   Frank Borzage

Idea Girl   JULIE BISHOP
UNIV   Will Jason

1947   *Cynthia*   ELIZABETH TAYLOR
       MGM   Robert Z. Leonard

Deception   BETTE DAVIS
WB   Irving Rapper

| | *Song Of Love* | | KATHARINE HEPBURN |
| | MGM | Clarence Brown | |

| 1950 | *Never a Dull Moment* | | IRENE DUNNE |
| | RKO | George Marshall | |

| | *Prisoners in Petticoats* | | VALENTINE PERKINS |
| | REP | Philip Ford | |

| | *September Affair* | | JOAN FONTAINE |
| | PARA | William Dieterle | |

| 1951 | *Honeychile* | | JUDY CANOVA |
| | REP | R. G. Springsteen | |

| | *Too Young To Kiss* | | JUNE ALLYSON |
| | MGM | Robert Z. Leonard | |

| 1957 | *Love In The Afternoon* | | AUDREY HEPBURN |
| | AA | Billy Wilder | |

While the cello student practices at home, her detective father's client requests that she stop that dreadful noise. She is shown twice rehearsing at the Paris Conservatory. In addition, she always carries her cello case wherever she goes, and, with its awkward size, the case serves as an amusing contrast to the slim, elfin Hepburn. She has an affair with a rich American and parks the cello case in the hall outside his hotel room because she does not want him to be able to identify her. She also packs her face-hiding hat and a "borrowed" fur coat in the case in order to further confuse her lover. In the end she is given a "life sentence in New York," and her father is left with the cello case. Presumably that is the end of her career.

| 1966 | *Harper* | | JULIE HARRIS |
| | WB | Jack Smight | |

| 1967 | *Counterpoint* | | KATHRYN HAYS |
| | UNIV | Ralph Nelson | |

NURSE

As is the case with so many other professions, romance
emerges as a more prevalent theme in nurse movies than the
professional functions of the women involved. Nursing, of
course, is seen as natural for women. They don't agonize
over their professional choices, as doctors often do; it is
the personal, i.e. romantic choices that matter.

Some nurses in the armed forces are included in this category
rather than under Military because their only function is
nursing and they have no military duties, and the main focus
of the plot is their love life.

| 1930 | *Little Accident* | | ZASU PITTS |
| | UNIV | William J. Craft | |

| | *Shooting Straight* | | MARY LAWLER |
| | RKO | George Archainbaud | |

| | *War Nurse* | | JANE WALKER |
| | MGM | Edgar Selwyn | |

| 1931 | *Arrowsmith* | | HELEN HAYES |
| | GOLDWYN/UA | John Ford | |

| | *Born To Love* | | CONSTANCE BENNETT |
| | RKO | Paul Stein | |

| | *The Last Parade* | | CONSTANCE CUMMINGS |
| | COL | Erle C. Kenton | |

| | *Night Nurse* | | BARBARA STANWYCK |
| | WB | William Wellman | |

| 1932 | *A Farewell To Arms* | | HELEN HAYES |
| | PARA | Frank Borzage | |

Hayes' Catherine is a romantic who had no idea what
war was like and remarks that if she had it to do over

again, she would have married. The nurses are told
that their personal lives are the Army's and
hospital's business, and they had better behave
themselves with unquestioned morality. Thus, she must
leave when she becomes pregnant. She sacrifices
all--her profession, and then her life--for the sake
of love. She is shown only once ministering to a
patient and once carrying a tray, which seems to have
a lunch rather than medicine on it. Even when her
lover is wounded, her caring for him consists of
caresses and kisses, not medical attention.

Exposed		BARBARA KENT
INVINCIBLE	Albert Herman	
Life Begins		ALINE MCMAHON
WB	J. Flood/E. Nugent	
The Man From Yesterday		CLAUDETTE COLBERT
PARA	Berthold Viertel	
Miss Pinkerton		JOAN BLONDELL
WB	Lloyd Bacon	
Unexpected Father		ZASU PITTS
UNIV	Thornton Freeland	
1933 *Ace of Aces*		ELIZABETH ALLEN
RKO	J. Walter Ruben	
A Bedtime Story		HELEN TWELVETREES
PARA	Norman Taurog	
Emergency Girl		WYNNE GIBSON
RKO	Edward Cohn	
International House		GRACIE ALLEN
PARA	Edward Sutherland	
The Mayor Of Hell		MADGE EVANS
WB	Archie Mayo	
1934 *Against the Law*		SALLY BLANE
COL	Lambert Hillyer	
Bedside		JEAN MUIR
WB	Robert Florey	

	Men In White MGM R. Boleslavsky	ELIZABETH ALLAN
	Mystery Liner MONO Willian Nigh	ASTRID ALLWYN
	Once To Every Woman COL Lambert Hillyer	FAY WRAY
	Registered Nurse WB Robert Florey	BEBE DANIELS
	The White Parade TCF Irving Cummings	LORETTA YOUNG
1935	*Death Flies East* COL Phil Rosen	FLORENCE RICE
	The Last Outpost PARA Charles Barton	GERTRUDE MICHAEL
	Our Little Girl TCF John Robertson	ERIN O'BRIEN-MOOR
	The Right To Live WB William Keighley	PEGGY WOOD
	Society Doctor MGM George B. Seitz	VIRGINIA BRUCE
	While The Patient Slept FN Ray Enright	ALINE MACMAHON
1936	*The Crime Patrol* EMPIRE Eugene Cummings	MARY PRENTISS
	Garden Murder Case MGM Edward L. Marin	BENITA HUME
	The Road To Glory TCF Howard Hawks	JUNE LANG
	The White Angel FN William Dieterle	KAY FRANCIS
1937	*A Doctor's Diary* PARA Charles Vidor	HELEN BURGESS

A Fight To The Finish COL C. C. Coleman, Jr.		ROSALIND KEITH
Between Two Women MGM George B. Seitz		MAUREEN O'SULLIVAN
Great Hospital Mystery TCF James Tinlin		JANE DARWELL
Green Light WB Frank Borzage		MARGARET LINDSAY
Mountain Justice WB Michael Curtiz		JOSEPHINE HUTCHINSON
Nobody's Baby MGM Gus Meins		PATSY KELLY
Oh Doctor UNIV Raymond B. McCarey		DONRUE LEIGHTON
Slim WB Ray Enright		MARGARET LINDSAY
Song of the City MGM Errol Taggart		MARGARET LINDSAY
They Gave Him A Gun MGM W. S. Van Dyke II		GLADYS GEORGE
Wife, Doctor and Nurse TCF Walter Lang		VIRGINIA BRUCE

1938   *Birth of a Baby*   RUTH MATTESON
         SPECFEAT   A. E. Christie

         King of Alcatraz   GAIL PATRICK
         PARA   Robert Florey

         Mystery House   ANN SHERIDAN
         WB   Noel Smith

         Nurse From Brooklyn   SALLY EILERS
         UNIV   S. Sylvan Simon

         Pacific Liner   WENDY BARRIE
         RKO   Lew Landers

The Patient In Room 18		ANN SHERIDAN
WB	B. Connolly/C. Wilbur	
Prison Nurse		MARIAN MARSH
REP	James Cruze	
Secrets of a Nurse		HELEN MACK
UNIV	Arthur Lubin	
Yellow Jack		VIRGINIA BRUCE
MGM	George B. Seitz	

1939	*Calling Dr. Kildare*	LARAINE DAY
	MGM W. S. Van Dyke II	
	Four Girls In White	FLORENCE RICE
	MGM S. Sylvan Simon	
	Mystery Of The White Room	HELEN MACK
	UNIV Otis Garrett	
	Nurse Edith Cavell	ANNA NEAGLE
	RKO Herbert Wilcox	
	The Secret Of Dr. Kildare	LARAINE DAY
	MGM Harold S. Bucquet	
	Strange Case Of Dr Meade	BEVERLY HOLT
	COL Lewis D. Collins	
	Undercover Doctor	JANICE LOGAN
	PARA Louis King	

1940	*Dr. Kildare Goes Home*	LARAINE DAY
	MGM Harold S. Bucquet	
	Dr. Kildare's Crisis	LARAINE DAY
	MGM Harold S. Bucquet	
	Dr. Kildare's Strange Case	LARAINE DAY
	MGM Harold S. Bucquet	
	Girl From God's Country	JANE WYATT
	REP Sidney Salkow	
	The Man With Nine Lives	JO ANN SAYERS
	COL Nick Grinde	

South To Karanga UNIV Harold Schuster		LULI DESTE
Vigil In The Night RKO George Stevens		CAROLE LOMBARD
Women In War REP John H. Auer		ELSIE JANIS
1941	*Dr. Kildare's Wedding Day* MGM Harold S. Bucquet	LARAINE DAY
	Fugitive Valley MONO S. Roy Luby	JULIE DUNCAN
	The Nurse's Secret WB Noel M. Smith	LEE PATRICK
	The People Vs. Dr. Kildare MGM Harold S. Bucquet	LARAINE DAY
	Private Nurse TCF David Burton	JANE DARWELL
	Remedy For Riches RKO Erle C. Kenton	DOROTHY LOVETT
	Tall, Dark and Handsome TCF H.B. Humberstone	VIRGINIA GILMORE
	West Point Widow PARA Robert Siodmark	ANNE SHIRLEY
1942	*Bullet Scars* WB D. Ross Ledermann	ADELE LONGMIRE
	Parachute Nurse COL Charles Barton	MARGUERITE CHAPMAN
1943	*Calling Dr. Death* UNIV Reginald LeBorg	PATRICIA MORISON
	I Walked With A Zombie RKO Jaques Tourneur	FRANCES DEE
1944	*The Story Of Dr. Wassell* PARA Cecil B. DeMille	LARAINE DAY

Three Russian Girls   ANNA STEN
UA   Fedor Ozep

1945   *First Yank Into Tokyo*   BARBARA HALE
       RKO   Gordon Douglas

       House Of Dracula   MARTHA O'DRISCOLL
       UNIV   Erle C. Kenton

       Isle Of The Dead   ELLEN DREW
       RKO   Mark Robson

       Miss Susie Slagle's   VERONICA LAKE
       PARA   John Berry

1946   *The Beast With Five Fingers*   ANDREA KING
       WB   Robert Florey

       My Darling Clementine   CATHY DOWNS
       TCF   John Ford

Here is a nurse who does not perform as a nurse until
the very last moment. Downs comes to the Western town
as the sweetheart Doc Holliday left behind in the
East. We do not know she is a nurse until her rival
Chihuahua the prostitute (Linda Darnell) is shot.
Then she abandons her demure Eastern clothing with
proper petticoats, which has been contrasted with
Chihuahua's off-the-shoulder Southwestern getup, and
puts on a nurse's uniform to assist in the attempt to
save Chihuahua's life. At the end, Clementine reveals
that she will stay in Tombstone as the teacher, a
profession for which she apparently has no training.
It is certainly not clear why she will be a teacher
rather than continue nursing; maybe she will do both,
as she is represented as the good woman who will
civilize the town.

Night And Day   ALEXIS SMITH
WB   Michael Curtiz

Shock   LYNN BARI
TCF   Alfred Werker

Sister Kenny   ROSALIND RUSSELL
RKO   Dudley Nichols

This screen biography portrays Kenny as admirable in
every way. While her father wonders why she went into

nursing, since "nursing is a career for a homely woman," her doctor friend protests that she is a "born nurse" and sees that the pinnacle of her profession could be to be matron at the local hospital some day. Instead she becomes an Australian bush nurse, running her own practice and doing things like setting broken bones that ordinarily only doctors would do. Then the film becomes a saga of her fight to convince doctors that her treatment for polio is proper and effective. She gives up everything, including the man she loves (because it is clearly stated that there are no married nurses in Australia), for this fight and the children she helps. The film not only emphasizes her personal courage and ability, it points out the class distinctions in the medical profession stating, "If Sister Kenny had been a doctor, this controversy would not have gone on for thirty-five years."

1947	*Possessed* WB	Curtis Bernhardt	JOAN CRAWFORD
	Seven Were Saved PARA	William H. Pine	CATHERINE CRAIG
	A Woman's Vengeance UNIV	Zoltan Korda	JESSICA TANDY
1948	*Buried Alive* PRODPIC	Victor Halperin	BEVERLY ROBERTS
	Four Faces West UA	Alfred E. Green	FRANCES DEE
1949	*Francis* UNIV	Arthur Lubin	ZASU PITTS
	Jolson Sings Again COL	Henry Levin	BARBARA HALE
	Pinky TCF	Elia Kazan	JEANNE CRAIN
1950	*Backfire* WB	Vincent Sherman	VIRGINIA MAYO
	Chain Lightning RKO	Stuart Heusler	ELEANOR PARKER

North of the Great Divide   PENNY EDWARDS
REP   William Witney

Outside The Wall   MARILYN MAXWELL
UNIV   Crane Wilbur

The Sleeping City   COLEEN GRAY
UI   George Sherman

Tarzan and the Slave Girl   DENISE DARCEL
RKO   Lee Sholam

1951   *The Blue Veil*   JANE WYMAN
       RKO   Curtis Bernhardt

       The Fat Man   JAYNE MEADOWS
       UI   William Castle

       Half Angel   LORETTA YOUNG
       TCF   Richard Sale

       Mr. Belvedere Rings The Bell   JOANNE DRU
       TCF   Henry Koster

       Queen For A Day   EDITH MEISER
       UA   Arthur Lubin

       Sealed Cargo   CARLA BELINDA
       RKO   Alfred Werker

       Target Unknown   JOYCE HOLDEN
       UNIV   George Sherman

1952   *Battle Zone*   LINDA CHRISTIAN
       AA   Lesley Selander

       Hangman's Knot   DONNA REED
       COL   Roy Huggins

       Torpedo Alley   DOROTHY MALONE
       MONO   Lew Landers

       With A Song In My Heart   THELMA RITTER
       TCF   Walter Lang

       You For Me   JANE GREER
       MGM   Don Weis

1953   *Bad For Each Other*   DIANNE FOSTER
        COL   Irving Rapper

        Mission Over Korea   AUDREY TOTTER
        COL   Fred F. Sears

        White Witch Doctor   SUSAN HAYWARD
        TCF   Henry Hathaway

1954   *The Atomic Kid*   ELAINE DAVIS
        REP   Leslie H. Martinson

        The Command   JOAN WELDON
        WB   David Butler

        Duffy Of San Quentin   JOANNE DRU
        AA   Walter Doniger

        Pushover   DOROTHY MALONE
        COL   Richard Quine

        Rear Window   THELMA RITTER
        PARA   Alfred Hitchcock

        The Seige At Red River   JOANNE DRU
        TCF   Rudy Mate

1955   *The Left Hand Of God*   GENE TIERNEY
        TCF   Edward Dmytryk

        Not As A Stranger   OLIVIA DE HAVILLAND
        UA   Stanley Kramer

Capable operating room nurse de Havilland is courted
by a medical student who needs her money to pay his
tuition. His fellow student is appalled that he is
taking advantage of a "squarehead who is afraid of
being an old maid" and marrying someone so socially
unsuited to the role of a doctor's wife. Explaining
that she wanted to be a nurse ever since she was six
years old and saw a nurse in a blue cape, de Havilland
is professionally proficient but always refers to
herself as stupid as well as unattractive and lacking
in social graces. She drills her husband in
practicing surgical techniques and remains his
assistant after he goes into practice in a small town.
Ever sacrificing for his sake, she finally makes her
statement of independence and tells him she no longer
needs him and will have their baby on her own. The

film ends as he finally acknowledges her expertise as a nurse and her wonderful qualities as a woman.

Violent Saturday   VIRGINIA LEITH
TCF   Richard Fleischer

1956   *Invasion Of The Body Snatchers*   DANA WYNTER
AA   Don Siegal

The Proud And Profane   DEBORAH KERR
PARA   George Seaton

1957   *Abandon Ship*   MAI ZETTERLING
PARA   Richard Sale

A Farewell To Arms   JENNIFER JONES
TCF   Charles Vidor

In this remake Catherine (Jones) is even more loyal and devoted to her lover, and she suffers even more because, as the lover philosophizes, "You never get away with anything." The audience must also suffer, through a more protracted labor, stillbirth, death scene, and his weeping.

Fear Strikes Out   NORMA MOORE
PARA   Robert Mulligan

The Girl In The Kremlin   ZSA ZSA GABOR
UNIV   Russell Birdwell

Hellcats Of The Navy   NANCY DAVIS
COL   Nathan Juran

Not Of This Earth   BEVERLY GARLAND
AA   Roger Corman

That Night   ROSEMARY MURPHEY
GALAHAD   John Newland

1958   *In Love And War*   FRANCE NUYEN
TCF   Philip Dunne

Jet Attack   AUDREY TOTTER
AIP   Edward L. Cahn

Macabre   JACQUELINE SCOTT
AA   William Castle

South Pacific   MITZI GAYNOR
MAGNA   Joshua Logan

Although a hometown newspaper refers to her as
"Arkansas's own Florence Nightingale," Nellie (Gaynor)
is not seen in a nurse's uniform or doing any kind of
nursing until nearly the end of the picture.
Otherwise she wears shorts and halter or Navy fatigue
blouse and skirt, and a lovely formal gown for Emile's
party. The sailors refer to her as "a nice little
girl," and the Captain, although he asks her to spy on
Emile, really sees her primary importance as a member
of the entertainment committee, putting together a
show which will boost morale. Overcoming her
prejudices, she shows her nurturing talents can also
be turned to marriage and motherhood as she takes a
motherly attitude toward Emile's Polynesian children;
and when he returns from a dangerous mission, she
greets him by passing him a bowl of soup!

1959   *The Alligator People*   BEVERLY GARLAND
       TCF   Roy Del Ruth

       Battle Of The Coral Sea   PATRICIA CUTTS
       COL   Paul Wendkas

       Five Gates To Hell   DOLORES MICHAELS
       TCF   James Clavell

       Operation Petticoat   JOAN O'BRIEN
       UNIV   Blake Edwards

1960   *Exodus*   EVA MARIE SAINT
       UA   Otto Preminger

Widow of a war correspondent, Saint has enough money
to live comfortably, but instead has been a public
health nurse in Greece. Not wanting to be one of
those women who go through life with no purpose, she
becomes involved with Jewish refugees on Cyprus and
accompanies them to Israel. When her Jewish lover is
wounded, she tends his wound and in one dramatic scene
injects a stimulant into his heart and saves his life.

Despite her feeling of being different, she decides to stay in Israel and in the end is wearing, not a nurse's uniform, but the garb of an Israeli soldier, complete with rifle.

Terror Is A Man		GRETA THYSSEN
VALIANT	Gerry DeLeon	
1961	*The Young Doctors*	INA BALIN
	UA Phil Karlson	
1962	*Adventures Of A Young Man*	SUSAN STRASBERG
	TCF Martin Ritt	
	Escape From Zahrain	MADLYN RHUE
	PARA Ronald Neame	
	It's Only Money	JOAN O'BRIEN
	PARA Frank Tashlin	
	Jessica	ANGIE DICKINSON
	UA Jean Negulesco	
1963	*The Caretakers*	JOAN CRAWFORD
	UA Hall Bartlett	CONSTANCE FORD
	Tammy and the Doctor	SANDRA DEE
	UI Harry Keller	
1964	*Man In The Middle*	FRANCE NUYEN
	TCF Guy Hamilton	
	The New Interns	STEPHANIE POWERS
	COL John Rich	
1965	*Doctor Zhivago*	JULIE CHRISTIE
	MGM David Lean	
	Thirty-Six Hours	EVA MARIE SAINT
	MGM George Seaton	
1967	*America, Texas Style*	ADRIENNE CORRI
	PARA Andrew Marion	
	The Honey Pot	SUSAN HAYWARD
	UA Joseph Mankiewicz	
1969	*The Student Nurses*	ELAINE GIFTOS
	NW Stephanie Rothman	

1970   *Catch 22*   PAULA PRENTISS
        PARA   Mike Nichols

This cockeyed look at men at war is just about men;
the few women have only the most minor roles.
Prentiss gets top billing among the women, but she
appears less than Yossarian's Italian lover. She
appears in three scenes; one is a dream in which
Yossarian is swimming toward a pier; she appears in
her nurse's uniform (but no cap, or anything
underneath), strips it off, and stands nude on the
pier waving him in. In the second she and another
nurse whisper as they switch the bottles on a totally
bandaged patient hooked up to tubes. In the third she
is wearing a demure white bathing suit and is with
some of the men on a beach, where they witness a
horrifying scene.

        The Honeymoon Killers   SHIRLEY STOLER
        CR   Leonard Kastle

1971   *The Hospital*   DIANA RIGG
        UA   Arthur Hiller

Rigg claims to be a nurse who works at her crazy
father's hospital in Mexico, but in the film she is
just visiting the hospital where her father is a
patient; and she provides the sexual interest for the
soul-searching doctor. She reveals that she never
finished nursing school because she had a "complete
breakdown" and was an "acid head." In one scene, she
helps with CPR, and that's it for the nursing.

        Johnny Got His Gun   DIANE VARSI
        AA   R. G. Springsteen

        Summertree   BRENDA VACCARO
        COL   Anthony Newley

1972   *Revengers*   SUSAN HAYWARD
        NG   Daniel Mann

        Top Of The Heap   INGEBORG SORENSEN
        FANFARE   Chris St. John

1973   *Coffy*   PAM GRIER
        AIP   Jack Hill

Where Does It Hurt?   JO ANN PFLUG
CINERAMA   Rod Amateau

1974 *The Crazy World of Julius Vrooder*   BARBARA SEAGULL
TCF   Arthur Hiller

1975 *One Flew Over The Cuckoo's Nest*   LOUISE FLETCHER
UA   Milos Forman

This film, which presents one of the most misogynistic
portraits in Hollywood history, is enough to set the
psychiatric nursing profession back a century. Nurse
Ratchett's (Fletcher) unsmiling visage and toneless,
flat voice are more sinister than anything ever
conjured up by Boris Karloff. Cruelly exercising her
authority over men, she treats her patients like
children and takes sadistic pleasure in their
distress. Although the doctors consider her one of
the best nurses the hospital has ever had, her quiet
threats lead one patient, McMurphy, to call her
"something of a cunt," saying, "She ain't honest; she
likes a rigged game." Because her insensitivity
results in the suicide of a young patient, McMurphy
almost chokes her to death; but she recuperates and in
the end she is still on the job, a brace on her neck,
but still the same horrific creature.

The Sunshine Boys   LEE MEREDITH
MGM   Herbert Ross

PILOT

Women pilots in the movies are strong and courageous, and flying is not projected as such a glamorous profession as many people think it might be.

1933   *Christopher Strong*   KATHARINE HEPBURN
        RKO   Dorothy Arzner

The eponymous male lead is not nearly so important or captivating as the well-known female pilot played by Hepburn. Claiming she had always wanted to fly, she says she would never give up flying, whether rich or poor. With ideas for creating a new plane, she hates to stop working on it even to go to a ball. Generally she dresses in tight pants for flying, or looser pants at home, but her attire becomes more "feminine" when she becomes Strong's lover. Previously she had thought herself sexually unattractive and thus chose the lonely life of a flier. The response to her decision to enter an around-the-world race is, "Don't tell me you would do that; you're only a girl." After making international headlines, she makes her lover promise that he will always let her do what she wants to do because that is the only way she can be happy, but then she gives up high-altitude test flight at his request. When her agent accuses her of resting on her laurels instead of following her instincts as a pioneer, she wants to fly again. What do other women do who won't risk their necks flying, she wonders. She complains to Strong, "I want to get oil on my hands; . . . You have your work; I have only you." When a young woman asks for her autograph, saying, "You gave us courage for everything; you were our heroine," she realizes she must follow the family motto, "Courage conquers death," and take her own life. Because she is pregnant and independent, she must pay the supreme price of non-conformity.

1935   *Ceiling Zero*   JUNE TRAVIS
       WB   Howard Hawks

       Wings In The Dark   MYRNA LOY
       PARA   James Flood

1938   *Too Hot To Handle*   MYRNA LOY
       MGM   Jack Conway

1939   *Tail Spin*   ALICE FAYE
       TCF   Roy Del Ruth

       Women In The Wind   KAY FRANCIS
       WB   John Farrow

1940   *Isle Of Destiny*   JUNE LANG
       RKO   Elmer Clifton

1940   *Mercy Plane*   FRANCES GIFFORD
       PRODPIC   Richard Harlan

1942   *Wings And The Woman*   ANNA NEAGLE
       RKO   Herbert Wilcox

1943   *Flight For Freedom*   ROSALIND RUSSELL
       RKO   Lothar Mendes

1944   *Tarzan's Magic Fountain*   EVELYN ANKERS
       RKO   Lee Sholem

1958   *The Lady Takes A Flyer*   LANA TURNER
       UI   Danny Arnold

As a ferry pilot during World War II, Turner put in
more hours in B-17s than many combat pilots. After
the war she is a partner with a male friend in a
flight school, and they later join another friend Mike
as partners in a ferrying service. She marries Mike,
and he carries her over the threshold into the plane
they are flying on their honeymoon. But dissension
rears its ugly head when she becomes pregnant,
grounded, and jealous of a young woman pilot Mike
hires. As a fulltime mother she says, "I am not just
one of the boys anymore." Yet when she rejoins the
firm, saying, "I am a pilot, in case you have
forgotten. I know all about carburetors and
generators and valves," Mike is furious because a baby
needs its mother. She insists on flying because she
is still one-third owner of the business. Lost in

with radio trouble, and only a little fuel left, she remains calm until she runs out of gas and cannot get the canopy open to parachute out. She makes it out, but is admonished, "If you had stayed home where you belong, this never would have happened." With a kiss and happy reconciliation, the film manages to show her as a rarity: both a good mother and a good pilot.

1966   *Way, Way Out*   CONNIE STEVENS
       TCF   Gordon   Douglas

PROSTITUTE

Prostitute is a popular Hollywood role, not surprising when you consider the aura of the forbidden which surrounds this profession. Because of various forms of censorship, the fact that a woman is a prostitute is often not made clear; she appears to be a nightclub hostess or something more legitimate, and, because that is how she is identified in a review, one cannot be sure what her real role is. However, there are a number of films where the prostitute is shown at work, sometimes realistically, sometimes romanticizing the life.

1930   *Anna Christie*   GRETA GARBO
        MGM   Clarence Brown

One of the most famous prostitute movies of them all ("Garbo talks!") never shows her as a prostitute. After Anna arrives in New York looking very world-weary for a 20-year old, more and more is revealed about her past, until finally she confesses to her father and suitor that she spent two years in a house, "Yes, that kind of house." When the two men fight over her, with Matt insisting she will take his orders now, she protests, "What do you think I am, a piece of furniture? Nobody owns me, except myself. No man can tell me what to do. I am my own boss. I will earn my own living one way or another." But when Matt still wants to marry her despite her past, she insists loving him has made her clean; and she will be happy to be a sailor's wife and the "nice, decent girl" the men are always referring to.

The Bad One   DOLORES DEL RIO
UA   George Fitzmaurice

Ladies Of Leisure   BARBARA STANWYCK
COL   Frank Capra

| | *The Man Who Came Back* | | JANET GAYNOR |
| | TCF | Raoul Walsh | |

| 1931 | *The Front Page* | | MARY BRIAN |
| | UA | Lewis Milestone | |

| | *Good Sport* | | GRETA NISSEN |
| | TCF | Kenneth MacKenna | |

| | *Safe In Hell* | | DOROTHY MACKAILL |
| | FN | William Wellman | |

| | *The Sin of Madelon Claudet* | | HELEN HAYES |
| | MGM | Edgar Selwyn | |

| | *Susan Lenox* | | GRETA GARBO |
| | MGM | Robert Z. Leonard | |

| | *Travelling Husbands* | | EVELYN BRENT |
| | RKO | Paul Sloane | |

| | *Waterloo Bridge* | | MAE CLARKE |
| | UNIV | James Whale | |

| 1932 | *Attorney For the Defense* | | EVELYN BRENT |
| | COL | Irving Cummings | |

| | *Rain* | | JOAN CRAWFORD |
| | UA | Lewis Milestone | |

| | *Red Dust* | | JEAN HARLOW |
| | MGM | Victor Fleming | |

Harlow is in a little trouble with the "gendarmes" in
this French Indochina outpost, so you know immediately
what she is. Tough, but fun, she is understanding and
sticks up for other women. She doesn't want to take
Clark Gable's money because she likes him; she waits
on him, pulls his boots off, and then helps him clean
out a bullet wound. At first she's angry when he
isn't really interested in her, though he finds her "a
cute little trick"; but she ends up in his arms
although there is nothing to indicate that this might
be a permanent arrangement.

| | *Shanghai Express* | | MARLENE DIETRICH |
| | PARA | Josef Von Sternberg | |

State's Attorney RKO George Archainbaud		HELEN TWELVETREES
1933	*Bed Of Roses* RKO Gregory LaCava	CONSTANCE BENNETT
	Convention City WB Archie Mayo	JOAN BLONDELL
	Frisco Jenny FN William A. Wellman	RUTH CHATTERTON
	She Done Him Wrong PARA Lowell Sherman	MAE WEST
	Song of Songs PARA Rouben Mamoulian	MARLENE DIETRICH
	What Price Decency EQUITABLE Arthur Gregor	DOROTHY BURGESS
1934	*Belle of the Nineties* PARA Leo McCarey	MAE WEST
	Gambling TCF Rowland V. Lee	WYNNE GIBSON
	Wharf Angel PARA Wm. Cameron Menzies	DOROTHY DELL
1935	*The Devil Is A Woman* PARA Josef Von Sternberg	MARLENE DIETRICH
1936	*The Gorgeous Hussy* MGM Clarence Brown	JOAN CRAWFORD
	Lady Be Careful PARA J. T. Reed	MARY CARLISLE
	Valiant Is The Word For Carrie PARA Wesley Ruggles	GLADYS GEORGE
1937	*The Last Train From Madrid* PARA James Hogan	DOROTHY LAMOUR
	Marked Woman WB Lloyd Bacon	BETTE DAVIS

1938   *The Shining Hour*   JOAN CRAWFORD
        MGM   Frank Borzage

1939   *The Light That Failed*   IDA LUPINO
        PARA   William A. Wellman

        Stagecoach   CLAIRE TREVOR
        UA   John Ford

Trevor, the victim of social prejudice, is hounded out
of town by the righteous ladies. "Haven't I got a
right to live," she inquires plaintively, and the
sympathies of the audience are with her. More
sympathy is aroused as she shows her courage and hides
her hurt as best she can when the other passengers,
particularly the pregnant lady, show her such disdain.
Only the convict Ringo treats her like a lady and
insists that the others do so as well. Her efficiency
and kindness during the delivery of a baby and her
tenderness with the baby finally redeem her in
everyone's eyes. Incredulous when Ringo proposes
marriage, she consults the doctor, "Is marriage all
right for a girl like me?" She refuses to run to
safety because she feels obligated to the mother and
baby. Yet, after bravely protecting the baby during
the Indian attack, she believes the only future for
her in the next town is the whorehouse. But Ringo's
love saves her.

1940   *Waterloo Bridge*   VIVIEN LEIGH
        MGM   Mervyn LeRoy

It's pretty far-fetched to swallow a story that
insists there is nothing a woman can do in wartime
England after she's been kicked out of a ballet
company except become a prostitute. Couldn't she have
joined the Red Cross? In this remake of the 1931
film, young, lovely Myra (Leigh), who has trained as a
dancer since she was twelve, is a defeatist who does
not expect much from life; so when she misses her
chance to marry the Army officer and loses her job,
virginal Myra walks on the bridge with suicide on her
mind. Instead she goes off with the first man who
approaches her and begins a second career that she is
not very good at. When she goes to meet a troop train
for business purposes, her missing fiance appears.
Rather than marry him and bring disgrace on his
family, she throws herself in front of a truck.

1941	*Man Hunt* TCF	Fritz Lang	JOAN BENNETT
1942	*Wild Bill Hickok Rides* WB	Ray Enright	CONSTANCE BENNETT
1944	*Christmas Holiday* UNIV	Robert Siodmak	DEANNA DURBIN
1945	*Hotel Berlin* WB	Peter Godfrey	FAYE EMERSON
	Kitty PARA	Mitchell Leison	PAULETTE GODDARD
1946	*The Killers* UI	Robert Siodmak	AVA GARDNER
	My Darling Clementine TCF	John Ford	LINDA DARNELL
1947	*Crossfire* RKO	Edward Dmytryk	GLORIA GRAHAME
	Forever Amber TCF	Otto Preminger	LINDA DARNELL
1948	*Arch Of Triumph* ENTERPRISE	Lewis Milestone	INGRID BERGMAN
	The Time Of Your Life W.CAGNEY	H. C. Potter	JEANNE CAGNEY

The titles introduce Kitty Duval (Cagney) as "a young woman with memories," but, despite her comparatively conservative dress, the minute she walks into Nick's bar and asks for a beer, you know she is a woman down on her luck. Nick identifies her as a B girl from the place up the street, but she insists that she used to be in burlesque, that European royalty sent her flowers and gifts, and wealthy young men took her to dinner. So "You can't push me around. Watch what you think of me, and don't call me any names." Although she has a prison record because she was mixed up with some gangsters in Chicago, Kitty dreams of a big house with big trees and time to read poetry. Her dreams will come true because a big stupid lug wants to marry her.

1949	*Anna Lucasta*	PAULETTE GODDARD
	COL Irving Rapper	
	Thieves Highway	VALENTINA CORTESA
	TCF Jules Dassin	
1954	*The Egyptian*	BELLA DARVI
	TCF Michael Curtiz	
1955	*Battle Cry*	ANNE FRANCIS
	WB Raoul Walsh	
1956	*Back From Eternity*	ANITA EKBERG
	RKO John Farrow	
	The Bold And The Brave	NICOLE MAUREY
	RKO Lewis Foster	
	Inside Detroit	TINA CARVER
	COL Fred F. Sears	
	Lust For Life	PAMELA BROWN
	MGM Vincente Minnelli	
	The Revolt of Mamie Stover	JANE RUSSELL
	TCF Raoul Walsh	
	Three Violent People	ANNE BAXTER
	PARA Rudolph Mate	
	Two-Gun Lady	MARIE WINDSOR
	ASSOCFILM Richard H. Butler	
1957	*The Strange One*	JULIE WILSON
	COL Jack Garfein	
	The Undead	PAMELA DUNCAN
	AIP Roger Corman	
1958	*The Badlanders*	KATY JURADO
	MGM Delmer Daves	
	I Want to Live	SUSAN HAYWARD
	UA Robert Wise	

Based on the life of Barbara Graham, who was executed for murder, the film begins with Graham's career as a prostitute. A tough broad, belligerent and sarcastic, but lots of fun with sailors, she seems to be having a

pretty good time at it. But she gets involved with
petty criminals and ends up with a perjury conviction.
Headlines announce "Goodtime Girl Gets Year for
Perjury." On probation, her next job is to bring
customers to a gambling joint, but she quits to get
married. When that fails, her situation quickly
deteriorates.

Lafayette Escadrille		ETCHIKA CHOUREAU
WB	William A. Wellman	
The Party Crashers		DORIS DOWLING
PARA	Bernard Girard	
Showdown on Boot Hill		CAROL MATTHEWS
TCF	Gene Fowler, Jr.	
Twilight For The Gods		CYD CHARISSE
UI	Joseph Pevney	

1959

Anna Lucasta		EARTHA KITT
UA	Arnold Laven	
Crime and Punishment, USA		MARY MURPHY
AA	Denis Sanders	
Cry Tough		LINDA CRISTAL
UA	Raul Stanley	
Vice Raid		MAMIE VAN DOREN
UA	Edward L. Cahn	

1960

The Angel Wore Red		AVA GARDNER
MGM	Nunnally Johnson	
Butterfield 8		ELIZABETH TAYLOR
MGM	Daniel Mann	

Although all reviews of this film refer to Taylor as
"a high-priced call girl," she insists that she does
not take money. She is insulted when a "client"
leaves her $250 and scribbles "No sale" on his mirror
with her lipstick. But she takes his wife's mink coat
to cover her torn dress. She lives with her mother,
whom she tells she is a model, and when the "client"
wants to set her up in an apartment, she insists, "I
earn my own money, modeling clothes." She takes pride
in maintaining that she chooses her own men and leaves

them when she is ready. A friend explains that her
father died when she was young and her mother had to
go to work. This appears to be the explanation for
her becoming a tramp! She goes to a psychiatrist and
believes there is something "bad" in her that makes
her go with lots of men. But when she falls in love
with her client, she says she no longer needs a
psychiatrist. Claiming again that she never took
money (although she kept the mink), she starts off for
a new life in Boston, but she pays the price society
demands and is killed in a car wreck. Taylor won an
Academy Award for this one.

Elmer Gantry		SHIRLEY JONES
UA	Richard Brooks	
Girl Of The Night		ANNE FRANCIS
WB	Joseph Cates	

1961   *Ada*   SUSAN HAYWARD
       MGM   Daniel Mann

Go Naked In The World   GINA LOLLOBRIGIDA
MGM   Ranald MacDougall

The True Gang Murders   VICTORIA SHAW
TEITEL   Sherman Rosenfield

Weekend Pass   SUZI CARNELL
PARA   John Howard

1962   *Gun Street*   JEAN WILLES
       UA   Edward L. Cahn

Nine Hours To Rama   DIANE BAKER
TCF   Mark Robson

Strangers In The City   CRETA MARCOS
EMBASSY   Rick Carrier

Walk On The Wild Side   CAPUCINE
COL   Edward Dymtryk

1963   *The Balcony*   SHELLEY WINTERS
       CP   Joseph Strick

Irma La Douce   SHIRLEY MACLAINE
UA   Billy Wilder

Proudly proclaiming that "This isn't a job; it's a profession," Irma is loyal to her pimp because "You've got to belong to someone, even if they kick you once in a while." Irma is following in the footsteps of her mother, who had the same good vocation, but who gave up her career for a man and, sadly, wound up a cashier. With her green stockings and see-through blouse, Irma is dressed for work, but this light-hearted comedy presents a very sanitized view of her life. When she has had free time, she has gone to cooking school, played solitaire, and knitted sweaters. She is determined to show off her success by keeping her new pimp supplied with money ("How would it look if you had to go to work?" she tells him) and fights with another girl who he thinks is after her man. All ends well as the about-to-give-birth--but clad in a white wedding gown--Irma is led to the altar so that the baby can be legitimate. "When I first met you, you were a streetwalker. Now you are going to be a wife and a mother. Isn't that a miracle?" is her lover's happy thought, since to his mind and the mind of this dumb movie, what better could a woman aspire to? Oh well, all this takes place in Paris, where, Americans think, this is acceptable and normal behavior.

| 1964 | *A House Is Not A Home* | SHELLEY WINTERS |
| | PARA   Russel Rouse | |

| | *The Naked Kiss* | CONSTANCE TOWERS |
| | AA   Samuel Fuller | |

| 1965 | *Andy* | SUDIE BOND |
| | UNIV   Richard C. Sarafia | |

| | *The Playground* | LORETTA LEVERSEE |
| | JERAND   Richard Hilliard | |

| | *Synanon* | STELLA STEVENS |
| | COL   Richard Quine | |

| | *Sylvia* | CARROLL BAKER |
| | PARA   Gordon Douglas | |

| 1966 | *Stagecoach* | ANN-MARGRET |
| | TCF   Gordon Douglas | |

Trevor, the victim of social prejudice, is hounded out of town by the righteous ladies. "Haven't I got a right to live," she inquires plaintively, and the sympathies of the audience are with her. More sympathy is aroused as she shows her courage and hides her hurt as best she can when the other passengers, particularly the pregnant lady, show her such disdain. Only the convict Ringo treats her like a lady and insists that the others do so as well. Her efficiency and kindness during the delivery of a baby and her tenderness with the baby finally redeem her in everyone's eyes. Incredulous when Ringo proposes marriage, she consults the doctor, "Is marriage all right for a girl like me?" She refuses to run to safety because she feels obligated to the mother and baby. Yet, after bravely protecting the baby during the Indian attack, she believes the only future for her in the next town is the whorehouse. But Ringo's love saves her.

Terror In The City AA	Allen Baron	LEE GRANT
1967 *Gunn* PARA	Blake Edwards	M.T. MARSHALL
1968 *Faces* MAURICE MC	John Cassavetes	GENA ROWLANDS
Uptight PARA	Jules Dassin	RUBY DEE
1969 *The Cheyenne Social Club* NG	Gene Kelly	SHIRLEY JONES
Gaily, Gaily UA	Norman Jewison	MELINA MERCOURI
The Grasshopper NG	Jerry Paris	JACQUELINE BISSET
The Kremlin Letter TCF	John Huston	BIBI ANDERSSON
Midnight Cowboy UA	John Schlesinger	SYLVIA MILES
The Model Shop COL	Jaques Demy	ANOUK AIMEE

Once Upon A Time In The West PARA Sergio Leone	CLAUDIA CARDINALE
The Reivers NG Mark Rydell	SHARON FARRELL

1970   *The Ballad Of Cable Hogue*   STELLA STEVENS
       WB   Sam Peckinpah

Dirty Dingus Magee   ANNE JACKSON
MGM   Burt Kennedy

The Last Of The Mobile Hot-Shots   LYNN REDGRAVE
S.LUMET   Sidney Lumet

Little Big Man   FAYE DUNAWAY
STOCKBRIDGE   Arthur Penn

Dunaway is the lead female, but she has a very small role. Seen first as the lascivious wife of the minister who "adopts" the film's protagonist Jack, she pops up again toward the end as a widow working in a bordello, explaining, "Yes this is a house of ill fame, and I am a fallen flower." She is dressed for the part and attempts to seduce Jack, considering him just another customer. Her complaint is, "This life is not only wicked and sinful; it isn't even any fun. If a woman was married and could come here once or twice a week, it might be fun, but every night . . ." But the money she receives from Wild Bill Hickok will "save" her.

Monte Walsh   JEANNE MOREAU
CINC   William A. Fraker

Moreau is a Frenchman in the American West who works in "a profession of diminishing returns." Her lover calls her Countess ("I thought all you foreign gals was countesses") and tells her she can do better. But when she moves to another town because her cowboy customers have left the area, she finds the job of waitress less attractive. When her lover mentions marriage, she likes the idea: "Marriage is a common ambition in my profession." She dies before the ambition is realized, but she leaves enough money for a nice funeral.

The Owl And The Pussycat   BARBRA STREISAND
COL   Herbert Ross

When her neighbor Felix calls her a whore, Doris
(Streisand) retorts, "I am not a whore; I am a model";
and when he refers to her as a "helpless, hopeless
hustler," she responds, "I am an actress; I have been
in three television commercials." Unlettered, an
incessant talker and gum chewer who wears Fredericks
of Hollywood creations to sleep and miniskirts, boots,
and net stockings to work, Doris insists that she has
"done it only a few times and then only with very
respectable people and under emergency conditions."
Though he bids her goodbye with a "happy
streetwalking," Felix cannot resist her and is
determined to make her see herself as she is. It is
difficult to measure his success when she replies to
his, "What do you do?" by maintaining, "I model; I am
an actress; I was formerly a hooker; plus I was in two
television commercials." Despite her resistance to
facing reality, they go off happily together.

Rabbit, Run   ANJANETTE COMER
WB   Jack Smight

Two Mules For Sister Sara   SHIRLEY MACLAINE
UNIV   Don Siegel

WUSA   JOANNE WOODWARD
PARA   Stuart Rosenberg

1971   *Born To Win*   PAULA PRENTISS
UA   Ivan Passer

Flap   SHELLEY WINTERS
WB   Joseph Strick

Klute   JANE FONDA
WB   Alan J. Pakula

Prostitutes seem to do pretty well in the Oscar
stakes, and Fonda won one for this role. She makes no
bones about the fact that she is a hard-boiled
businesswoman who has spent some time in jail, but she
does try to get modeling and acting jobs and does have
some training as an actress. She satisfies her
customers but does not enjoy her work; yet she tells
her psychiatrist she likes it because she is in
control and it's really like acting. With a good

reputation in the business, she has offers from madams at swank places, but she prefers independence. When the detective offers her $200 to help him, she laughs that she can make that much on her lunch break. Eventually she attempts suicide, "to get away from a world I knew was not good for me," but she also refuses the detective's offer to leave with him. "I cannot set up housekeeping in Tuscarora," she admits; "I cannot be darning socks; I would go crazy." So her future is left open; she is what she is.

The Last Run   COLLEEN DEWHURST
MGM   Richard Fleisher

McCabe And Mrs. Miller   JULIE CHRISTIE
WB   Robert Altman

Christie is impressive in this impressionistic view of the old West, and her characterization of madam, businesswoman, and whore is convincingly real. After McCabe buys three whores to set up business in a remote mining town, Mrs. Miller comes along and insists he needs her for a partner because "I am a whore, and I know a lot about whorehouses." Knowing how to deal with whores, understanding their problems, she convinces McCabe he needs her expertise. She makes him build a fancy sportin' house and imports more attractive whores from Seattle. She sees customers herself, and even McCabe has to pay her expensive $5.00 fee, but when not otherwise engaged, she reads in bed. Better at arithmetic than her partner, with whom she generally disagrees on business matters, she makes plenty of money for them.

The Panic In Needle Park   KITTY WINN
GADD   Jerry Schatzberg

Romance Of A Horsethief   LAINIE KAZAN
AA   Abraham Polonsky

1972   *The Cowboys*   COLLEEN DEWHURST
       WB/SANFORD   Mark Rydell

       The Mechanic   JILL IRELAND
       UA   Michael Winner

1973   *Black Mama, White Mama*   PAM GRIER
       AIP   George Romero

Cinderella Liberty   MARSHA MASON
TCF   Mark Rydell

Jesus Christ Superstar   YVONNE ELLIMAN
UNIV   Norman Jewison

Steelyard Blues   JANE FONDA
WB   Alan Myerson

The Sting   EILEEN BRENNAN
UNIV   George Roy Hill

Willie Dynamite   DIANA SANDS
UNIV   Gilbert Moses

1974 *California Split*   ANN PRENTISS
COL   Robert Altman

The Front Page   CAROL BURNETT
UNIV   Billy Wilder

The Last Detail   CAROL KANE
COL   Hal Ashby

The Pyx   KAREN BLACK
CINERAMA   Harvey Hart

Road Movie   REGINA BAFF
GROVEPRESS   Joseph Strick

Super Cops   SHEILA E. FRAZIER
CINEMATION   Gordon Parks

Truck Stop Women   CLAUDIA JENNINGS
LT FILMS   Mark L. Lester

1975 *Bite The Bullet*   CANDICE BERGEN
COL   Richard Brooks

The Drowning Pool   LINDA HAYES
WB   Stuart Rosenberg

The Happy Hooker   LYNN REDGRAVE
DOUBLE H   Nicholas Sgarro

Hustle   CATHERINE DENEUVE
PARA   Robert Aldrich

Undercover Hero   LILA KEDROVA
UA   Roy Boulting

QUEEN

Queen is a popular role for women in Hollywood films. Except
for famous entertainers, queens are the most likely subjects
of biographical films. After all, they are about the only
women in history books or encyclopedias. I have tried to
list only those roles in which the queen is actually ruling,
in which she has at least some kind of royal job to do. I
therefore leave out such well-known films as *The Lion in
Winter*, where Katharine Hepburn, as Eleanor of Acquitaine, is
shut up in a castle, no longer on a throne. It would be
useless to try to comment on the historical accuracy of the
films; the point is what the film shows about a woman
wielding power.

1931	*A Connecticut Yankee In King Arthur's Court*	MYRNA LOY
	PARA Tay Garnett	
	Ambassador Bill	MARGUERITE CHURCHILL
	TCF Sam Taylor	
	Command Performance	HELEN WARE
	TIFFANY Walter Lang	
	The Royal Bed	NANCE O'NEIL
	RKO Lowell Sherman	
1932	*Rasputin And The Empress*	ETHEL BARRYMORE
	MGM R. Boleslavsky	
1933	*The King's Vacation*	FLORENCE ARLISS
	PARA John Adolfi	
	Queen Christina	GRETA GARBO
	MGM Rouben Mamoulian	

Although there is at first a hint of lesbianism in her
jealous attachment to a young woman of the court,
Cristina soon shows herself to be "really a woman" by

falling in love with the Spanish Ambassador. "I was
not a queen--just a woman in a man's arms," she
croons. An intellectual, she shows that being a queen
is hard work. With a war on her hands, she wants
beauty, gaiety and freedom in her country, not just
the power of the sword. She is busy with papers,
politics, and public appearances. When the people
storm the palace to protest her affair with the
Ambassador, she bravely faces them with, "My business
is governing. I have the knack of it, just as you do
in your business, by inheritance. Go back to work and
leave me to mine." Although she is admonished to give
up her life to her duty, because "greatness demands
all," she abdicates to go with her lover. She is,
however, fated to die, as she predicted, not as an
"old maid," but as a "bachelor."

Tonight Is Ours		CLAUDETTE COLBERT
PARA	Stuart Walker	
The Warrior's Husband		MARJORIE RAMBEAU
TCF	Walter Lang	
1934	*Cleopatra*	CLAUDETTE COLBERT
PARA	Cecil B. de Mille	
The Scarlet Empress		MARLENE DIETRICH
PARA	J. Von Sternberg	
1935	*All The King's Horses*	MARY ELLIS
PARA	Frank Tuttle	
Cardinal Richlieu		VIOLET COOPER
TCF	Rowland V. Lee	
She		HELEN GALLAGHER
RKO	I. Pachel/I. Holden	
1936	*Mary Of Scotland*	KATHARINE HEPBURN
RKO	John Ford	
1937	*Victoria The Great*	ANNA NEAGLE
RKO	Herbert Wilcox	

1938   *Marie Antoinette*   NORMA SHEARER
        MGM   W. S. Van Dyke II

        Sixty Glorious Years   ANNA NEAGLE
        RKO   Herbert Wilcox

1939   *The Devil Is An Empress*   FRANCOISE ROSAY
        COL   Jean Dreville

        Juarez   BETTE DAVIS
        WB   William Dieterle

        The Private Lives Of Elizabeth and Essex   BETTE DAVIS
        WB   Michael Curtiz

The main concern here is not Elizabeth as a ruler, but an older Elizabeth in love with the young Essex. She signs a few papers, but spends most of her time storming around in extravagant costumes, ranting jealously, breaking mirrors that reveal her aging face. Called a king in petticoats, she agonizes over the conflicts between being a queen and being a woman (a problem that rarely seems to bother kings). Wanting peace, but attempting to make wise decisions concerning the various wars England is engaged in, she worries, "I am only a woman. Must I carry the agony of the world on my shoulders alone?" Despite her mooning over love, she shows herself to be courageous and strong-willed. Rather than share the throne with Essex, she sends him to his death.

        Tower of London   BARBARA O NEIL
        UNIV   Rowland V. Lee

1940   *The Mad Empress*   MEDEA NOVARA
        WB   Miguel C. Torres

        The Sea Hawk   FLORA ROBSON
        WB   Michael Curtiz

1942   *The Prime Minister*   FAY COMPTON
        WB   Thorold Dickinson

        A Royal Scandal   TALLULAH BANKHEAD
        TCF   Otto Preminger

        Song Of The Sarong   NANCY KELLY
        UNIV   Harold Young

	Sudan		MARIA MONTEZ
	UNIV	John Rawlins	
1948	*Adventures Of Don Juan*		VIVECA LINDFORS
	WB	Vincent Sherman	
	Sirens Of Atlantis		MARIA MONTEZ
	UA	Greg C. Tallas	
	The Three Musketeers		ANGELA LANSBURY
	MGM	George Sidney	
1949	*Black Magic*		NANCY GUILD
	E.SMALL	Gregory Ratoff	
	Christopher Columbus		FLORENCE ELDRIDGE
	UI	David MacDonald	
	The Pirates of Capri		BINNIE BARNES
	FILMCLASS	Edgar Ulmer	
1951	*David and Bathsheba*		SUSAN HAYWARD
	TCF	Henry King	
1952	*At Sword's Point*		GLADYS COOPER
	RKO	Lewis Allen	
1953	*The Diamond Queen*		ARLENE DAHL
	WB	John Brahm	
	Roman Holiday		AUDREY HEPBURN
	PARA	William Wyler	
	Salome		JUDITH ANDERSON
	COL	William Dieter	
	Serpent of the Nile		RHONDA FLEMING
	COL	William Castle	
	The Sword And The Rose		ROSALIE CRUTCHLEY
	RKO	Kenneth Annakin	
	Young Bess		JEAN SIMMONS
	MGM	George Sidney	
1955	*The Virgin Queen*		BETTE DAVIS
	TCF	Henry Koster	

1956	*The Swan*	AGNES MOOREHEAD
	MGM Charles Vidor	

1957	*The Story Of Mankind*	VIRGINIA MAYO
	WB Irwin Allen	AGNES MOOREHEAD

1958	*The Story Of Vickie*	ROMY SCHNEIDER
	BV Ernst Marischka	

1959	*The Big Fisherman*	CHARLOTTE FLETCHER
	CENTURION Frank Borzage	

John Paul Jones   BETTE DAVIS
WB   John Farrow

Solomon And Sheba   GINA LOLLOBRIGIDA
UA   King Vidor

1961	*Legions Of The Nile*	LINDA CRISTAL
	TCF Signor Cottafavi	

Snow White And The Three Stooges   PATRICIA MEDINA
TCF   Walter Lang

1963	*Cleopatra*	ELIZABETH TAYLOR
	TCF J. Mankiewicz	

Lancelot and Guinevere   JEAN WALLACE
UNIV   Cornel Wilde

Seven Seas to Calais   IRENE WORTH
MGM   Rudolph Mate

Sword of Lancelot   JEAN WALLACE
UNIV   Cornel Wilde

1965	*She*	URSULA ANDRESS
	RKO Robert Day	

1967	*Camelot*	VANESSA REDGRAVE
	WB Joshua Logan	

1970	*Start The Revolution Without Me*	BILLIE WHITELAW
	WB Bud Yorkin	

1971	*Macbeth*	FRANCESCA ANNIS
	COL Roman Polanski	

Trojan Women		KATHARINE HEPBURN
J.SHAFTEL	Michael Cacoyannis	
1972	*Everything You Always Wanted*	
	to Know About Sex	LYNN REDGRAVE
	UA Woody Allen	
1973	*Westworld*	VICTORIA SHAW
	MGM Michael Crichton	

RADIO/TELEVISION

Most women involved in radio and television are shown as
entertainers, usually singers. It is too early to see women
as broadcast journalists before 1975. The women listed here
are primarily involved in production.

1930   *Remote Control*   MARY DORAN
        MGM   Malcolm St. Clair

1933   *Professional Sweethearts*   GINGER ROGERS
        RKO   William Seiter

1934   *Gift of Gab*   GLORIA STUART
        UNIV   Karl Freund

1935   *Thanks A Millions*   ANN DVORAK
        TCF   Roy Del Ruth

1936   *Big Broadcast of 1937*   GRACIE ALLEN
        PARA   Mitchell Leisen

1938   *Five of a Kind*   CLAIRE TREVOR
        TCF   Herbert I. Leeds

        Safety In Numbers   SPRING BYINGTON
        TCF   Malcolm St. Clair

1940   *Charter Pilot*   LYNN BARI
        TCF   Eugene Ford

1941   *Adventure In Washington*   VIRGINIA BRUCE
        COL   Alfred E. Green

        The Great American Broadcast   ALICE FAYE
        TCF   Archie Mayo

        Pot O' Gold   PAULETTE GODDARD
        UA   George Marshall

Too Many Blondes   HELEN PARRISH
UNIV   Thornton Freeland

1942   *The Lady Has Plans*   PAULETTE GODDARD
       PARA   Sidney Lanfield

       Little Tokyo, U.S.A.   BRENDA JOYCE
       TCF   Otto Brower

1943   *Reveille With Beverly*   ANN MILLER
       COL   Charles Barton

1945   *People Are Funny*   HELEN WALKER
       PARA   Sam White

       Tokyo Rose   LOTUS LONG
       PARA   Lew Landers

1947   *Something In The Wind*   DEANNA DURBIN
       UNIV   Irving Pichel

1948   *I Surrender Dear*   GLORIA JEAN
       COL   Arthur Dreifuss

       Rovin' Tumbleweeds   MARY CARLISLE
       REP   George Sherman

1950   *Champagne For Caesar*   CELESTE HOLM
       UA   Richard B. Whorf

1952   *We're Not Married*   GINGER ROGERS
       TCF   Edmund Goulding

1957   *A Face In The Crowd*   PATRICIA NEAL
       WB   Elia Kazan

A "roving reporter" for an Arkansas radio station, Marsha (Neal) discovers Rhodes, a singer-guitar player in jail and makes him a radio, then television personality. He refers to her as "my little gal Friday, not to mention Monday, Tuesday, Wednesday and Thursday," and knows she has created him and that he needs her on the way up. He also appreciates her sexuality, commenting, "You cold fish respectable girls. Inside you crave the same thing as the rest of them." At the pinnacle of his success and power, megalomaniac that he is, he still admits that she made him, that he owed it all to her. He calls her the boss lady of the show, and she is the show's coordinator; the staff goes to pieces and cannot put the show together the one time she fails to be there. Though she demands 50% as her share of what becomes a commercial empire based on Rhodes's personality, she exposes him for the hypocrite he is. Understanding that he has married his public, she refuses to act like a "female" over the drum majorette wife he brings back from Arkansas, but the feelings of hurt show when he introduces the wife. Rhodes claims he was afraid to marry Marsha because "You know more than I do; you're so critical; you do not really approve of me; the bigger I get the smaller you make me feel." He cannot tolerate her superiority, but he goes totally to pieces when she finally leaves for good. She is obviously morally superior as well. The film never leaves any doubt as to her ability, importance and professionalism; her only weakness is loving the wrong man for too long.

| 1970 | *My Lover, My Son* | PATRICIA BRAICE |
| | MGM   John Newland | |

| 1971 | *The Last Picture Show* | SYBIL SHEPHERD |
| | COL   Peter Bogdanovich | |

| 1973 | *Cancel My Reservation* | EVA MARIE SAINT |
| | WB   Paul Bogart | |

| 1974 | *The Parallax View* | PAULA PRENTISS |
| | PARA   Alan J. Pakula | |

| 1975 | *Nashville* | GERALDINE CHAPLIN |
| | PARA   Robert Altman | |

RANCHER/FARMER

Here the attempt has been to identify those films in which
the woman owns the ranch or farm and makes it a business
(rather than just living off the farm). If she just works
alongside her husband, that doesn't count.

1930	*The Light Of Western Star* PARA Otto Brower		MARY BRIAN
	The Texan PARA John Cromwell		EMMA DUNN
	Way Out West MGM Fred Niblo		LEILA HYAMS POLLY MORAN
1931	*The Conquering Horde* PARA Edward Sloman		FAY WRAY
1932	*Mystery Ranch* TCF David Howard		CECILIA PARKER
1937	*It Happened Out West* TCF Howard Bretherton		JUDITH ALLEN
	Springtime In The Rockies REP Joseph Kane		POLLY ROWLES
1938	*Roll Along, Cowboy* TCF Gus Meins		CECILIA PARKER
1939	*Heaven With A Barbed-Wire Fence* TCF Ricardo Cortez		MARJORIE RAMBEAU
	Rio Grande COL Sam Nelson		ANN DORAN
	Singing Cowgirl GN Samuel Diege		DOROTHY PAGE

	Water Rustlers		DOROTHY PAGE
	GN	Samuel Diege	
1940	*Bullets For Rustlers*		LORNA GRAY
	COL	Sam Nelson	
	Ride, Tenderfoot, Ride		JUNE STOREY
	REP	Frank McDonald	
	Texas Stagecoach		IRIS MEREDITH
	COL	Joseph Lewis	
1941	*Texas Rangers Ride Again*		MAY ROBSON
	PARA	James Hogan	
1942	*The Forest Rangers*		SUSAN HAYWARD
	PARA	George Marshall	
1943	*Harvest Melody*		ROSEMARY LANE
	PRC	Sam Newfield	
1944	*Tall In The Saddle*		ELLA RAINES
	RKO	Edwin L. Marin	
1945	*Utah*		DALE EVANS
	REP	John English	
1946	*Smoky*		ANNE BAXTER
	TCF	Louis King	
1947	*Ramrod*		VERONICA LAKE
	UA	Andre DeToth	
	Shadow Valley		JENNIFER HOLT
	EL	Ray Taylor	
1948	*Blood On The Moon*		BARBARA BEL GEDDES
	RKO	Robert Wise	
	Northwest Stampede		JOAN LESLIE
	EL	Albert S. Rogell	
	Oklahoma Badlands		MILDRED COLES
	REP	Yakima Canutt	
1949	*The Big Sombrero*		ELENA VERDUGO
	COL	Frank McDonald	

Brothers In The Saddle RKO Lesley Selander		VIRGINIA COX
Riders of the Range RKO Lesley Selander		JACQUELINE WHITE
1950	*Cow Town* COL John English	GAIL DAVIS
	Montana WB Ray Enright	ALEXIS SMITH
	The Palomino COL Ray Lazarro	BEVERLY TYLER
	Please Believe Me MGM Norman Taurog	DEBORAH KERR
	Summer Stock MGM Charles Walters	JUDY GARLAND
1951	*Cattle Queen* UA Robert Tansey	MARIA HART
	Silver City Bonanza REP George Blair	MARY ELLEN KAY
	The Whip Hand RKO Stuart Gilmore	JOAN DIXON
1952	*Aaron Slick From Punkin Crick* PARA Claude Binyon	DINAH SHORE
	Rancho Notorious RKO Fritz Lang	MARLENE DIETRICH
	Trail Guide RKO Lesley Selander	LINDA DOUGLAS
1953	*The Lady Wants Mink* REP William A. Seiter	RUTH HUSSEY
	So Big WB Robert Wise	JANE WYMAN
1954	*Black Horse Canyon* UNIV Jesse Hibbs	MARI BLANCHARD

    Cattle Queen Of Montana   BARBARA STANWYCK
    RKO   Allan Dwan

1955   *The Man From Laramie*   ALINE MACMAHON
    COL   Anthony Mann

    Man Without A Star   JEANNE CRAIN
    UI   King Vidor

The new owner of a ranch is coming from the East and has already shocked everyone by having an indoor bathroom installed in the ranch house. Only one ranch hand (Kirk Douglas) is amazed to learn the new owner is a woman; the other ranch hands greet her with equanimity, just wanting to know if she is going to be a "working boss." She claims to know cattle and wants to run her cattle over government land, with ruthless disregard for her rancher neighbors. Crain is femininity masking villainy; she is always dressed in a skirt, even wears an unsuitably dressy hat while out on the range, does not ride a horse, although she handles the horses who pull her trap well. She cannot pay Douglas enough to be her foreman, except with her body; and once she has done that, he has only contempt for her, threatening to wrap barbed wire around her pretty neck.

    The Vanishing American   AUDREY TOTTER
    REP   Joseph Kane

1956   *The Maverick Queen*   BARBARA STANWYCK
    REP   Joe Kane

1957   *The Black Scorpion*   MARA CORDAY
    WB   Edward Ludwig

    Forty Guns   BARBARA STANWYCK
    TCF   Samuel Fuller

    Gun Duel In Durango   ANN ROBINSON
    UA   Sidney Salkow

    The Oklahoman   BARBARA HALE
    AA   Francis D. Lyon

    Utah Blaine   SUSAN CUMMINGS
    COL   Fred F. Sears

1958	*The Big Country* UA William Wyler	JEAN SIMMONS
	Fort Dobbs WB Gordon Douglas	VIRGINIA MAYO
	The Proud Rebel BV Michael Curtiz	OLIVIA DE HAVILLAND
	This Angry Age COL Rene Clement	JO VAN FLEET
	Wild Heritage UNIV Charles Haas	MAUREEN O'SULLIVAN
1959	*King Of The Wild Stallions* AA R. G. Springsteen	DIANE BREWSTER
	Mustang UA Peter Stephens	MADALYN TRAHEY
	The Sad Horse TCF James B. Clark	PATRICE WYMORE
1960	*Guns of the Timberland* WB Robert D. Webb	JEANNE CRAIN
1961	*Tess of the Storm Country* TCF Paul Guilfoyle	DIANE BAKER
1965	*Tickle Me* AA Norman Taurog	JULIE ADAMS
1966	*The Rare Breed* UNIV Andrew McLaglen	MAUREEN O'HARA
	Smoky TCF George Sherman	DIANA HYLAND
1967	*The Ballad Of Josie* UNIV Andrew McLaglen	DORIS DAY
	The Fox WB Mark Rydell	SANDY DENNIS
1974	*Castaway Cowboy* BV Vincent McEveely	VERA MILES

RELIGIOUS WORKER

This category includes evangelists, lay missionaries, and nuns. Lay teachers who teach in missionary schools but are not intimately involved in missionary work are classified under teachers.

Hollywood seems fascinated with nuns; perhaps producers felt it incumbent upon them to inform the world that nuns are real people, that they have ordinary everyday problems and emotions. Also, nuns are very mysterious, especially to non-Catholics. There was a time when people wondered what was really under those habits. They're a safe topic for Hollywood because there is no worry about how to deal with matters of sex; it was possible to humanize nuns while still keeping them sexless.

1930	*Madonna Of The Streets*		EVELYN BRENT
	SU	John Robertson	
	Not Damaged		LOIS MORAN
	TCF	Chandler Sprague	
1931	*Laughing Sinners*		JOAN CRAWFORD
	MGM	Harry Beaumont	
	The Miracle Woman		BARBARA STANWYCK
	COL	Frank Capra	
	Salvation Nell		HELEN CHANDLER
	TIFFANY	James Cruze	
1933	*Cradle Song*		DOROTHEA WIECK
	PARA	Mitchell Leison	
	The White Sister		HELEN HAYS
	MGM	Victor Fleming	
1936	*Klondike Annie*		HELEN GEROME EDDY
	PARA	Raoul Walsh	

1938   *Tarnished Angel*   SALLY EILERS
        RKO   Leslie Goodwins

1944   *The Keys Of The Kingdom*   ROSA STRADNER
        TCF   John M. Stahl

        Til We Meet Again   BARBARA BRITTON
        PARA   Frank Borzage

1945   *The Bells Of St. Mary's*   INGRID BERGMAN
        RKO   Leo McCarey

The new pastor of a parochial school, whose
predecessor says, "You don't know what it's like to be
up to you neck in nuns," doesn't know how to act when
he is the only priest among a group of nuns. Bergman,
who was nominated for an Academy Award for this role,
is beatific, but knows how to laugh with the other
nuns; she is very much a part of her order and in
charge. She was a tomboy as a child and still likes
to play baseball, but she is naive about worldly
matters. It seems a man is needed to take care of the
business aspects of the school; as he says, "On the
outside it's a man's world." The nun is the one most
concerned with moral education and is rigid in
upholding standards. With a mind of her own, she is
still not very practical and thinks God will provide a
miracle to save the school, but the miracle is the way
she charms an old greedy man into donating money.
When one of the students says, "I want to be a nun
like you," her reply is "You don't become a nun to run
away from life; it is not because you lost something
but because you found something." Her simple
explanation of a nun's vocation is reinforced by the
ecstatic prayer she offers before she leaves the
school.

1948   *Citizen Saint*   CARLA DARE
        RKO   Harold Young

        Joan Of Arc   INGRID BERGMAN
        RKO   Victor Fleming

1949   *Come To The Stable*   CELESTE HOLM
        TCF   Henry Koster

1950   *Angels Of The Streets*   RENEE FAURE
        MGM   Robert Bresson

The Red Danube   ETHEL BARRYMORE
MGM   George Sidney

1951   The African Queen   KATHARINE HEPBURN
       UA   John Huston

Rosie the missionary was one of Hepburn's Oscar-
nomination roles. She is first seen playing the organ
and singing lustily in her brother's mission church.
Although referred to as "not comely among the maidens"
by her brother and excoriated as a "crazy, psalm-
singing, skinny old maid" by the boatman, she proves
attractive as well as intelligent, clever and
courageous. Prudish at first, she learns to live with
a man on the boat and is sexually stimulated by the
thrill of going through the rapids. Love makes her
"human," and she learns to laugh and quits reading the
Bible; and the boatman-turned-lover finally stops
calling her "Miss."

       Appointment With Danger   PHYLLIS CALVERT
       PARA   Lewis Allen

       Thunder On The Hill   CLAUDETTE COLBERT
       UI   Douglas Sirk

1952   The Belle Of New York   VERA ELLEN
       MGM   Charles Walters

1953   Little Boy Lost   GABRIELLE DORZIAT
       PARA   George Seaton

1955   Fort Yuma   JOAN VOHS
       UA   Lesley Selander

       Guys And Dolls   JEAN SIMMONS
       S GOLDWYN   Joseph Mankiewicz

Simmons runs the Save-A-Soul Mission in New York but
considers herself a failure because the mission does
not have enough souls to save. In her tightly
buttoned up uniform, she denies that she is sexually
repressed or perversely attracted to sinners. She
allows a gambler to take her to Havana for dinner
because he has made a deal with her to save the
mission. In Havana she gets drunk, loosens up, dances
wildly, gets in a fist fight and falls in love. When
she later turns against the gambler, he wonders "What
kind of doll are you?" and she angrily replies, "I am

a daytime doll, a mission doll." But in the end she marries the gambler, still wearing her tightly buttoned uniform.

The Prodigal LANA TURNER
MGM Richard Thorpe

1957 *Heaven Knows, Mr. Allison* DEBORAH KERR
TCF John Huston

Marooned on a Pacific island with a U.S. Marine during World War II, this nun shows faith, bravery and affection for her protector who, she realizes, will be her "dear companion always" in her thoughts and prayers. Because the Marine is ignorant of Catholicism, the Sister explains about nuns and their dedication; she must also explain, when he makes a comb for her, that nuns do not use them but that she will treasure it always as a keepsake. He understands her vocation when he explains his own: "I am a Marine like you are a nun; you got your cross; I got my globe and anchor; I got the Corps like you got the Church." The nun is also naive; she believes that if she turns herself in to the Japanese, they will respect her vocation. When the Marine asks her to marry him, she is moved, but explains that she has given her heart to Christ. His desire for her is so strong that, when he is drunk, he lunges for her and attacks her innocence ("Do you think this is the Garden of Eden?"). She runs away, more in fear of what she later calls "the truth" than fear of him. However, when they leave the island, it is clear she will carry on her life as a nun.

1958 *Inn of the Sixth Happiness* INGRID BERGMAN
TCF Mark Robson

Bergman plays Gladys Aylwood, an English housemaid who is determined to go to China as a missionary. She is turned down because she is not considered qualified for missionary work, but she manages to get to China on her own. She works with an elderly missionary and takes over her inn, which has served as the base for mission work, upon the woman's death. Eventually she earns the respect of the local mandarin and the people and becomes a Chinese citizen. Despite her protestation that she is "not attractive in that way," a Eurasian soldier falls in love with her. She demonstrates incredible courage in entering villages to enforce laws, in dealing with bandits, and in quelling a prison riot; but her most courageous act is leading a group of 100 children over a dangerous mountain route to safety after the Japanese attack. Bergman portrays Gladys as sincere in her belief that she is doing God's work and as an indomitable, but very real, woman.

1959   *Girls Town*   MAGGIE HAYS
        MGM   Charles Haas

        The Miracle   CARROLL BAKER
        WB   Irving Rapper

        The Nun's Story   AUDREY HEPBURN
        WB   Fred Zinnemann

This is one attempt to grapple with the thoughts, feelings, beliefs, and conscience of a nun; so there is a lot of music and facial expressions (especially since much of the time the nun must be silent). The film is a guide to becoming a nun; it takes us through the various steps of the postulant and then novice and nurse's training. Because her father is a doctor and she worked in his lab, she is an excellent student and nurse. A frustrated scientist, she works so hard in the lab in the Congo she has little time for her religious duties, and the doctor tells her, "You are not in the mold; you never will be; you have your own ideas; you will never be the kind of nun the order wants you to be." She is therefore sent home to Belgium to renew her spiritual life. When her father is killed by the Germans, she realizes she no longer belongs in a convent; she cannot forgive, and she cannot continue to sacrifice. The camera, which so reverently followed the ceremony in which her nun's garments were placed upon her head and body, now slowly observes her removal of these garments and her silent departure from the convent. This role netted Hepburn an Academy Award.

1960   *Crack In The Mirror*   CATHERINE LACEY
        TCF   Richard Fleisher

        Elmer Gantry   JEAN SIMMONS
        UA   Richard Brooks

Gantry is stunned by his first glimpse of Sister Sharon in her peasant dress and bonnet, carrying a

milk pail to collect the donations. Idolized, she
manipulates her audience but has no time for
individuals. Shrewd, and not to be conned, she also
somehow is not a hypocrite; she manages to impress the
doubters and scoffers with her quiet sincerity and her
pure white robe. She has the courage to fight back
when attacked by a newspaper and also the courage to
love Gantry, who wants to "tear those wings off you
and make a real woman of you." Thriving on the
adulation of her flock, Sharon believes the people
need her and so she refuses to leave her burning
tabernacle.

1961	*Angel Baby* MADERA	Paul Wendkos	SALOME JENS
	Francis of Assisi TCF	Eugene Vale	DOLORES HART
	The Sins of Rachel Cade WB	Gordon Douglas	ANGIE DICKINSON
1962	*The Nun And The Sergeant* UA	Peter Adreon	ANNA STEN
1963	*Lilies Of The Field* UA	Ralph Nelson	LILIA SKALA

In their rundown desert convent a group of East German
refugee nuns thinks God has sent them Homer, the
strong black handyman who happens by. The moral force
of the Mother Superior keeps the handyman there
against his better judgment. She bosses him around
and bawls him out, and he in turns says, "That old
lady has a mean streak," and refers to her as a
regular Hitler. She is wily and pretends her English
is very poor when Homer keeps asking for his pay.
Though cunning and manipulative, she is full of faith
and sincerely believes God will build her a chapel;
therefore she cares nothing about Homer's feelings and
his desire to build the chapel by himself. The
closest she can come to thanking him is to tell him to
sit up front during the inaugural mass. Her methods
may not be admirable, but her determination is. It is
clear that she is foreign, with no understanding of
American or Hispanic-American culture. The
implication is that an American nun would not behave
in this way.

	Stolen Hours		GWEN NELSON
	UA	Daniel M. Petrie	

1966	*The Singing Nun*		DEBBIE REYNOLDS
	MGM	Henry Koster	

	The Trouble With Angels		ROSALIND RUSSELL
	COL	Ida Lupino	

A very severe Reverend Mother, Russell enforces the rules of her convent school but understands the psychology of teenage girls. Although she has a sense of humor, she is opposed to "progressive" education, and in her argument with the headmaster of a progressive school who says, "The finest minds in education are on our side," she smirks, "God is on our side." The challenge of molding an independent spirit without breaking it is what keeps her going despite exasperation. She is intelligent and "human" (she weeps over the death of an old nun), but other than saying she gave up a budding career as a seamstress in a Parisian couturier firm because she "found something better," there is no attempt at understanding the character and feelings of a nun.

1967	*A Time For Killing*		INGER STEVENS
	COL	Phil Karlson	

1968	*Where Angels Go, Trouble Follows*		ROSALIND RUSSELL
	COL	Jamer Nelson	

1969	*Change Of Habit*		MARY TYLER MOORE
	UNIV	William Graham	

	The Trygon Factor		BRIGITTE HORNEY
	WB	Cyril Frankel	

1970	*Madron*		LESLIE CARON
	FOUR STAR	Jerry Hopper	

1971	*The Devils*		VANESSA REDGRAVE
	WB	Ken Russell	

1972	*Pope Joan*		LIV ULLMANN
	COL	Michael Anderson	

1974	*Murder On The Orient Express*		INGRID BERGMAN
	PARA	Sidney Lumet	

1975   *Day Of The Locust, The*   GERALDINE PAGE
        PARA   John Schlesinger

SALESWOMAN

Hollywood women characters sell everything from Fuller brushes to apples, but they are generally seen selling flowers, perfume or other more "feminine" items. As usual, sales is not a profession, but a stopgap job until a man comes along.

1930	*Our Blushing Brides* MGM Harry Beaumont	JOAN CRAWFORD
	Dough Boys MGM Edward Sedgewick	SALLY EILERS
	Life of the Party WB Roy Del Ruth	WINNIE LIGHTNER
	Lord Byron of Broadway MGM Wm. Nigh/H. Beaumont	MARION SCHILLING
	Not Damaged TCF Chandler Sprague	LOIS MORAN
1931	*City Lights* UA Charlie Chaplin	VIRGINIA CHERRILL
	The Cuban Love Song MGM W. S. Van Dyke II	LUPE VELEZ
	Easiest Way MGM Jack Conway	CONSTANCE BENNETT
	Girl Habit PARA Eddie Cline	TAMARA GEVA
	Hush Money TCF Sidney Lanfield	JOAN BENNETT
	Kiss Me Again FN William Seiter	BERNICE CLAIRE

No Limit   CLARA BOW
PARA   Frank Tuttle

One Heavenly Night   EVELYN LAYE
UA   George Fitzmaurice

Paid   JOAN CRAWFORD
MGM   Sam Wood

Women Go On Forever   MARION NIXON
TIFFANY   Walter Lang

1932   *Ladies of the Big House*   SYLVIA SIDNEY
PARA   Marion Gering

Play Girl   LORETTA YOUNG
WB   Ray Enright

Shop Angel   MARION SCHILLING
TOWER   E. M. Hopper

1933   *Cynara*   PHYLLIS BARRY
MGM   King Vidor

Gigolettes of Paris   MADGE BELLAMY
EQUITABLE   Alphonse Martel

Hold Me Tight   SALLY EILERS
TCF   David Butler

Lady For A Day   MAY ROBSON
COL   Frank Capra

1934   *The Cat's Paw*   UNA MERKEL
TCF   Sam Taylor

Sadie McKee   JOAN CRAWFORD
MGM   Clarence Brown

1935   *Great Hotel Murder*   MADGE BELLAMY
TCF   Eugene Forde

One In A Million   DOROTHY WILSON
CHESTERF   Frank Strayer

Traveling Saleslady   JOAN BLONDELL
FN   Ray Enright

1936	*The Big Noise* WB	Frank McDonald	MARIE WILSON
	The Longest Night MGM	Errol Taggert	FLORENCE RICE
	Sing Me a Love Song FN	Ray Enright	PATRICIA ELLIS
	Star For a Night TCF	Lewis Seiler	CLAIRE TREVOR
1937	*Along Came Love* PARA	Bert Lytrell	IRENE HERVEY
	Turn of the Moon PARA	Lewis Seiler	ELEANOR WHITNEY
1938	*Hold That Kiss* MGM	Edwin L. Marin	MAUREEN O'SULLIVAN
	My Lucky Star TCF	Roy Del Ruth	SONJA HENIE
	Saleslady MONO	Arthur G. Collins	ANNE NAGEL
	There Goes My Heart UA	Norman Z. McLeod	VIRGINIA BRUCE
	You and Me PARA	Fritz Lang	SYLVIA SIDNEY
	Youth Takes a Fling UNIV	Archie Mayo	ANDREA LEEDS
1939	*Bachelor Mother* RKO	Garson Kanin	GINGER ROGERS

A toy department clerk loses her job on Christmas Eve, and jobs are hard to get; but she is rehired when the owner's son thinks she is the mother of a baby she has accidentally found. She shows appropriate motherly instincts toward the baby, and her boss, as if to prove that only women know how to handle babies, is a klutz around the baby. She gets pay raises in order to support the baby, and of course she gets the boss.

Within The Law   RUTH HUSSEY
MGM   Gustav Machaty

The Women   JOAN CRAWFORD
MGM   George Cukor

Norma Shearer is the lead here, if anyone in this
ensemble piece can be said to be the star. But it is
worth noting that the only member of the bevy of
bitchy females created by Clare Booth Luce who works
is Crystal (Crawford), and hers is the most
unsympathetic role. Crystal sells perfume and uses
her position to get herself a sugar daddy. Obviously
below the other women in class, she is viewed as
contemptible because she has to work. Rather than
work she prefers to have a rich man to support her.
She is unworthy of the husband she steals and so loses
him. The film presents the most negative picture
possible of working women.

1940 *Irene*   ANNA NEAGLE
      RKO   Herbert Wilcox

      Lady In Question   RITA HAYWORTH
      COL   Charles Vidor

      Lucky Partners   GINGER ROGERS
      RKO   Lewis Milestone

      The Shop Around The Corner   MARGARET SULLAVAN
      MGM   Ernst Lubitsch

1941 *The Devil And Miss Jones*   JEAN ARTHUR
      RKO   Sam Wood

      Model Wife   JOAN BLONDELL
      UNIV   Leigh Jason

      Unexpected Uncle   ANNE SHIRLEY
      RKO   Peter Godfrey

      Weekend In Havana   ALICE FAYE
      TCF   Walter Lang

1942 *Rings On Her Fingers*   GENE TIERNEY
      TCF   Rouben Mamoulian

1944 *Reckless Age*   GLORIA JEAN
      UNIV   Felix K. Keist

1945   *River Gang*   GLORIA JEAN
        UNIV   Charles David

        Tell It To A Star   RUTH TERRY
        REP   Frank McDonald

        Those Endearing Young Charms   LARAINE DAY
        RKO   Lewis Allen

1946   *The Bachelor's Daughters*   GAIL RUSSELL
        UA   Andrew Stone

        From This Day Forward   JOAN FONTAINE
        RKO   John Berry

1948   *Every Girl Should Be Married*   BETSY DRAKE
        RKO   Don Hartman

A baby clothes saleswoman sets her cap for a
pediatrician and finally succeeds in breaking down all
his defenses. All she yearns to be is a wonderful
wife and mother, but she refuses a proposal from the
department store owner because she wants love as well
as wealth. Everyone refers to her as "a little
salesgirl" when her picture is in the paper. There
are three scenes of her at work, one selling booties
to the doctor, one where she seems to have been
demoted to shipping clerk, and one where she is in the
boss's office being fired. She thinks women should be
able to ask men for dates and speak to them the way
they woo women. Instead she must trap a husband,
using subterfuges and wiles women have used for
centuries. Even Cary Grant's light touch cannot save
this insulting "comedy," which depicts the salesgirl
as interested only in marriage, willing to do any
conniving thing to trap a man, preferably one who can
support her comfortably, so she can settle down in her
dream house and have babies.

        Relentless   MARGUERITE CHAPMAN
        COL   George Sherman

1949   *Chinatown At Midnight*   JEAN WILLES
        COL   Seymour Friedman

        The Doctor and the Girl   JANET LEIGH
        MGM   Curtis Bernhardt

In The Good Old Summertime MGM Robert Z. Leonard		JUDY GARLAND
Traveling Saleswoman COL Charles F. Reisner		JOAN DAVIS

1950 *The Fuller Brush Girl*   LUCILLE BALL
     COL   Lloyd Bacon

1956 *Bundle Of Joy*   DEBBIE REYNOLDS
     RKO   Norman Taurog

In this musical remake of Bachelor Mother Reynolds is so self-confident and eager as a saleswoman that she is chastised for overselling. The same plot unfolds, and in the end the happy couple are pushing the baby stroller through the store.

The First Travelling Saleslady   GINGER ROGERS
     RKO   Arthur Lubin

1958 *Bell, Book and Candle*   KIM NOVAK
     COL   Richard Quine

King Creole   DOLORES HART
     PARA   Michael Curtiz

Lost, Lonely and Vicious   BARBARA WILSON
     STATERIGHT   Frank Myers

Vertigo   KIM NOVAK
     PARA   Alfred Hitchcock

1961 *Pocketful Of Miracles*   BETTE DAVIS
     UA   Frank Capra

Apple Annie (Davis) sells apples on Broadway to support her daughter in Spain. An old drunk whose kidneys are failing, she is referred to as an old bag, a creature of the pavements and a filthy hag; but she has many loyal friends and customers. When the daughter decides to show up in New York with a titled fiance, Annie's friends transform her into the grande dame she has pretended to be in her letters to the daughter. Coiffed, made up and dressed in finery, she not only looks like a dowager, she speaks and acts like one; and, despite many comic misadventures, they pull off the deception. Then we can assume she will be back selling apples.

1963   *Love With A Proper Stranger*   NATALIE WOOD
        PARA   Robert Mulligan

1964   *My Fair Lady*   AUDREY HEPBURN
        WB   George Cukor

        Eliza Doolittle (Andrews) does not sell flowers after
        she meets Professor Higgins, though he threatens to
        send her back to her old job if she misbehaves. At
        least she made a modest living selling flowers; so she
        rightly worries about what she will be qualified to do
        once Prof. Higgins has taught her to speak properly.

1967   *Games*   SIMONE SIGNORET
        UNIV   Curtis Harrington

1968   *Did You Hear The One About The Travelling*
        Saleslady?   PHYLLIS DILLER
        UNIV   Don Weis

1969   *John and Mary*   MIA FARROW
        TCF   Peter Yates

MADAME CURIE

SCIENTIST

Most celluloid women scientists appear in science fiction films, as if any realistic portrayal of scientific activity could not plausibly include women, with the exception of Madame Curie.

1933	*It's Great To Be Alive* TCF Alfred Werker	EDNA MAY OLIVER
	Silver Cord RKO John Cromwell	IRENE DUNNE
1936	*Moonlight Murder* MGM Edwin L. Marin	MADGE ADAMS
	The Walking Dead WB Michael Curtiz	MARGUERITE CHURCHILL
1937	*Under Cover Of Night* SVENSK Gustaf Morlander	SARA HADEN
1939	*Exile Express* GN Otis Garrett	ANNA STEN
	Homicide Bureau COL C. C. Coleman, Jr.	RITA HAYWORTH
1940	*The Man With Nine Lives* COL Nick Grinde	JO ANN SAGERS
	The Mummy's Hand UNIV Christy Cabanne	PEGGY MORAN
1941	*The Kid From Kansas* UNIV William Nigh	ANN DORAN
	Our Wife COL James M. Stahl	RUTH HUSSEY

| | *Shining Victory* | GERALDINE FITZGERALD |
| | WB | Irving Rapper |

1942 *Kid Glove Killer*   MARSHA HUNT
     MGM   Fred Zimmerman

1943 *Madame Curie*   GREER GARSON
     MGM   Mervyn LeRoy

1944 *Her Primitive Man*   LOUISE ALLBRITTON
     UNIV   Charles Lamont

     The Lady And The Monster   VERA RALSTON
     REP   George Sherman

1946 *Strange Conquest*   JANE WYATT
     COL   John Rawlins

1948 *Jungle Jim*   VIRGINIA GREY
     COL   William Berke

     Sofia   SIGRID GURIE
     FILMCLASS   John Reinhardt

     Walk A Crooked Mile   LOUISE ALLBRITTON
     COL   Gordon Douglas

1949 *The Lady Takes a Sailor*   JANE WYMAN
     WB   Michael Curtiz

     On the Town   ANN MILLER
     MGM   Gene Kelly/Stanley Donen

Miller is the second lead, but is mentioned here because he takes pride in being a scientist and is a part of the ensemble of three employed women who match up with the ensemble of three sailors.

1950 *Rocketship XM*   OSA MASSEN
     LIPPERT   Kurt Neumann   LISA VAN HORN

     The Tattooed Stranger   PATRICIA WHITE
     RKO   Edward Montagne

1951 *Flight To Mars*   VIRGINIA HUSTON
     MONO   Lesley Selander

     The Second Woman   BETSY DRAKE
     UA   James V. Kern

	The Thing	MARGARET SHERIDAN
	RKO Christian Nyby	
1952	*Belles On Their Toes*	MYRNA LOY
	TCF Henry Levin	
	Jungle Jim In The Forbidden Land	ANGELA GREENE
	COL Lew Landers	
	Red Planet Mars	ANDREA KING
	UA Harry Horner	
	When Worlds Collide	BARBARA RUSH
	PARA Rudolph Mate	
1953	*Beast From 20,000 Fathoms*	PAULA RAYMOND
	WB Eugene Lourie	
	Invaders From Mars	HELENA CARTER
	TCF W. C. Menzies	
	Phantom From Space	NOREEN NASH
	UA W. Lee Wilder	
	Project Moonbase	DONNA MARTEL
	LIPPERT Richard Talmadge	
	Spaceways	EVA BARTOK
	LIPPERT Terence Fisher	
	War Of The Worlds	ANN CODEE
	PARA B. Haskin	
1954	*Cat Women Of The Moon*	MARIE WINDSOR
	ASTOR Arthur Hilton	
	Creature From The Black Lagoon	JULIE ADAMS
	UI Jack Arnold	
	Hell And High Water	BELLA DARVI
	TCF Samuel Fuller	

	Riders To The Stars UA Richard Carlson	MARTHA HYER
	Them! WB Gordon Douglas	JOAN WELDON
1955	*It Came From Beneath The Sea* COL R. Gordon	FAITH DOMERGUE
	King Dinosaur LIPPERT Bert I. Gordon	WANDA CURTIS
	Revenge of the Creature UNIV Jack Arnold	LORI NELSON
	Tarantula UNIV Jack Arnold	MARA CORDAY
	This Island Earth UNIV J. M. Newman	FAITH DOMERGUE
1956	*Curucu, Beast of the Amazon* UNIV Curt Siodmak	BEVERLY GARLAND
	Forbidden Planet MGM Fred M. Wilcox	ANNE FRANCIS
	The Gamma People COL John Gilling	EVA BARTOK
1957	*Attack of the Crab Monsters* AA Roger Corman	BEVERLY GARLAND
	From Hell It Came AA Dan Milner	TINA CARVER
	Love Slaves of the Amazon UNIV Curt Siodmak	GIANNA SEGALE
	The Night The World Exploded COL Fred F. Sears	KATHRYN GRANT
	Two Grooms For A Bride TCF Henry Cass	VIRGINIA BRUCE
	The Unearthly REP B. L. Peters	MARILYN BUFERD

1958   Night Of The Blood Beast   ANGELA GREENE
        AIP   B. Kowalski

        Wink Of An Eye   DORIS DOWLING
        UA   Winston Jones

1959   Have Rocket, Will Travel   ANNA-LISA
        COL   D. L. Rich

1960   12 To The Moon   ANNA-LISA
        COL   D. Bradly

1961   The Flight That Disappeared   PAULA RAYMOND
        UA   Reginald LeBorg

        Seven Women From Hell   PATRICIA OWENS
        TCF   Robert Webb

1962   The Underwater City   JULIE ADAMS
        COL   Frank McDonald

1963   Call Me Bwana   ANITA EKBERG
        UA   George Douglas

        X-the Man With X-ray Eyes   DIANA VAN DER VLIS
        AIP   Roger Corman

1964   The Time Travelers   MERRY ANDERS
        AIP   Ib Melchior

1965   Clarence The Cross-eyed Lion   BETSY DRAKE
        MGM   Andrew Marton

        Crack In The World   JANETTE SCOTT
        PARA   Andrew Marton

        Mutiny In Outer Space   DOLORES FAITH
        AA   H. Grimaldi

1966   Around The World Under The Sea   SHIRLEY EATON
        MGM   Andrew Marton

        Destination Inner Space   SHEREE NORTH
        MAGNA   Francis D. Lyon

Fantastic Voyage	RAQUEL WELCH
TCF R. Fleischer	
Way, Way Out	CONNIE STEVENS
TCF G. Douglas	
Women of the Prehistoric Planet	MERRY ANDERS
REALART Arthur Pierce	

1968 *The Bamboo Saucer*   LOIS NETTLETON
      WE   Frank Telford

      Journey To The Center Of Time   GIGI PERREAU
      BOREALIS&D   D. Hewitt

      The Power   SUZANNE PLESHETTE
      MGM   Byron Baskin

1969 *Planet of the Apes*   KIM HUNTER
      TCF   Franklin Schaffner

      Queen Of Blood   JUDI MEREDITH
      AIP   Curtis Harrington

1970 *Beneath The Planet Of The Apes*   KIM HUNTER
      TCF   Ted Post

      The Forbin Project   SUSAN CLARK
      UNIV   Joseph Sargent

      Skullduggery   SUSAN CLARK
      UNIV   Gordon Douglas

1971 *The Andromeda Strain*   KATE REID
      UNIV   Robert Wise

      Escape From The Planet Of The Apes   NATALIE TRUNDY
      TCF   Don Taylor

      Horror Of The Blood Monsters   VICKI VOLANTE
      II   A. Adamson

      A New Leaf   ELAINE MAY
      PARA   Elaine May

The caricature of the unworldly scientist is carried
to extremes as Henrietta (May), described as lacking
in social grace ("no taste, no wit, no conversation,
no spirit, has to be vacuumed every time she eats,

primitive, positively feral, a menace to
civilization"), is courted by Henry so that he can
murder her and inherit her money. An incurable klutz,
Henrietta wears ridiculous hats and glasses which keep
slipping down her nose. Upon learning of her
millionaire status, Henry inquires, "Is she engaged?"
and his friend disdainfully replies, "No. She's a
botanist." Who would court such a woman, for whom
science, not love, is paramount and whose ambition is
to discover a new variety of fern that has never been
identified and classified? Henrietta's attempts at
housewifely duties are pathetic, but she does find her
fern, which she names for Henry, thus giving up her
name, her identity and her place in the scientific
atlas. She wins Henry's love with her tenderness, and
thus is not murdered, and wants to depend on Henry for
the rest of her life.

Zeppelin		ELKE SOMMER
WB	Etienne Perier	
1973	*The Day of the Dolphin*	TRISH VAN DEVERE
	AE Mike Nichols	
	Night of the Lupus	JANET LEIGH
	MGM William F. Claxton	
1974	*Young Frankenstein*	TERI GARR
	TCF Mel Brooks	

SECRETARY/OFFICE WORKER

By 1930, 96% of secretaries were women, and though office jobs were difficult to get during the `30s, the movies of the decade feature secretaries as the most typical of working women. Over 70 feature films of the decade had the leading actress in such a role. Since 1940 office workers have constituted the single largest occupational category for American women, and this is reflected in the long list of secretary films. Such films dropped off during the `60s, although the number of women employed in the United States as secretaries continued to rise. More and more of these women were married and mothers, but the movies never showed married secretaries, and usually by the end of the film the secretary has been "successful" and is about to marry the boss, or someone else, and quit work.

1930   *Children of Pleasure*   HELEN JOHNSON
          MGM   Harry Beaumont

          The Girl Said No   LEILA HYAMS
          GN   Sam Wood

          The Golden Calf   SUE CAROL
          TCF   Millard Webb

          Ladies Must Play   DOROTHY SEBASTIAN
          COL   Raymond Cannon

          The Locked Door   BARBARA STANWYCK
          UA   George Fitzmaurice

          The Office Wife   DOROTHY MACKAILL
          WB   Lloyd Bacon

          Party Girl   JEANETTE LOFF
          TIFFANY   Edward Halperin

          Playing Around   ALICE WHITE
          FN   Mervyn LeRoy

Queen High   GINGER ROGERS
PARA   Fred Newmeyer

Remote Control   MARY DORAN
MGM   Malcolm St.Clair

Sin Takes A Holiday   CONSTANCE BENNETT
SU   Sam Wood

Temple Tower   MARCELINE DAY
TCF   Donald Gallaher

Way For A Sailor   LEILA HYAMS
MGM   Sam Wood

1931   *The Age For Love*   BILLIE DOVE
UA   Frank Lloyd

Bachelor Apartment   IRENE DUNNE
RKO   Lowell Sherman

Behind Office Doors   MARY ASTOR
RKO   Melville Brown

Big Business Girl   LORETTA YOUNG
FN   William A. Seiter

Five Star Final   MARIAN MARSH
WB   Mervyn LeRoy

Marsh is the secretary to the managing editor of a
newspaper. Although in love with him, she says she is
happy to be his secretary instead of marrying him.
Efficient, she just takes orders, but she is cynical
about the newspaper business. Finally, she comes into
the office slightly drunk and tells off the boss,
asserting that he should be ashamed of his sleazy
tactics. Whereupon he calls her his "visible
conscience."

The Flood   ELEANOR BOARDMAN
COL   James Tinling

Honor Among Lovers   CLAUDETTE COLBERT
PARA   Dorothy Arzner

It Pays To Advertise   MARY GRAYSON
PARA   Frank Tuttle

Lonely Wives   PATSY RUTH MILLER
PATHE   Russell Mack

Lover Come Back   CONSTANCE CUMMINGS
COL   Erle C. Kenton

Morals For Women   BESSIE LOVE
TIFFANY   Mort Blumenstock

Naughty Flirt   IRENE DUNNE
FN   Edward Cline   ALICE WHITE

Party Husband   DOROTHY MACKAILL
FN   Clarence Badger

Peach O'Reno   DOROTHY LEE
RKO-PATHE   William Seiter

Secrets Of A Secretary   CLAUDETTE COLBERT
PARA   George Abbott

The Single Sin   KAY JOHNSON
TIFFANY   William Nigh

Three Girls Lost   LORETTA YOUNG
TCF   Sidney Lanfield

1932   *Attorney For The Defense*   CONSTANCE CUMMINGS
        COL   Irving Cummings

        The Big Broadcast   GRACIE ALLEN
        PARA   Frank Tuttle

        Blessed Event   RUTH DONNELLY
        WB   Roy Del Ruth

        The Dark Horse   BETTE DAVIS
        WB   Alfred E. Green

        Discarded Lovers   SHARON LYNN
        TOWER   Fred Newmeyer

        Down To Earth   DOROTHY JORDAN
        TCF   David Butler

        Grand Hotel   JOAN CRAWFORD
        MGM   Edmund Goulding

Hot Saturday PARA William Seiter		NANCY CARROLL
Is My Face Red? RKO William Seiter		ARLINE JUDGE
Lawyer Man WB William Dieterle		JOAN BLONDELL
Okay America UNIV Tay Garnett		MAUREEN O'SULLIVAN
A Private Scandal INDEP Charles Hutchinson		MARION NIXON
Red Headed Woman MGM Jack Conway		JEAN HARLOW
Skyscraper Souls WB Edgar Selwyn		MAUREEN O'SULLIVAN
Strangers In Love PARA Lothar Mendes		KAY FRANCIS
The Tenderfoot FN Ray Enright		GINGER ROGERS

1933   *Baby Face*   BARBARA STANWYCK
       WB   Alfred E. Green

       Corruption   EVALYN KNAPP
       IMPERIAL   C. Edward Roberts

       Counsellor-At-Law   BEBE DANIELS
       UNIV   William Wyler

       Footlight Parade   JOAN BLONDELL
       WB   Lloyd Bacon

       Goodbye Again   JOAN BLONDELL
       WB   Lloyd Bacon

       His Private Secretary   EVELYN KNAPP
       SHOWMEN   Philip H. Whiteman

       Pleasure Cruise   GENEVIEVE TOBIN
       TCF   Frank Tuttle

Private Jones GLORIA STUART
UNIV   Russell Mack

Second Hand Wife SALLY EILERS
TCF   Hamilton McFadden

Stage Mother ALICE BRADY
MGM   Charles R. Brabin

The Working Man BETTE DAVIS
WB   John Adolfi

1934 *Black Moon* FAY WRAY
COL   Roy W. Hill

Friends of Mr. Sweeney ANN DVORAK
WB   Peter Collinson

He Couldn't Take It VIRGINIA CHERRILL
MONO   William Nigh

Kiss and Make Up HELEN MACK
PARA   Harlan Thompson

Man Of Iron MARY ASTOR
FN   William McGann

A Man's Game EVALYN KNAPP
COL   D. Ross Lederman

Private Scandal ZASU PITTS
PARA   Ralph Murphy

Public Stenographer LOLA LANE
SHOWMEN   Lew Collins

Richest Girl In The World FAY WRAY
RKO   William A. Seiter

Springtime For Henry HEATHER ANGEL
TCF   Frank Tuttle

Stand Up And Cheer MADGE EVANS
TCF   Hamilton McFadden

Success at Any Price COLLEEN MOORE
RKO   J. Walter Ruben

Such Women Are Dangerous   ROSEMARY AMES
TCF   James Flood

Take the Stand   THELMA TODD
LIBERTY   Phil Rosen

Ticket to Crime   LOLA LANE
BEACON   Lewis D. Collins

What Every Woman Knows   HELEN HAYES
MGM   Gregory LaCava

1935   *Accent On Youth*   SYLVIA SIDNEY
       PARA   Wesley Ruggles

       Age of Indiscretion   MADGE EVANS
       MGM   Edward Ludwig

       Behind The Green Lights   JUDITH ALLEN
       TWICKENHAM   Christy Cabanne

       Broadway Gondolier   JOAN BLONDELL
       WB   Lloyd Bacon

       The Case of The Lucky Legs   GENEVIEVE TOBIN
       WB   Archie L. Mayo

       The Case of the Curious Bride   CLAIRE DODD
       FN   Michael Curtiz

       Confidential   EVALYN KNAPP
       REP   Edward L. Cahn

       Dangerous Corner   VIRGINIA BRUCE
       RKO   Phil Rosen

       Four Hours To Kill   HELEN MACK
       PARA   Mitchell Leisen

       The Gay Deception   FRANCES DEE
       TCF   William Wyler

       The Gilded Lily   CLAUDETTE COLBERT
       PARA   Wesley Ruggles

Guard That Girl   FLORENCE RICE
COL   Lambert Hillyer

His Night Out   IRENE HERVEY
UNIV   Chas. Christensen

Maybe It's Love   GLORIA STUART
WB   William McGann

Mr. Dynamite   JEAN DIXON
UNIV   Alan Crosland

The Nitwits   BETTY GRABLE
RKO   George Stevens

One Hour Late   HELEN TWELVETREES
PARA   Ralph Murphy

She Married Her Boss   CLAUDETTE COLBERT
COL   Gregory LaCava

Two For Midnight   JOAN BENNETT
PARA   Frank Tuttle

Vagabond Lady   EVELYN VENABLE
MGM   Sam Taylor

The Whole Town's Talking   JEAN ARTHUR
COL   John Ford

1936   *Absolute Quiet*   IRENE HERVEY
MGM   George Seitz

Below the Deadline   CECILIA PARKER
GN   Charles Lamont

The Case of the Black Cat   JUNE TRAVIS
WB   William McGann

The Case of the Velvet Claws   CLAIRE DODD
WB   William Clemens

Dracula's Daughter   MARGUERITE CHURCHILL
UNIV   Lambert Hillyer

Easy Money   KAY LINAKER
INVINCIBLE   Phil Rosen

Four Day Wonder   MARTHA SLEEPER
UNIV   Sidney Salkow

Gold Diggers of 1937   JOAN BLONDELL
WB   Lloyd Bacon

Here Comes Carter   GLENDA FARRELL
WB   William Clemens

Hot Money   BEVERLY ROBERTS
WB   William McGann

Lady in Scarlet   PATRICIA FARR
CHESTERF   Charles Lamont

More Than A Secretary   JEAN ARTHUR
COL   Alfred E. Green

Muss Em Up   MARGARET CALLAHAN
RKO   Charles Vidor

Strike Me Pink   SALLY EILERS
UA   Norman Taurog

Two Against the World   BEVERLY ROBERTS
WB   William McGann

Wife Vs. Secretary   JEAN HARLOW
MGM   Clarence Brown

Harlow is sensible and discreet and, although in love
with her boss, decides to do nothing to entice him
away from his jealous wife (Myrna Loy).

The Witness Chair   ANN HARDING
RKO   George Nicholls, Jr.

1937   *As Good As Married*   DORIS NOLAN
UNIV   Edward Buzzell

The Case of the Stuttering Bishop   ANN DVORAK
WB   William Clemens

Country Gentleman   JOYCE COMPTON
REP   Ralph Staub

Dance, Charlie, Dance   JEAN MUIR
WB   Frank McDonald

Easy Living   JEAN ARTHUR
PARA   Mitchell Leison

Ever Since Eve   MARION DAVIES
WB   Lloyd Bacon

Headline Crasher   MURIEL EVANS
GUARANTEED   Les Godwins

Her Husband's Secretary   BEVERLY ROBERTS
WB   Frank McDonald

Married Before Breakfast   FLORENCE RICE
MGM   Edwin Marin

Missing Witness   JEAN DALE
WB   William Clemens

Mr. Dodd Takes the Air   JANE WYMAN
WB   Alfred E. Green

Outlaws of the Orient   MAE CLARKE
COL   Ernest Schoedsack

She's Got Everything   ANN SOTHERN
RKO   Joseph Santley

Super-Sleuth   ANN SOTHERN
RKO   Ben Stoloff

That Certain Woman   BETTE DAVIS
WB   Edmund Goulding

The Thirteenth Man   INEZ COURTNEY
MONO   William Nigh

Turn Off The Moon   MARJORIE GATESON
PARA   Lewis Seiler

Wake Up And Live   PATSY KELLY
TCF   Sidney Lanfield

1938 *Alibi For Murder*   MARGUERITE CHURCHILL
COL   D. Ross Lederman

Cipher Bureau   CHARLOTTE WYNTERS
GN   Charles Lamont

Fast Company MGM Edward Buzzell		FLORENCE RICE
Having A Wonderful Time RKO Alfred Santell		GINGER ROGERS
Hold That Co-Ed TCF George Marshall		MARJORIE WEAVER
Island in the Sky TCF Herbert I. Leeds		GLORIA STUART
It's All Yours COL Elliot Nugent		MADELEINE CARROLL
Keep Smiling TCF Herbert I. Leeds		GLORIA STUART
Men Are Such Fools WB Busby Berkeley		PRISCILLA LANE
The Mysterious Mr. Moto TCF Norman Foster		MARY MAGUIRE
Personal Secretary UNIV Otis Garrett		JOY HODGES
Rich Man, Poor Girl MGM Reinheld Schunzel		RUTH HUSSEY
Squadron of Honor COL C. C. Coleman, Jr.		MARY RUSSELL
Trade Winds UA Tay Garnett		ANN SOTHERN
Tropic Holiday PARA Theodore Reed		MARTHA RAYE
Unashamed CINE-GRAND Allan Stuart		RAE KIDD
1939	*The Amazing Mr. Williams* COL Alexander Hall	JOAN BLONDELL
	Ambush PARA Kurt Neumann	GLADYS SWARTHOUT

Daytime Wife	WENDY BARRIE
TCF Gregory Ratoff	JOAN DAVIS
For Love Or Money	JUNE LANG
UNIV Albert Rogell	
Grand Jury Secrets	GAIL PATRICK
PARA James Hogan	
Hero For A Day	ANITA LOUISE
UNIV Harold Young	
Mr. Smith Goes To Washington	JEAN ARTHUR
COL Frank Capra	

When is a secretary not a secretary? When she's
administrative assistant, legislative assistant,
constituent liaison, office manager and press
secretary all rolled into one. Saunders the secretary
fulfills all these functions for Senator Smith, as
well as selecting a new wardrobe for him and "wiping
his nose." Saunders (Arthur), always addressed only
by her last name, is the cynical old Washington hand
juxtaposed against Smith's innocence. But she finally
admits corrupt Washington is no place for a woman. "A
lady wouldn't be working for this outfit," she says as
she determines to get out. But first she must open
Smith's eyes and help him win his fight. Smith has
never met anyone as "capable and intelligent" as she,
and he follows her coaching and tactics in order to
win the day in the Senate. He gets the credit and
will presumably be reelected; she will presumably get
to be Senator's wife.

Risky Business	DOROTHEA KENT
UNIV Arthur Lubin	

1940	*Escape To Glory*	JOAN BENNETT
	COL John Brahm	
	Gambling On The High Seas	JANE WYMAN
	WB George Amy	
	The Golden Fleecing	RITA JOHNSON
	MGM Leslie Fenton	
	Hired Wife	ROSALIND RUSSELL
	UNIV William A. Seiter	

We Who Are Young   LANA TURNER
MGM   Harold S. Bucquet

1941   *Andy Hardy's Private Secretary*   KATHRYN GRAYSON
MGM   George B. Heltz

Blonde Inspiration   VIRGINIA GREY
MGM   Busby Berkeley

Ellery Queen And The Murder Ring   MARGARET LINDSAY
COL   James Hogan

Ellery Queen And The Perfect Crime   MARGARET LINDSAY
COL   James Hogan

Ellery Queen's Penthouse Mystery   MARGARET LINDSAY
COL   James Hogan

The Feminine Touch   KAY FRANCIS
MGM   W. S. Van Dyke II

Flying Blind   JEAN PARKER
PARA   Frank McDonald

A Girl, A Guy, And A Gob   LUCILLE BALL
RKO   Richard Wallace

Honeymoon For Three   ANN SHERIDAN
WB   Lloyd Bacon

Kitty Foyle   GINGER ROGERS
RKO   Sam Wood

Murder Among Friends   MARJORIE WEAVER
TCF   Ray McCarey

Murder By Invitation   MARIAN MARSH
MONO   Phil Rosen

The Night Of January 16th   ELLEN DREW
PARA   William Clemens

Secret Evidence   MARJORIE REYNOLDS
PRC   William Nigh

She Knew All The Answers   JOAN BENNETT
COL   Richard Wallace

Tillie The Toiler   KAY HARRIS
COL   Sidney Salkow

The Trail Of Mary Dugan   LARAINE DAY
MGM   Norman Z. McLeod

1942   *A Close Call For Ellery Queen*   MARGARET LINDSAY
COL   James Hogan

Enemy Agents Meet Ellery Queen   MARGARET LINDSAY
COL   James Hogan

Eyes Of The Underworld   WENDY BARRIE
UNIV   Roy William Neill

The Magnificent Dope   LYNN BARI
TCF   Walter Lang

The Man Who Came To Dinner   BETTE DAVIS
WB   William Keighley

Obliging Young Lady   RUTH WARRICK
RKO   Richard Wallace

Sweetheart Of The Fleet   JOAN DAVIS
COL   Charles Barton

That Other Woman   VIRGINIA GILMORE
TCF   Ray McCarey

Treat 'Em Rough   PEGGY MORAN
UNIV   Ray Taylor

1943   *Dixie Dugan*   LOIS ANDREWS
TCF   Otto Brower

Get Going   GRACE MCDONALD
UNIV   Jean Yarbrough

He Hired The Boss   EVELYN VENABLE
TCF   Thomas Z. Loring

A Lady Takes A Chance   JEAN ARTHUR
RKO   William A. Seiter

A Stranger In Town   JEAN ROGERS
REP   Roy Rowland

Here Comes Elmer REP Joseph Santley		DALE EVANS
High Explosive PARA Frank McDonald		JEAN PARKER
The More The Merrier COL George Stevens		JEAN ARTHUR
1944	*Crime By Night* WB William Clemens	JANE WYMAN
	The Doughgirls WB James V. Kern	ANN SHERIDAN
	Government Girl RKO Dudley Nichols	OLIVIA DE HAVILLAND
	Phantom Lady UNIV Robert Siodmak	ELLA RAINES
	Pin Up Girl TCF Bruce Humberstone	BETTY GRABLE
	Practically Yours PARA Mitchell Leisen	CLAUDETTE COLBERT
	Shadows Of Suspicion MONO William Beaudine	MARJORIE WEAVER
	Standing Room Only PARA Sidney Lanfield	PAULETTE GODDARD
	The Suspect UNIV Robert Siodmak	ELLA RAINES
	The Whistler COL William Castle	GLORIA STUART
1945	*The Beautiful Cheat* UNIV Charles Barton	BONITA GRANVILLE
	The Clock MGM Vincente Minnelli	JUDY GARLAND

There is mention here of the fact that Garland is a secretary, but she is never shown working, and the plot revolves completely around her attempt to be with a soldier on furlough for one day.

Danger Signal   FAYE EMERSON
WB   Robert Florey

The Horn Blows At Midnight ALEXIS SMITH
WB   Raoul Walsh

Jungle Captive   AMELITA WARD
UNIV   Harold Young

Men In Her Diary   PEGGY RYAN
UNIV   Charles Barton

My Name Is Julia Ross   NINA FOCH
COL   Joseph H. Lewis

Pillow Of Death   BRENDA JOYCE
UNIV   Wallace Fox

Roughly Speaking   ROSALIND RUSSELL
WB   Michael Curtiz

Weekend At The Waldorf LANA TURNER
MGM   Robert Z. Leonard

1946 *Blonde For A Day*   KATHRYN ADAMS
PRC   Sam Newfield

The Dark Corner   LUCILLE BALL
TCF   Henry Hathaway

Ding Dong Williams   MARCY MCGUIRE
RKO   William Berke

The Inner Circle   ADELE MARA
REP   Phil Ford

One Way To Love   JANIS CARTER
COL   Ray Enright

Step By Step   ANNE JEFFREYS
RKO   Phil Rosen

Up Goes Maisie   ANN SOTHERN
MGM   Harry Beaumont

Young Widow   JANE RUSSELL
UA   Edwin L. Marin

1947   *Always Together*   JOYCE REYNOLDS
        WB   Fred DeCordova

        The Beginning Or The End   AUDREY TOTTER
        MGM   Norman Taurog

        The Case Of The Babysitter   PAMELA BLAKE
        S GOLDWYN   Lambert Hillyer

        The Hatbox Mystery   PAMELA BLAKE
        S GOLDWYN   Lambert Hillyer

        Miracle On 34th Street   MAUREEN O'HARA
        TCF   George Seaton

        The Shocking Miss Pilgrim   BETTY GRABLE
        TCF   George Seaton

        An odd footnote here is that a trailor for this
        musical contains no reference to the fact that Grable
        portrays one of the earliest pioneers in the office.
        It focusses only on the music and the love affair.

        They Won't Believe Me   SUSAN HAYWARD
        RKO   Irving Pichel

        Three On A Ticket   CHERYL WALKER
        PRC   Sam Newfield

        Too Many Winners   TRUDY MARSHALL
        PRC   William Beaudine

        The Web   ELLA RAINES
        UI   Michael Gordon

1948   *Bodyguard*   PRISCILLA LANE
        RKO   Richard O. Fleisher

        Daredevils Of The Clouds   MAE CLARKE
        REP   George Blair

        Grand Canyon Trail   JANE FRAZEE
        REP   William Witney

        Hollow Triumph   JOAN BENNETT
        EL   Steve Sekely

        One Touch Of Venus   EVE ARDEN
        UNIV   William A. Seiter

Panhandle   ANNE GWYNNE
AA   Lesley Selander

1949 *Caught*   BARBARA BEL GEDDES
MGM   Max Ophuls

The Lucky Stiff   CLAIRE TREVOR
UA   Lewis R. Foster

Miss Grant Takes Richmond   LUCILLE BALL
COL   Lloyd Bacon

My Dear Secretary   LARAINE DAY
MGM   Charles Martin

An aspiring novelist takes a job as secretary to a
well-known novelist, but he is more interested in
making romantic advances. She, however, resists these
advances with "You've got the wrong girl. But they
marry, and she continues as his secretary. When his
book is a failure, he decides he needs another
secretary, and she becomes secretary to another
writer. She has written a novel, but is willing to
sacrifice her writing career for her husband's.
However, when his jealousy drives her away, she
publishes her novel and wins a prize. After their
reconciliation, she gets herself a male secretary. It
looks like one of the few films of the period in which
the woman does get to have it all.

My Friend Irma   DIANA LYNN
PARA   George Marshall

Slattery's Hurricane   VERONICA LAKE
TCF   Andre De Toth

1950 *D.O.A.*   PAMELA BRITTON
CARDINAL   Rudolph Mate

The Duchess of Idaho   PAULA RAYMOND
MGM   Robert Z. Leonard

The Flying Missile   VIVECA LINDFORS
COL   Henry Levin

The Hills of Oklahoma   ELISABETH FRASER
REP   H. G. Springsteen

Mr. Music PARA	Richard Hadyn	NANCY OLSON
Outrage FM	Ida Lupino	MALA POWERS
Pretty Baby WB	Bretaigne Windust	BETSY DRAKE
The Second Fall EL	Jack Bernhardt	ELLA RAINES
Stella TCF	Claude Binyon	ANN SHERIDAN
Union Station PARA	Rudolph Mate	NANCY OLSON

1951
Criminal Lawyer COL	Seymour Friedman	JANE WYATT
The Family Secret COL	Henry Levin	JODY LAWRENCE
A Millionaire For Christy TCF	George Marshall	ELEANOR PARKER
Sunny Side Of The Street COL	Richard Quine	TERRY MOORE

1952
Bal Tabarin REP	Phillip Ford	MURIEL LAWRENCE
Big Jim McLain WB	Edward Ludwig	NANCY OLSON
Harem Girl COL	Edward Bernds	JOAN DAVIS
Just Across The Street UI	Joseph Pevney	ANN SHERIDAN
The Marrying Kind COL	George Cukor	JUDY HOLLIDAY
Monkey Business TCF	Howard Hawks	MARILYN MONROE

No Time For Flowers   VIVECA LINDFORS
RKO   Don Diegel

The Turning Point   ALEXIS SMITH
PARA   William Dieterle

Woman Of Sin   TRACEY ROBERTS
UA   Ben Hecht

1953   *Paris Model*   PAULETTE GODDARD
COL   Alfred E. Green

Vicki   JEANNE CRAIN
TCF   Harry Horner

1954   *Executive Suite*   SHELLEY WINTERS
MGM   Robert Wise

Night People   RITA GAM
TCF   Nunnally Johnson

1955   *Angela*   MARA LANE
TCF   Dennis O'Keefe

The Big Bluff   EVE MILLER
UA   W. Lee Wilder

The Big Tip Off   CONSTANCE SMITH
AA   Frank McDonald

Sincerely Yours   JOANNE DRU
WB   Gordon Douglas

Summertime   KATHARINE HEPBURN
UA   David Lean

Hepburn is shown only on vacation in Venice. When
asked what she does for a living, she identifies her
position as "administrative assistant," but then
admits that she's "just a fancy secretary, really."
She never discusses her work with the Italian antiques
dealer with whom she has an affair.

Trial   DOROTHY MCGUIRE
MGM   Mark Robson

1956   *Lisbon*   YVONNE FURNEAUX
REP   Ray Milland

Miracle In The Rain   JANE WYMAN
WB   Rudolph Mate

Slightly Scarlet   ARLENE DAHL
RKO   Allan Dwan

That Certain Feeling   EVA MARIE SAINT
WB   Norman Panama

Saint is private secretary to a cartoonist, Larkin,
and is "on the bench" to be Mrs. Larkin Number Four.
When Larkin tells her ex-husband, another cartoonist,
that she is his secretary, he is impressed; but when
Saint tells her ex-husband that she and Larkin are
going to be married, he considers her a gold digger.
Always very nicely dressed, Saint is efficient in
running her boss's life, and she is shown working at a
desk in Larkin's apartment, and she even types a
little. She has the authority to hire her ex-husband
as Larkin's assistant, and then she fires him; but in
the end they go off together and nothing is said about
being his secretary.

Toward The Unknown   VIRGINIA LEITH
WB   Mervyn LeRoy

1957   *Calypso Heat Wave*   MERRY ANDERS
       COL   Fred F. Sears

       Destination 60,000   COLEEN GRAY
       AA   George Waggner

       Ghost Diver   AUDREY TOTTER
       TCF   Robert Einfeld

       The Great Man   JOANNE GILBERT
       UNIV   Jose Ferrer

       Mr. Rock and Roll   LOIS O'BRIEN
       PARA   Charles Dubin

       Naked Paradise   BEVERLY GARLAND
       AIP   Roger Corman

       Voodoo Island   BEVERLY TAYLOR
       UA   Reginald Leborg

1958   *Auntie Mame*   PEGGY CASS
       WB   Morton Da Costa

The Big Beat   ANDRA MARTIN
UI   Will Cowan

The Girl Most Likely   JANE POWELL
RKO   Mitchell Leison

Hong Kong Affair   MAY WYNN
AA   Paul F. Heard

I Was a Teenage Frankenstein   PHYLLIS COTES
AIP   Herbert L. Strock

Paris Holiday   MARTHA HYER
UA   Gerd Oswald

1959   *Anatomy Of A Murder*   EVE ARDEN
COL   Otto Preminger

Ask Any Girl   SHIRLEY MACLAINE
MGM   Charles Walters

But Not For Me   CARROLL BAKER
PARA   Walter Lang

Middle Of The Night   KIM NOVAK
COL   Delbert Mann

1960   *Because They're Young*   VICTORIA SHAW
COL   Paul Wendkos

The Third Voice   LARAINE DAY
TCF   Hubert Cornfield

1962   *The Couch*   SHIRLEY KNIGHT
WB   Owen Crump

That Touch Of Mink   DORIS DAY
UI   Delbert Mann

Day is described as a "girl who operates a computing
machine," but she spends almost all of the film
unemployed, and, of course since this is Day,
protecting her virginity. At one point the
millionaire who tried to seduce her gets her a job,
and she is shown sorting key punch cards. She likes
the job and hopes she will do well, but when she finds
out how she got it, she is upset and protests, "You do
not have to feel sorry for me. I will get my own job.
And if I never work again, at least I will have done

it on my own!" She then accidentally causes the computer to go haywire, and the millionaire complains, "She cannot hold a job; no company can afford her; she destroys everything. Why doesn't she get married?" She does.

1963	*Beach Party* AIP	William Asher	DOROTHY MALONE
	Who's Been Sleeping In My Bed? PARA	Daniel Mann	CAROL BURNETT
1964	*Paris When It Sizzles* PARA	Richard Quine	AUDREY HEPBURN
	The Patsy PARA	Jerry Lewis	INA BALIN
	The Pleasure Seekers TCF	Jean Negulesco	CAROL LYNLEY
1966	*Paradise, Hawaiian Style* PARA	Michael Moore	SUZANNA LEIGH
	Walk, Don't Run COL	Charles Walters	SAMANTHA EGGAR
1967	*Doctor, You've Got To Be Kidding* MGM	Peter Tewksbury	SANDRA DEE
	Fitzwilly UA	Delbert Mann	BARBARA FELDON
	How To Succeed In Business Without Really Trying UA	David Swift	MICHELE LEE

Despite a musical number which proclaims "A Secretary Is Not a Toy," the secretaries are regarded as such by the all-male executives of the company. Lee is very eager to help the new man in the company and is not shy about getting him to invite her out. At first he thinks it won't be good for his career to get serious about a secretary, but in the end he proposes, then turns around and pleads with her to be his secretary because now he is a vice president and needs her. Once Lee is grabbed by one of the executives, but she pushes him away and says no in no uncertain terms. She is presented in contrast to the chorus girl who is the boss's tootsie and thus hired as a totally incompetent secretary. Chorus-girl-turned-secretary shows off her boobs while Lee impresses her beau with the fact that she likes to curl up in bed with *Fortune* and *Business Week*. She has ambition, but it is only for the man in her life.

Thoroughly Modern Millie	JULIE ANDREWS
UNIV George Roy Hill	

In this musical about the `20s, women are purportedly gaining independence. Andrews is modern with her bobbed hair and short skirts and the fact that she has come to the city to be a "stenog." She interviews bosses to find an eligible bachelor because she intends to marry her boss. She finds the right boss, and he calls her "John" because she is so efficient, even while wearing her flapper's cloche in the office. She refuses to marry the young man she falls in love with because she thinks he is poor, but when he turns out to be rich, she is delighted. "Be my stenog," he proposes, but she maintains, "Oh no. I don't want to be equal anymore. I want to be a woman!"

Warning Shot	STEPHANIE POWERS
PARA Buzz Kulik	

1968	*Hot Millions*	MAGGIE SMITH
	MGM Eric Till	

The Love Bug	MICHELE LEE
BV Robert Stevenson	

Paper Lion	LAUREN HUTTON
UA Alex March	

The Secret Cinema	AMY VANE
TAMBELLINI Paul Bartel	

1969	*The Big Bounce*	LEIGH TAYLOR-YOUNG
	WB Alex March	

Cactus Flower	INGRID BERGMAN
COL Gene Saks	

Popi	BARBARA DANA
UA Arthur Hiller	

1973	*Charley Varrick* UNIV Don Siegal	FELICIA FARR
1974	*How To Seduce A Woman* CINERAMA Charles Martin	ANGEL TOMPKINS
	Longest Yard PARA Robert Aldrich	BERNADETTE PETERS
1975	*The Black Bird* COL David Giles	LEE PATRICK
	Hearts Of The West UA Howard Zieff	BLYTHE DANNER
	Sheila Levine Is Dead & Living *In New York* PARA Gene Marum	JEANNIE BERLIN

SOCIAL WORKER

It is surprising that there are so few social worker movies. Here is a traditional role for women which film makers could have portrayed without stepping out of bounds, and the cases these women deal with make for great soap opera.

1933   *Ann Vickers*   IRENE DUNNE
       RKO   John Cromwell

      Ann (Dunne) works in a settlement house, has "a passion for helping people," and is highly regarded professionally. Not ready for love, she considers her work the most important thing in her life. The setting is World War I, and Ann is portrayed as one of the new independent women; refusing a proposal from an Army officer, she claims, "I have set out on a career . . . I have a very important job." Still she gives up a career move in order to be with him, a decision which leaves her pregnant. She resigns her position in order to have the baby, expects a girl whom she will train for a career, and decides to work in a prison, writes an expose of the barbaric treatment to which women prisoners are subjected, and becomes a prison superintendent. Her next affair is with a judge, with whom she has a son. But where does this feminist non-conformity get her? Nowhere, since she loses her job and writes articles to make a living. She considers herself to have been locked in the "prison of ambition, the prison of desire of praise for myself." So she gives up that "misery" for love of the judge and her son.

1936   *Pennies From Heaven*   MADGE EVANS
       COL   Norman Z. McLeod

1942   *Journey For Margaret*   FAY BAINTER
       MGM   W. S. Van Dyke II

1943	*Crime Doctor*		MARGARET LINDSAY
	COL	Michael Gordon	

1944	*White Cliffs of Dover*		IRENE DUNNE
	MGM	Clarence Brown	

1948	*The Search*		ALINE MCMAHON
	MGM	Fred Zimmerman	

1949	*Mr. Soft Touch*		EVELYN KEYES
	COL	H. Lewis/D. Gordon	

1950	*Deported*		MARTA TOREN
	UNIV	Robert Siodmark	

1951	*Gambling House*		TERRY MOORE
	RKO	Ted Tetzlaff	

1952	*Meet Me At The Fair*		DIANA LYNN
	UNIV	Douglas Sirk	

1953	*Trouble Along The Way*		DONNA REED
	WB	Michael Curtiz	

1955	*Target Zero*		PEGGY CASTLE
	WB	Harmon Jones	

1956	*Dance With Me Henry*		MARY WICKES
	UA	Charles Barton	

1957	*The Man Who Turned To Stone*		CHARLOTTE AUSTIN
	COL	Leslie Kardos	

1958	*The Tunnel Of Love*		GIA SCALA
	MGM	Gene Kelly	

1962	*Follow That Dream*		JOANNA MOORE
	UA	Gordon Douglas	

	Requiem For A Heavyweight		JULIE HARRIS
	COL	Ralph Nelson	

Harris plays a sterotypical lonely-spinster social
worker who, implausibly, falls for the brutish,
brain-damaged fighter. At first she merely wants to
help someone she views as misunderstood, but
compassion is detrimental to her good judgment. Her
loosening up as she has a beer in a bar with the
punch-drunk fighter is intended to show the audience

that such a woman can have "real" emotion, but it is irrelevant to the film. Her only believable moment comes when, frightened, she resists the advances she has naively encouraged.

1964   *The New Interns*   INGER STEVENS
        COL   John Rich

1965   *The Pawnbroker*   GERALDINE FITZGERALD
        LANDAU-UNGER   Sidney Lumet

Here is another loveless, lonely social worker, shy and plain. The pawnbroker she tries to befriend finds her tedious and incapable of understanding his post-Holocaust pain. He tells her to stay out of his life, but at his most depressed he goes to talk to her. She realizes she can do nothing for him; she literally holds out her hand to him, but he does not take it. Realistically, she provides no bright light in this unrelievedly grim film.

        Synanon   EARTHA KITT
        COL   Richard Quine

        A Thousand Clowns   BARBARA HARRIS
        UA   Fred Coe

Presumably a Ph.D. in psychology, this Child Welfare Board caseworker is referred to and addressed as Miss Markowitz. She considers herself unsuited to her profession because she gets too involved in her cases. Mousy at first, she turns on her partner (and fiance) and asserts herself. After falling in love with the nonconformist she is investigating, she loosens up and moves in with him; her next step is to clean his apartment and decorate it with flowers. At first worried about keeping her job, she is happy to give it up for a life of enjoyment and total uncertainty.

1969   *The Lost Man*   JOANNA SHIMKUS
        UNIV   Robert A. Arthur

        Pieces of Dreams   LAUREN HUTTON
        UA   Daniel Haller

1971   *Marriage Of A Young Stock*broker   PATRICIA BARRY
        TCF   Lawrence Turman

1973   *Blume In Love*   SUSAN ANSPACH
        WB   Paul Mazursky

        Willie Dynamite   DIANA SANDS
        UNIV   Gilbert Moses

SPY

It is difficult to tell who fits in this category, because often the woman has another profession, but is enlisted as a spy. It is rarely the primary occupation of any of the characters. Also, in many war films, ordinary civilians are enlisted as spies; but they are doing it simply as patriotic duty and not for pay, so they are not included in this listing.

1930	*Inside The Lines* SU	Roy Pomeroy	BETTY COMPSON
	Renegades TCF	Victor Fleming	MYRNA LOY
	Three Faces East WB	Roy Del Ruth	CONSTANCE BENNETT
	Young Eagles PARA	William Wellman	JEAN ARTHUR
1931	*A Woman Of Experience* RKO	Harry Joe Brown	HELEN TWELVETREES
	Dishonored PARA	J. Von Sternberg	MARLENE DIETRICH
	The Gay Diplomat RKO	Rich Boleslavsky	BETTY COMPSON GENEVIEVE TOBIN
	Men of the Sky FN	Alfred E. Green	IRENE DELROY
	The Seas Beneath TCF	John Ford	MARION LESSING
1932	*Mata Hari* MGM	George Fitzmaurice	GRETA GARBO

	Million Dollar Legs PARA Edward Cline	LYDA ROBERTI
1933	*After Tonight* RKO George Archainbaud	CONSTANCE BENNETT
1934	*British Agent* WB Michael Curtiz	KAY FRANCIS
	Madame Spy UNIV Karl Freund	FAY WRAY
	Operator Thirteen MGM Rich Boleslavsky	MARION DAVIES
	Stamboul Quest MGM Sam Wood	MYRNA LOY
1935	*Rendezvous* MGM William K. Howard	ROSALIND RUSSELL
1936	*The General Died At Dawn* PARA Lewis Milestone	MADELEINE CARROLL
	Til We Meet Again PARA Robert Florey	GERTRUDE MICHAEL
1937	*Bulldog Drummond* REP Norman Lee	DOROTHY MACKAILL
	The Firefly MGM Robert Z. Leonard	JEANETTE MACDONALD
	Lancer Spy TCF Gregory Ratoff	DOLORES DEL RIO
	Soldier and the Lady RKO George Nicholls, Jr.	MARGOT GRAHAME
1938	*Blockade* W.WANGER William Dieterle	MADELEINE CARROLL
	I Married a Spy GN Edmond Greville	BRIGITTE HORNEY
	Mr. Moto Takes a Chance TCF Norman Foster	ROCHELLE HUDSON

	Mr. Wong, Detective MONO William Nigh	EVELYN BRENT
	Spy Ring UNIV Joseph H. Lewis	JANE WYMAN
1940	*British Intelligence* WB Terry Morse	MARGARET LINDSAY
	Murder In The Air WB Lewis Seiler	LYA LEYS
1941	*Criminals Within* PRC Joseph Lewis	CONSTANCE WORTH
	International Lady UA Tim Whelan	ILONA MASSEY
	Mr. Dynamite UNIV John Rawlins	IRENE HERVEY
	Paris Calling UNIV Edwin L. Marin	ELISABETH BERGNER
1942	*Dangerously They Live* WB Robert Florey	NANCY COLEMAN
	Escape From Hong Kong UNIV William Nigh	MARJORIE LORD
	Hitler - Dead Or Alive CHAS.HOUSE Nicke Grinde	DOROTHY TREE
	Invisible Agent UNIV Edwin L. Marin	ILONA MASSEY
	Madame Spy UNIV Roy William Neill	JOAN BENNETT
	My Favorite Blonde PARA Sidney Lanfield	MADELEINE CARROLL

Carroll plays a British agent trying to get a warplane
schedule in code from New York to Los Angeles, all the
while chased by enemy agents. Hiding in a theatre,
she enlists the aid of a vaudevillian. Through many

comic misadventures they outwit the other agents and complete the mission. She is the clever, experienced one, and the real hero of the day; but she is proud of her partner, with whom she has fallen in love, and gives him credit, predicting that the British government will decorate him.

| *My Favorite Spy* | | ELLEN DREW |
| RKO | Tay Garnett | JANE WYMAN |

| *Once Upon a Honeymoon* | | GINGER ROGERS |
| RKO | Leo McCarey | |

An ex-stripper from Brooklyn marries a German Baron who arranges for the capitulation of various countries early in World War II. An American reporter fakes the stripper's death so she can get away from the Baron, but, because she has exchanged passports with a Jewish maid, she is arrested as a Jew. After another escape she is enlisted as a spy and sent back to her husband to learn Hitler's plans. Although she is not too expert ("She couldn't spy her way through a knothole"), she accidentally photographs a secret code and does away with the Baron.

| *Salute To Courage* | | ANN AYARS |
| MGM | Jules Dassin | |

| *Secret Agent Of Japan* | | LYNN BARI |
| TCF | Irving Pechel | |

| *Ship Ahoy* | | ELEANOR POWELL |
| MGM | Edward Buzzell | |

| *Spy Ship* | | IRENE MANNING |
| WB | B. Reaves Eason | |

| 1943 | *Background To Danger* | | BRENDA MARSHALL |
| | WB | Raoul Walsh | |

| | *The Fallen Sparrow* | | MAUREEN O'HARA |
| | RKO | Richard Wallace | |

| | *First Comes Courage* | | MERLE OBERON |
| | COL | Dorothy Arzner | |

| | *Miss V From Moscow* | | LOLA LANE |
| | PRC | Albert Herman | |

Secret Enemies   FAYE EMERSON
WB   Ben Stoloff

1944   *Action in Arabia*   VIRGINIA BRUCE
        RKO   Leonide Moguy

        The Hour Before Dawn   VERONICA LAKE
        PARA   Frank Tuttle

        Storm Over Lisbon   VERA RALSTON
        REP   George Sherman

1945   *Blood On The Sun*   SYLVIA SIDNEY
        UA   Frank Lloyd

        The House On Ninety-Second Street   SIGNE HASSO
        TCF   Henry Hathaway

        Salome, Where She Danced   YVONNE DE CARLO
        UNIV   Charles Lamont

1946   *Notorious*   INGRID BERGMAN
        RKO   Alfred Hitchcock

Because her father was imprisoned for treason, Bergman
considers herself a marked woman. When the FBI offers
her a job, her cynical response is, "There is only one
job you coppers would want me for, but I am no stool
pigeon." She is sent to Brazil to find out
information from Germans who paid her father.
Considering herself a crook and a tramp, she goes, not
for patriotism, but to help her father. As
instructed, she marries a German agent and pumps him
for information. When he realizes what she is, he
tries to kill her, but she is rescued.

O.S.S.   GERALDINE FITZGERALD
PARA   Irving Pichel

A sculptor who studied in Paris is hired by the O. S.
S. to spy in France because of her contacts there and
knowledge of the language. Her work as a sculptor
serves as an appropriate cover for her activities.

Rendezvous 24   MARIA PALMER
TCF   James Tinling

1948   *Old Los Angeles*   CATHERINE MCLEOD
        REP   Joseph Kane

The Paleface   JANE RUSSELL
PARA   Norman Z. McLeod

In exchange for a pardon, outlaw Calamity Jane agrees
to spy for the government and find out who is passing
contraband arms to the Indians. She joins a wagon
train posing as a "lady." She is clever and
resourceful, as well as a crack shot. After her
quickly-acquired husband saves her from the Indians,
they catch the villains and she ends up in fancy
feminine attire, a happy wife with no more guns under
her apron.

Rogue's Regiment   MARTA TOREN
UI   Robert Florey

1949   *Francis*   PATRICIA MEDINA
        UNIV   Arthur Lubin

1950   *Abbott & Costello in the*
        Foreign Legion   PATRICIA MEDINA
        UI   Charles Lamont

        Davis Harding, Counterspy   AUDREY LONG
        COL   Ray Nazarro

        The Redhead and the Cowboy   RHONDA FLEMING
        PARA   Leslie Fenton

        Spy Hunt   MARTA TOREN
        UNIV   George Sherman

1951   *Drums In The Deep South*   BARBARA PAYTON
        RKO   Wm. Cameron Menzies

        I Was An American Spy   ANN DVORAK
        MONO   Lesley Selander

        My Favorite Spy   HEDY LAMARR
        PARA   Norman Z. McLeod

        When The Redskins Rode   MARY CASTLE
        COL   Lew Landers

1952   *Diplomatic Courier*   PATRICIA NEAL
        TCF   Henry Hathaway   HILDEGARDE NEFF

        Five Fingers   DANIELLE DARRIEUX
        TCF   Jos. L. Mankiewicz

The Pathfinder HELENA CARTER
COL   Sidney Salkow

Walk On East Beacon VIRGINIA GILMORE
COL   Alfred Werker

1953 *Arrowhead* KATY JURADO
PARA   Charles M. Warren

Charge of the Lancers PAULETTE GODDARD
COL   William Castle

Fort Algiers YVONNE DE CARLO
UA   Lesley Selander

Pickup On South Street JEAN PETERS
TCF   Samuel Fuller

1954 *Betrayed* LANA TURNER
MGM   Gottfried Reinhard

Fire Over Africa MAUREEN O'HARA
COL   Richard Sale

Gog CONSTANCE DOWLING
IVAN TORS   Herbert L. Strock

The Iron Glove URSULA THEISS
COL   William Castle

Night People ANITA BJORK
TCF   Nunnally Johnson

1955 *The Sea Chase* LANA TURNER
WB   John Farrow

1957 *Jet Pilot* JANET LEIGH
H.HUGHES   J. Von Sternberg

Stopover Tokyo JOAN COLLINS
TCF   Richard L. Breen

1958 *Count Five and Die* ANNAMARIE DURINGER
TCF   Victor Vicas

Space Master X-7 LYNN THOMAS
TCF   Edward Bernds

1959   *North by Northwest*   EVA MARIE SAINT
       MGM   Alfred Hitchcock

As the mistress of a foreign agent, Saint is enlisted
by the CIA; she claims she accepted because it was the
first time anyone asked her to do anything worthwhile.
She does not appear until one-third of the way through
the film, when she is sent to seduce Thornhill, an
advertising man who has inadvertently gotten mixed up
in spy shenanigans. Meeting him on a train, she
claims to be an industrial designer. Originally she
saves him from the villains, but in the end it is he
who must save her. The reward for her loyal service?
She gets to be Mrs. Thornhill.

1960   *The House Of Intrigue*   DAWN ADDAMS
       AA   Duilio Coletti

       I Aim At The Stars   GIA SCALA
       COL   J. Lee Thompson

1961   *Armored Command*   TINA LOUISE
       AA   Byron Haskin

       The Last Time I Saw Archie   FRANCE NUYEN
       UA   Jack Webb

1962   *The Counterfeit Traitor*   LILLI PALMER
       PARA   George Seaton

       The Road To Hong Kong   JOAN COLLINS
       UA   Norman Panama

1964   *A Global Affair*   LILO PULVER
       MGM   Jack Arnold

       Advance To The Rear   STELLA STEVENS
       MGM   George Marshall

1966   *Ambush Bay*   TISA CHANG
       COL   Ron Winston

       Batman   LEE MERIWETHER
       TCF   Leslie H. Martinson

       I Deal In Danger   CHRISTINE CARERE
       TCF   Walter Grauman

Murderer's Row		CAMILLA SPARV
COL	Henry Levin	
Our Man Flint		GILA GOLAN
TCF	Daniel Mann	
The Silencers		DALIAH LAVI
COL	Phil Karlson	
The Spy With My Face		SENTA BERGER
MGM	John Newland	
That Man In Istanbul		SYLVA KOSCINA
COL	Anthony Isasi	

1967	*The Ambushers*		SENTA BERGER
	COL	Henry Levin	
	Caprice		DORIS DAY
	TCF	Frank Tashlin	

In this tale of industrial espionage, Day, who passes herself off as an industrial designer, sells the secret of a new roll-on deodorant, then tries to steal the formula for changing the consistency of animal hair to that of human hair. She bungles the spying with her clumsiness, and when the police are after her, she worries about losing her new hat. It turns out that, although she has worked hard to earn the money she is paid, she is really doing it to find out who killed her father, an Interpol agent. She accomplishes her goal, while also accidentally uncovering a big international narcotics ring. All this nonsense is difficult to figure out.

Deadlier Than The Male		ELKE SOMMER
UNIV	Ralph Thomas	
In Like Flint		ANNA LEE
TCF	Gordon Douglas	
The Venetian Affair		ELKE SOMMER
MGM	Jerry Thorpe	

1968	*In Enemy Country*		ANJANETTE COMER
	UNIV	Harry Keller	
1970	*Darling Lili*		JULIE ANDREWS
	PARA	Blake Edwards	

1971 *Mrs. Polifax - Spy*   ROSALIND RUSSELL
      UA   Leslie Martinson

TEACHER/EDUCATOR

Teacher is one occupational category which realistically parallels the large proportion of employed women who were teachers. They are never married and are often stereotypically shown as sexually frustrated spinsters. Their classroom efforts, however, are generally lauded.

1930	*Mountain Justice* UNIV　　　　Harry J. Brown	KATHRYN CRAWFORD
1931	*Daybreak* MGM　　　　Jacques Feyder	HELEN CHANDLER
	Palmy Days UA　　　　Edward Sutherland	CHARLOTTE GREENWOOD
1932	*Night After Night* PARA　　　　Archie Mayo	ALISON SKIPWORTH
	The Penguin Pool Murder RKO　　　　George Archainbaud	EDNA MAY OLIVER
1933	*Ann Carver's Profession* COL　　　　Eddie Buzzell	FAY WRAY
	King Of The Jungle PARA　　　　H. B. Humberstone	FRANCES DEE
	Meet The Baron MGM　　　　Walter Lang	EDNA MAY OLIVER
1934	*Eight Girls in a Boat* PARA　　　　Richard Wallace	KAY JOHNSON
	Finishing School RKO　　　　George Nicholls	BEULAH BONDI
	Four Frightened People PARA　　　　Cecil B. DeMille	CLAUDETTE COLBERT

Have a Heart   JEAN PARKER
MGM   David Butler

I'll Fix It   MONA BARRIE
COL   Roy William Neill

Love Birds   ZASU PITTS
UNIV   William Seiter

Murder on the Blackboard   EDNA MAY OLIVER
RKO   George Archainbaud

This Side Of Heaven   MAE CLARKE
MGM   William K. Howard

1935   *Chasing Yesterday*   ELIZABETH PATTERSON
      RKO   George Nichols

      Freckles   CAROL STONE
      RKO   Edward Killy/William Hamilton   VIRGINIA WEIDLER

      Grand Old Girl   MAY ROBSON
      RKO   John Robertson

      Life Begins At Forty   ROCHELLE HUDSON
      TCF   George Marshall

      Murder on a Honeymoon   EDNA MAY OLIVER
      RKO   Lloyd Corrigan

      Shipmates Forever   RUBY KEELER
      WB   Frank Borzage

      Silk Hat Kid   MAE CLARKE
      TCF   H. B. Humberstone

1936   *Collegiate*   BETTY JANE COOPER
      PARA   Ralph Murphy   FRANCES LANGFORD

      Cowboy and the Kid   DOROTHY REVIER
      UNIV   Ray Taylor

      Girls' Dormitory   RUTH CHATTERTON
      TCF   Irving Cummings

      Little Red School House   ANN DORAN
      CHESTERF   Charles Lamont

Man Hunt		MARGUERITE CHURCHILL
WB	William Clemens	

The Plot Thickens		ZASU PITTS
RKO	Ben Holmes	

Silly Billies		DOROTHY LEE
RKO	Fred Guiol	

These Three		MIRIAM HOPKINS
S GOLDWYN	William Wyler	MERLE OBERON

Two college graduates decide to start a boarding
school. Having no family, they must support
themselves, and teaching seems the only respectable
thing they can do because they have not been educated
to do anything specific at their women's college.
Oberon is the conscientious administrator who tries to
be understanding but who punishes the girls when
necessary. Hopkins teaches Latin and other subjects;
she is clever and does not permit the girls to
outsmart her. Both women fall in love with the local
doctor; he becomes engaged to Oberon, but a malicious
student accuses Hopkins of having an affair with him.
This forces the closure of the school, which means the
loss not only of their source of income and something
they have built, but also the loss of their
self-respect. The women and the doctor sue the
student's grandmother for libel; they lose, but
eventually the truth comes out. Although the school
has fallen into ruins, the friendship has remained
intact. It must be noted that in the play the scandal
was an accusation of lesbianism, but Hollywood
censorship forbade such a plot. The film serves as a
good example of female bonding even though Oberon goes
off to join the doctor.

Three On The Trail		MURIEL STEVENS
PARA	Howard Bretherton	

1937	*The Great O'Malley*		ANN SHERIDAN
	WB	William Dieterle	

Hoosier Schoolboy		ANNE NAGEL
MONO	William Nigh	

The Outcasts of Poker Flat		JEAN MUIR
RKO	Christy Cabanne	

Quality Street   KATHARINE HEPBURN
RKO   George Stevens

Thin Ice   SONJA HENIE
TCF   Sidney Langfield

We Have Our Moments   SALLY EILERS
UNIV   Alfred L. Worker

1938 *Beloved Brat*   DOLORES COSTELLO
WB   Arthur Lubin

Coconut Grove   HARRIET HILLIARD
PARA   Alfred Santell

The Frontiersmen   EVELYN VENABLE
PARA   Lesley Selander

Girl's School   GLORIA HOLDEN
COL   John Brahm

Girls on Probation   DOLORES COSTELLO
WB   Arthur Lubin

Goodby Broadway   ALICE BRADY
UNIV   Ray McCarey

Shadow Over Shanghai   LINDA GRAY
GN   Charles Lamont

South Riding   EDNA BEST
UA   Victor Saville

1939 *Andy Hardy Gets Spring Fever*   CECILIA PARKER
MGM   W. S. Van Dyke II

Back Door To Heaven   ALINE MCMAHON
PARA   William K. Howard

The Cisco Kid and the Lady   MARJORIE WEAVER
TCF   Herbert I. Leeds

The Marshall of Mesa City   VIRGINIA VALE
RKO   David Howard

Second Fiddle   SONJA HENIE
TCF   Sidney Lanfield

1940	*Anne Of Windy Poplars* RKO Jack Hively	ANNE SHIRLEY
	Escape MGM Mervyn LeRoy	NORMA SHEARER
	Forty Little Mothers MGM Busby Berkeley	JUDITH ANDERSON
	Let's Make Music RKO Leslie Goodwins	ELIZABETH RISDON
	Rainbow Over The Range MONO Al Herman	DOROTHY FAY
1941	*Cheers For Miss Bishop* PARA Tay Garnett	MARTHA SCOTT
	Hold Back The Dawn PARA Mitchell Leisen	OLIVIA DE HAVILLAND
	The Lady From Cheyenne UNIV Frank Lloyd	LORETTA YOUNG
	Remember The Day TCF Henry King	CLAUDETTE COLBERT
	Rise And Shine TCF Allan Dwan	LINDA DARNELL
	Scattergood Baines RKO Christy Cabanne	CAROL HUGHES
1942	*Heart Of The Rio Grande* REP William Morgan	FAY MCKENZIE
	The Powers Girl UA Norman Z. McLeod	ANNE SHIRLEY
	The Talk Of The Town COL George Stevens	JEAN ARTHUR
1943	*The Amazing Mr. Holiday* UNIV Bruce Manning	DEANNA DURBIN
	China PARA John Farrow	LORETTA YOUNG

China Girl	GENE TIERNEY
TCF Henry Hathaway	
Crash Dive	ANNE BAXTER
TCF Archie Mayo	
Girls In Chains	ARLINE JUDGE
PRC Edgar L. Ulmer	
In Old Oklahoma	MARTHA SCOTT
REP Albert S. Rogell	
This Land Is Mine	MAUREEN O'HARA
RKO Jean Renoir	

1944	*An American Romance*	ANN RICHARDS
	MGM King Vidor	
	Bathing Beauty	ESTHER WILLIAMS
	MGM George Sidney	
	Nine Girls	ANN HARDING
	COL Leigh Jason	
	South Of Dixie	ANNE GWYNNE
	UNIV Jean Yarbrough	
	Tomorrow The World	BETTY FIELD
	UA Leslie Fenton	
1945	*The Corn Is Green*	BETTE DAVIS
	WB Irving Rapper	

This is one teacher film where we get to see the woman practicing her profession at length, and there is no question that teaching is the only thing in her life. Davis is the only teacher in a Welsh village and much of the film is taken up with her preparation of one of her students for the Oxford entrance examination.

Our Vines Have Tender Grapes	FRANCES GIFFORD
MGM Roy Rowland	
Salty O'Rourke	GAIL RUSSELL
PARA Raoul Walsh	
Thrill Of A Romance	ESTHER WILLIAMS
MGM Richard Thorpe	

The Brute Man   JANE ADAMS
PRC   Jean Yarbrough

Do You Love Me   MAUREEN O'HARA
TCF   Grogory Ratoff

She Wrote The Book   JOAN DAVIS
UNIV   Charles Lamont

1947   *Driftwood*   RUTH WARRICK
REP   Allan Dwan

It Happened In Brooklyn   KATHRYN GRAYSON
MGM   Richard Whorf

The Pilgrim Lady   LYNNE ROBERTS
REP   Lesley Selander

Welcome Stranger   JOAN CAULFIELD
PARA   Elliot Nugent

1948   *An Old-Fashioned Girl*   GLORIA JEAN
EL   Arthur Dreifuss

The Boy With Green Hair   BARBARA HALE
RKO   Joseph Losey

Moonrise   GAIL RUSSELL
REP   Frank Borzage

1949   *The Accused*   LORETTA YOUNG
PARA   William Dieterle

Arson, Inc.   ANNE GWYNNE
S GOLDWYN   William Berke

The Girl From Jones Beach   VIRGINIA MAYO
WB   Peter Godfrey

Undertow   DOROTHY HART
UI   William Castle

1950   *A Woman Of Distinction*   ROSALIND RUSSELL
COL   Edward Buzzell

The credits show the Dean of Benton College on the
cover of Time as one of the country's most
distinguished educators. The Dean claims that there
is no room for romance in a career, and she dismisses

one of her professors who tries to woo her. Her father constantly nags her about the need for romance, maintaining, "A woman in not complete without a man, a home, and children." She believes her life to be complete with her work and the French orphan she adopted. Romance does arrive in the person of a British astronomer, who expects a college dean to be an old maid, a "crusty spinster who looks under the bed every night, hoping there is a man." He finds her to be the coldest woman he has ever met; he should have brought her a suit of long underwear. But the newspapers link the two romantically, and this causes a scandal on campus. Russell sports her usual severe business suits and leads an antiseptic life, although she is loving to her adopted daughter. Her idea of weekend fun is bicycle riding with "the girls." Still she is offended when a young boy calls her an older woman, and she wears a glamorous strapless formal gown to the prom, though she never dances at these affairs. The President is worried that the scandal will hurt the college, but her father considers this her opportunity to become a woman. "I sent you to college to come home with a man, but you came home with degrees. You look like a woman, but you don't think and feel like one. It is time you had a man in your life," lectures her father. Despite the importance of her career, she resigns because she is tired of self-denial. Evidently you cannot have both a career and a man, and the film's clear message is that a career does not make you a woman.

Destination Big House		DOROTHY PATRICK
REP	George Blair	
Girls' School		JULIA DEAN
MACDONALD	Lew Landers	
Love That Brute		RUTH MANNING
TCF	Alexander Hall	
The Pretty Girl		JOAN CAULFIELD
COL	Henry Levin	
1951 *According To Mrs. Hoyle*		SPRING BYINGTON
MONO	Jean Yarbrough	
Bannerline		SALLY FORREST
MGM	Don Weis	

The Bushwackers RKO Rod Amateau		DOROTHY MALONE
I Was A Communist For The FBI WB Gordon Douglas		DOROTHY HART
The Lady Pays Off UNIV Douglas Sirk		LINDA DARNELL
Man In The Saddle COL Andre DeToth		ELLEN DREW
Two Tickets To Broadway RKO James V. Kern		JANET LEIGH
1952	*Arctic Flight* MONO Lew Landers	LOLA ALBRIGHT
	Atomic City PARA Jerry Hopper	NANCY GATES
	Hong Kong PARA Lewis R. Foster	RHONDA FLEMING
	Just For You PARA Elliott Nugent	ETHEL BARRYMORE
	Love Is Better Than Ever MGM Stanley Donen	ELIZABETH TAYLOR
	The Man Behind The Gun WB Felix Feist	PATRICE WYMORE
	My Pal Gus TCF Robert Parrish	JOANNE DRU
	One Big Affair UA Peter Godfrey	EVELYN KEYES
1953	*A Lion Is In The Streets* WB Raoul Walsh	BARBARA HALE

Hale plays a northern college graduate who is teaching in a rural southern school. In the first scene she is shown teaching, but then she is wooed by an itinerant peddler who says he has never met a pretty girl who was a college graduate. She first assists him with his peddling, then she is devoted to his career as he studies law and goes into politics. As he says, "Marry a college girl, and up you go in the world."

Bright Road   DOROTHY DANDRIDGE
MGM   Gerald Mayer

Dandridge goes to teach in an all-black rural school,
and from then on it's trite treacle. Although
apprehensive about her first day on the job,
Dandridge, properly dressed, proves capable, wise, and
understanding. She takes a special interest in a
"backward" child and corrects his behavior; she
teaches Sunday school and leads hymn-singing; she
helps nurse a sick child and comforts the mother. All
the teachers in the school are women, but the
principal is a man, and guess who gets him?

It Came From Outer Space   BARBARA RUSH
UNIV   Jack Arnold

Problem Girls   HELEN WALKER
COL   E. A. Dupont

The Story Of Three Loves   LESLIE CARON
MGM   Vincente Minnelli

1954   *Her Twelve Men*   GREER GARSON
MGM   Robert Z. Leonard

Tanganyika   RUTH ROMAN
UNIV   Andre DeToth

Three Coins In The Fountain   DOROTHY MCGUIRE
TCF   Jean Negulesco

1955   *The Blackboard Jungle*   ANNE FRANCIS
MGM   Richard Brooks

Bring Your Smile Along   CONSTANCE TOWERS
COL   Blake Edwards

Daddy Long Legs   LESLIE CARON
TCF   Jean Negulesco

Good Morning Miss Dove   JENNIFER JONES
TCF   Henry Koster

The Kentuckian   DIANA LYNN
UA   Burt Lancaster

Las Vegas Shakedown   COLEEN GRAY
AA   Sidney Salkow

Marty   BETSY BLAIR
UA   Delbert Mann

"You're not such a dog as you think you are" has
become one of the classic film lines, and Clara
(Blair) is the stereotypical teacher--shy, no
personality, plain looking, a "dog," a twenty-
nine-year-old spinster who Marty's friends and mother
think looks forty or fifty. One of the nicest touches
in the film is when Marty's mother returns home,
almost catching them kissing, and Marty immediately
introduces Clara: "This is Miss Clara Snyder. She is
a graduate of New York University. She teaches
chemistry at Benjamin Franklin High School." The
mother worries about "these college girls; they're
just one step from the street." Marty is shown
working in the butcher shop, but we do not see Clara
in her classroom. Clara has been offered a job as
head of the science department, in a suburban school,
something she could never hope to attain in New York
City schools, but she is too fearful and homebound to
take it. It will take Marty the butcher to rescue her
from her drab life.

You're Never Too Young   DIANA LYNN
PARA   Norman Taurog

1956   *Everything But The Truth*   MAUREEN O'HARA
        UNIV   Jerry Hopper

        The King And I   DEBORAH KERR
        TCF   Walter Lang

This musical version of Anna and the King of Siam
portrays the same spirited Anna (Kerr); the only
difference seems to be more hint of romantic
attachment between Anna and the King. Kerr received
an Academy Award nomination for the role.

Our Miss Brooks   EVE ARDEN
WB   Al Lewis

The Unguarded Moment   ESTHER WILLIAMS
UNIV   Harry Keller

1957   *Copper Sky*   COLEEN GRAY
        TCF   Charles M. Warren

Don't Go Near The Water MGM Charles Walters		GIA SCALA
The Monolith Monsters UI John Sherwood		LOLA ALBRIGHT
Spring Reunion UA Robert Pirosh		IRENE RYAN
This Could Be The Night MGM Robert Wise		JEAN SIMMONS
1958	*As Young As We Are* PARA Bernard Girard	PIPPA SCOTT
	High School Confidential MGM Jack Arnold	JAN STERLING
	Johnny Rocco AA Paul Landres	COLEEN GRAY
	Kings Go Forth UA Delmer Daves	NATALIE WOOD
	The Long Hot Summer TCF Martin Ritt	JOANNE WOODWARD
	Man of the West UA Anthony Mann	JULIE LONDON
	Teacher's Pet PARA George Seaton	DORIS DAY

"A frustrated old biddy" is what a hard-boiled editor expects to meet when he learns that E. R. Stone (Day), who teaches a night school journalism class, is a woman. Though he thinks it is terrible that now "dames are teaching unsuspecting suckers journalism," he attends the class and learns that E. R. knows more than the stuff in books. Her father was a famous small-town editor, and she has had practical experience on a newspaper. There are several scenes of E. R. in the classroom and her office, and she is competent and effective. In addition she's a good dancer, showing off her legs and a bouncy rear end which the editor admires. She learns more about the practical aspects of the newspaper business from him, and he learns more about the value of an education and about idealism and thoughtfulness in journalism from her.

1960	*The Crowning Experience* MORALREARM		MURIEL SMITH
	High Time TCF	Blake Edwards	NICOLE MAUREY
	Studs Lonigan UA	Irving Lerner	HELEN WESTCOTT
1961	*The Children's Hour* UA	William Wyler	AUDREY HEPBURN SHIRLEY MACLAINE
	Two Loves MGM	Charles Walters	SHIRLEY MACLAINE
1962	*Five Weeks In A Balloon* TCF	Irving Allen	BARBARA EDEN
	The Miracle Worker UA	Arthur Penn	ANNE BANCROFT

This stunning biography of Annie Sullivan, Helen Keller's teacher, won an Oscar for Anne Bancroft. In the film Annie must prove herself to the Keller family because she is considered too young and inexperienced to teach the barbaric child Helen has become. Visually impaired, Annie grew up in a horrible asylum and realizes that she can have no future of her own. Teaching the blind is the only way she can earn a living, and she will not let the Kellers get rid of her because she has nothing else to do and nowhere to go. She calls herself a governess, but the family considers her a hireling. However, she is insistent upon the family's not interfering with her methods. She is stubborn and persistent; giving up is her idea of original sin. When Helen finally catches on to Annie's sign language, to identify her she does not spell "Annie"; instead, she spells "teacher."

	Two For The See-Saw UA	Robert Wise	SHIRLEY MACLAINE
	Zotz COL	William Castle	JULIA MEADE
1963	*A Child Is Waiting* UA	Stanley Kramer	JUDY GARLAND

| | *Ladybug, Ladybug* | JANE CONNELL |
| | UA Frank Perry | |

| 1964 | *Cheyenne Autumn* | CARROLL BAKER |
| | WB John Ford | |

| | *Father Goose* | LESLIE CARON |
| | UI Ralph Nelson | |

| 1965 | *Saturday Night In Apple Valley* | MIMI HINES |
| | EMERSON John Myhers | |

| | *What's New Pussycat?* | ROMY SCHNEIDER |
| | UA Clive Donner | |

| 1966 | *Cat Ballou* | JANE FONDA |
| | COL Eliot Silverstein | |

| | *The Sand Pebbles* | CANDICE BERGEN |
| | TCF Robert Wise | |

Although she is first seen with a missionary on her way to a mission in China, Bergen maintains that she is a teacher, not a missionary. She is never shown teaching, but she is shown at the mission, claiming she likes her teaching job and is learning Chinese. She and the head of the mission become stateless persons in order not to be involved with the American-Chinese political disagreement. Her love for an American sailor and her undelineated character add nothing to the central theme.

| 1967 | *Eight On The Lam* | SHIRLEY EATON |
| | UA George Marshall | |

| | *Hurry, Sundown* | DIAHANN CARROLL |
| | PARA Otto Preminger | |

| | *Luv* | NINA WAYNE |
| | COL Clive Donner | |

| | *Never a Dull Moment* | DOROTHY PROVINE |
| | Disney Jerry Paris | |

In this Walt Disney spoof of gangster movies, Provine plays a famous gangster's art teacher, calling herself "head of the mob's fine arts division." She insists their relationship is strictly teacher-pupil, and there is a funny scene in which she teaches him to

take out his aggressions on the canvas. When one of
the gangster's henchmen gets fresh, Provine socks him
and points out that she is the art teacher and nothing
else. She reveals that she had an exhibit in the
Village and the gangster bought three of her
paintings, then asked her to be his teacher. In the
end she helps foil his theft of a famous painting.

The Perils of Pauline	PAMELA AUSTIN
UNIV Herbert B. Leonard	

Up The Down Staircase	SANDY DENNIS
WB Robert Mulligan	

This film is a rarity in that it shows the lead
character only at work; any life she has outside of
work is not mentioned. As a graduate of an exclusive
women's college, Dennis is naive and out of place in
the New York public school. Her first problems are
with discipline, and she has to deal with the
principal and the bureaucracy as well as unruly
students, some of whom are bright, some stupid. There
is also an incident in which a student thinks she is
dying to have sex with him. She gets a little harried
at first, but she manages to handle it all with aplomb
and with what appears to be wisdom beyond her years
and experience. The inner-city school culture is
sanitized somewhat for the film, but otherwise it is
refreshing in that it does attempt to present the
everyday activities of a teacher.

Valley of Mystery	JULIE ADAMS
UNIV Joseph Leytes	

1968	*Blackbeard's Ghost*	SUZANNE PLESHETTE
	BV Robert Stevenson	

Charly	CLAIRE BLOOM
SELMUR/ROBERTSON Ralph Nelson	

Although at one point a colleague refers to her as a
psychologist, Mrs. Kenyon (Bloom) only seems to be
performing the role of a special education teacher who
is working on her doctorate. At first she is shown in
a night class for adult retardates; after that she has
only one student, Charly. A clinic team performs
experimental surgery on Charly, considering him a good
candidate because he is close to his teacher and will
have her support. As she works with him, he grows

more and more intelligent, and she teaches him everything from chemistry to the American government system. Soon she worries that the student has begun to surpass the teacher. The more normal he becomes, the more he eyes her buttocks and breasts and stylishly short skirts; and she refuses to answer his personal questions. At one point she wants to resign from the project because they are becoming emotionally involved, and one doctor wants to let her go because she is not expert enough. Finally, she and Charly have a happy love affair (despite a previous attempted rape!), but she refuses to marry him. Then, when she realizes that the results of the operation are temporary, she provides a salient example of a woman's heart getting the better of her head and she wants to marry him.

Maryjane   DIANE MCBAIN
AIP   Maury Dexter

Rachel, Rachel   JOANNE WOODWARD
WB   Paul Newman

Rachel personifies every stereotypical quality that has been fostered with respect to spinster schoolteachers. She is plain, wears a plain dress with plain shoes, has a plain hairstyle, and leads a plain vanilla life. Retiring and shy, under the authority of her whining mother, Rachel is uncomfortable in the presence of others, apart from her elementary schoolchildren. Lonely and inhibited, the school is her only outlet, yet it is also her cage. Teaching young children is not sufficient to satisfy her motherly longings, and she yearns for a child of her own. There is no indication that her decision to leave the small town will liberate her into a life of fulfillment. This was Woodward's first Academy Award nomination after winning an Oscar for *The Three Faces of Eve* in 1957.

1969   *Butch Cassidy And The Sundance Kid*   KATHARINE ROSS
        TCF   George Roy Hill

"Keep going, teacher lady," Sundance insists as Ross undresses. Otherwise, who would know she is a teacher? She is not seen teaching, and her only other reference to her profession is when she decides to throw in her lot with Sundance and Butch and become an outlaw: "I am twenty-six and single and a schoolteacher and that is the bottom of the pit." Her promise to the men is "I will go with you, and I will sew your sox and stitch your underwear, and I won't whine." Apparently she finds this menage-a-trois much more exciting than teaching school.

The Chairman		ANNE HEYWOOD
TCF	J. Lee Thompson	

Halls Of Anger		JANET MACLACHLAN
UA	Paul Bogart	

Tell Them Willie Boy Is Here		SUSAN CLARK
UNIV	Abraham Polonsky	KATHARINE ROSS

1971	*The Beguiled*	ELIZABETH HARTMAN
	UNIV Don Siegel	GERALDINE PAGE

A wounded Union soldier takes refuge in a Southern school for girls during the Civil War, and the headmistress (Page) and teacher (Hartman) and all the students crave his affection and his body. After nursing, protecting and hiding him, and even amputating his leg, they hold him prisoner and fight over him and eventually murder him. This school seems to teach very little besides Bible study and the social graces, and the headmistress knows there will be no money for tuition after the war. This psychological film contains some stereotypical touches of the frustration of spinster teachers.

Billy Jack		DELORES TAYLOR
WB	T. C. Frank	

The Hunting Party		CANDICE BERGEN
UA	Don Medford	

Pretty Maids All In a Row		ANGIE DICKINSON
MGM	Roger Vadim	

The Steagle		JEAN ALLISON
AE	Paul Sylbert	

1973	*Gentle People*	PATSY MCBRIDE
	COMMERCIAL Richard H. Bartlett	

1974	*Conrack*	MADGE SINCLAIR
	TCF Martin Ritt	

The Trial of Billy Jack   DELORES TAYLOR
TAYLORLAUG   Frank Laughlin

TELEPHONE

This occupation, dominated for most of its history by women, is obviously not that popular as a cinematic occupation, even though conversations overheard or participated in by the operator can have numerous possibilities. It is an opportunity for adventure or mystery or even love that only a few film makers took advantage of. The nosy operator is a stock comedy figure, but, with a few exceptions, she is always only a minor character.

1931	*The Secret Call*		PEGGY SHANNON
	PARA	Stuart Walker	
	The Secret Witness		ZASU PITTS
	COL	Thornton Freeland	
1932	*Is My Face Red?*		ZASU PITTS
	RKO	William Seiter	
1934	*I've Got Your Number*		JOAN BLONDELL
	WB	Ray Enright	
	Ladies Should Listen		FRANCES DRAKE
	PARA	Frank Tuttle	
	Looking For Trouble		CONSTANCE CUMMINGS
	TCF	William Wellman	
	Murder in the Private Car		UNA MERKEL
	MGM	Harry Beaumont	
	Private Scandal		JUNE BREWSTER
	PARA	Ralph Murphy	
1935	*The Mysterious Mr. Wong*		ARLINE JUDGE
	MONO	William Nigh	
	One New York Night		UNA MERKEL
	MGM	Jack Conway	

1938	*Telephone Operator*	JUDITH ALLEN
	MONO Scott Pembroke	
1941	*Pacific Blackout*	MARTHA O'DRISCOLL
	PARA Ralph Murphy	
	Tom, Dick And Harry	GINGER ROGERS
	RKO Garson Kanin	
1942	*Star Spangled Rhythm*	BETTY HUTTON
	PARA George Marshall	
1944	*Adventures Of Kitty O'Day*	JEAN PARKER
	MONO William Beaudine	
	Between Two Women	MARIE BLAKE
	MGM Willis Goldbeck	
1948	*For The Love Of Mary*	DEANNA DURBIN
	UI Fred De Cordova	
1953	*The Blue Gardenia*	ANNE BAXTER
	WB Fritz Lang	
1957	*Bernardine*	TERRY MOORE
	TCF Henry Levin	
1960	*Bells Are Ringing*	JUDY HOLLIDAY
	MGM Vincente Minnelli	

An operator at a telephone answering service is so motherly-- nurturing her customers, giving advice, playing matchmaker--that one of them, a playwright, even calls her "Mom." A complete klutz when she is out with men, shy and with nothing to say, she cannot deal with the fact that the playwright falls in love with her. He has fallen in love with a fictional character she has created for him in person, as she has done for all her customers over the phone. She inspires him to write a play, but it seems it is her motherly gesture of bringing him coffee and danish that makes him want her around forever. Meanwhile, she is just a "dumb broad" to a bookie whose scheme for avoiding the police she cleverly manages to ruin.

WAITRESS

Waiting on tables in a restaurant or serving drinks at a bar is hardly a glamorous occupation, and in general the movies do not try to glamorize it. On the contrary, being a waitress is shown, not as a career, as it is for something like four percent of American working women, but as something temporary to do until something better comes along. Movies often depict actresses or singers working as waitresses while waiting for that big break, or better still, while waiting for the right man to rescue her, preferably through marriage.

1930	*Behind the Makeup*	FAY WRAY
	PARA Robert Milton	
	Girl of the Port	SALLY O'NEIL
	RKO Burt Glennon	
	A Lady To Love	VILMA BANKY
	MGM Victor Seastrom	
	Love Among The Millionaires	CLARA BOW
	PARA Frank Tuttle	
	True to the Navy	CLARA BOW
	PARA Frank Tuttle	
1931	*Her Majesty Love*	MARILYN MILLER
	FN William Dieterle	
	Safe In Hell	NINA MAE MCKINNEY
	FN William A. Wellman	
1932	*The Age Of Consent*	ARLINE JUDGE
	RKO Gregory LaCava	
	The Country Fair	MARION SCHILLING
	MONO Louie King	

Dr. Jekyll and Mr. Hyde   MIRIAM HOPKINS
PARA   Rouben Mamoulian

Heart of New York   ALINE MACMAHON
WB   Mervyn LeRoy

Me And My Gal   JOAN BENNETT
TCF   Raoul Walsh

Virtue   CAROLE LOMBARD
COL   Edward Buzzell

Weekends Only   JOAN BENNETT
TCF   Alan Crosland

1933   *My Lips Betray*   LILIAN HARVEY
        TCF   John Blystone

1934   *Men of the Night*   JUDITH ALLEN
        COL   Lambert Hillyer

        The Most Precious Thing   JEAN ARTHUR
        COL   Lambert Hillyer

        Of Human Bondage   BETTE DAVIS
        RKO   John Cromwell

The waitress is considered fair game by men customers
in the restaurant, and she likes them for sex and
support. There are two early scenes in which she is
seen working; afterwards she is only shown coming off
work. After she has been abandoned by the father of
her child, she puts the baby out to nurse, excusing
her action with, "I can't do anything else if I am
going to work." However, the expected deterioration
and degradation ensue, and later it is obvious that
her work is prostitution.

Shopworn   BARBARA STANWYCK
COL   Nicholas Grinde

St. Louis Kid   PATRICIA ELLIS
WB   Ray Enright

1935   *Alias Mary Dow*   SALLY EILERS
        UNIV   Kurt Neumann

        Devil Dogs Of The Air   MARGARET LINDSAY
        WB   Lloyd Bacon

False Pretenses   IRENE WARE
CHESTERF   Charles Lamont

She Gets Her Man   ZASU PITTS
UNIV   William Nigh

1936   *Night Waitress*   MARGOT GRAHAME
        RKO   Lew Landers

        The Petrified Forest   BETTE DAVIS
        WB   Archie L. Mayo

Daughter of the owner of a cafe-gas station on the edge of the desert, Davis serves as the bookkeeper and also does the waitressing and clears dishes off the table, but she does not wear a uniform. There is a Mexican cook, but Davis also prepares the food for serving. A dreamer, she paints and reads poetry and dreams of getting a job in Hollywood, or going to France and finding something beautiful. When a wandering intellectual drifts in, she asks him many questions about the world, in return explaining Bar-B-Q to him. She confesses that she does not want to marry because she always wants to be free. The stranger sacrifices his life in order to enable her dreams to come true.

        Under Two Flags   CLAUDETTE COLBERT
        TCF   Frank Lloyd

1937   *London By Night*   VIRGINIA FIELD
        MGM   William Thiele

        That I May Live   ROCHELLE HUDSON
        TCF   Allan Dwan

        What Price Vengeance   WENDY MARRIE
        RIALTO PRO   Del Lord

1938   *Boy Meets Girl*   MARIE WILSON
        WB   Lloyd Bacon

        City Girl   PHYLLIS BROOKS
        TCF   Alfred Werker

        Painted Trail   ELEANORE STEWART
        MONO   Robert Hill

Ranger's Roundup   CHRISTINE MCINTYRE
SPECTRUM   Sam Newfield

1939   *Good Girls Go To Paris*   JOAN BLONDELL
        COL   Alexander Hall

        Sweepstakes Winner   MARIE WINDSOR
        WB   William McGann

        When Tomorrow Comes   IRENE DUNNE
        UNIV   John M. Stahl

1940   *Little Old New York*   ALICE FAYE
        TCF   Henry King

        Street Of Memories   LYNNE ROBERTS
        TCF   Shepard Traube

        They Drive By Night   ANN SHERIDAN
        WB   Mark Hellinger

Sheridan's waitressing activities are limited to one
early scene where she is behind the counter of a truck
stop, indulging in amusing, sexually explicit repartee
with her customers. She soon quits because her boss
wouldn't keep his hands off of her and hitches a ride
with the truck drivers. In San Francisco she refers
to working in a store, but she does not say what kind
of store or what she does.

        They Knew What They Wanted   CAROLE LOMBARD
        RKO   Garson Kanin

1941   *Dr. Jekyll And Mr. Hyde*   INGRID BERGMAN
        MGM   Victor Fleming

Dr. Jekyll rescues the barmaid as she is struggling
with a masher, and she unsuccessfully attempts to
seduce him. As Hyde, he finds her happily performing
her functions as barmaid, singing and joking with the
customers. When Hyde gets her fired, she loudly
protests the loss of her job. She is repelled by Hyde
but allows him to set her up in a apartment and
support her so that she will have the luxuries she
never enjoyed before. Her life turns into a hell as
she is a prisoner in the apartment, and she realizes
that she will die at Hyde's hands. In her attempts to
support herself and be supported, she is
representative of the very limited opportunities for a
working-class woman in nineteenth-century London.

	Moon Over Miami TCF Walter Lang	BETTY GRABLE
	Reaching For The Sun PARA William A. Wellman	ELLEN DREW
	Son Of Fury TCF John Cromwell	ELSA LANCHESTER
	We Go Fast TCF William McGann	LYNN BARI
1942	*Call Out The Marines* RKO F. Ryan/W. Hamilton	BINNIE BARNES
	Joan Of Paris RKO Robert Stevenson	MICHELE MORGAN
	Moontide TCF Archie Mayo	IDA LUPINO
1943	*Slightly Dangerous* MGM Wesley Ruggles	LANA TURNER
	True To Life PARA George Marshall	MARY MARTIN
	The Unknown Guest MONO Kurt Neuman	PAMELA BLAKE
	Where Are Your Children MONO William Nigh	GALE STORM
1944	*Blonde Fever* MGM Richard Whorf	GLORIA GRAHAME
	End Of The Road REP George Blair	JUNE STOREY
1945	*Anchors Aweigh* MGM George Sidney	PAMELA BRITTON
1946	*Because Of Him* UA Richard Wallace	DEANNA DURBIN

The Fabulous Suzanne   BARBARA BRITTON
REP   Steve Sekely

Fallen Angel   LINDA DARNELL
TCF   Otto Preminger

The Harvey Girls   JUDY GARLAND
MGM   George Sidney

Fred Harvey's "winsome waitresses" are identified as
unsung heroines and "civilizing forces" of the West.
The women on their way to become Harvey Girls are
informed that a Harvey Girl is more that a waitress;
she is a symbol and promise of the order that is to
come.   The trainees were teachers or something else
and wanted a more exciting life, but when they arrive
in the West they are horrified to see dance hall
girls.   Garland comes West as a mail order bride but
eschews marriage in favor of becoming a Harvey Girl.
Some of the women are scared out of town by the saloon
owners, but Garland and others spunkily stick it out,
working in the vegetable and flower gardens as well as
serving meals when the trains come through.   They live
in a nicely appointed dormitory, full of ruffles, and
introduce the waltz to the town.   Always respectable,
they can't avoid getting into a brawl with the saloon
girls while dressed in their starched uniforms.   They
are the ones courted by the local men.

Of Human Bondage   ELEANOR PARKER
WB   Edmund Goulding

1947 *Wake Up And Dream*   JUNE HAVER
TCF   Lloyd Bacon

1949 *It's A Great Feeling*   DORIS DAY
WB   David Butler

Makebelieve Ballroom   VIRGINIA WELLES
COL   Joseph Santley

1950 *The Asphalt Jungle*   JEAN HAGEN
MGM   John Huston

1951 *Decision Before Dawn*   HILDEGARDE NEFF
TCF   Anatole Litvak

Once Upon A Thief   JUNE HAVOC
UA   W. Lee Wilder

| | *The Scarf* | | MERCEDES MCCAMBRIDGE |
| | UA | E. A. Dupont | |

| | *Vengeance Valley* | | SALLY FORREST |
| | MGM | Richard Thorpe | |

| 1952 | *The Devil Makes Three* | | PIER ANGELI |
| | MGM | Andrew Marton | |

| | *A Girl In Every Port* | | MARIE WILSON |
| | RKO | Chester Erskine | |

| | *Steel Town* | | ANN SHERIDAN |
| | UNIV | George Sherman | |

| | *Untamed Frontier* | | SHELLEY WINTERS |
| | UNIV | Hugo Fregonese | |

| 1953 | *The Bigamist* | | IDA LUPINO |
| | FM | Ida Lupino | |

| | *One Girl's Confession* | | CLEO MOORE |
| | COL | Hugo Haas | |

| | *The Wild One* | | MARY MURPHY |
| | COL | Laslo Benedek | |

| 1954 | *Bait* | | CLEO MOORE |
| | COL | Hugo Haas | |

| | *The Egyptian* | | JEAN SIMMONS |
| | TCF | Michael Curtiz | |

| | *Return From The Sea* | | JAN STERLING |
| | AA | Lesley Selander | |

| | *The Student Prince* | | ANN BLYTH |
| | MGM | Richard Thorpe | |

| | *Wicked Woman* | | BEVERLY MICHAELS |
| | UA | Russell Rouse | |

| 1955 | *Night Freight* | | BARBARA BRITTON |
| | AA | Jean Yarbrough | |

| 1956 | *Crime Against Joe* | | JULIE LONDON |
| | UA | Lee Sholem | |

	Shack Out On 101	TERRY MOORE
	AA Edward Dein	
1957	*3:10 To Yuma*	FELICIA FARR
	COL Delmer Daves	
	The Way To The Gold	SHEREE NORTH
	TCF Robert D. Webb	
1958	*Live Fast, Die Young*	MARY MURPHY
	UNIV Paul Henreid	
1964	*Kiss Me, Stupid*	KIM NOVAK
	UA Billy Wilder	
1968	*The Counterfeit Killer*	SHIRLEY KNIGHT
	UNIV Josef Leytes	
1970	*Cowards*	SUSAN SPARLING
	JAYLO Simon Nuchtern	
	Machine Gun McCain	BRITT EKLAND
	COL Giuliano Montaldo	
	Monte Walsh	JEANNE MOREAU
	CINC William A. Fraker	
1972	*Hammersmith Is Out*	ELIZABETH TAYLOR
	CINERAMA Peter Ustinov	

Taylor is a foul-mouthed waitress in a diner, sporting a blond wig, a miniskirt, eye-catching cleavage and the name of Jimmie Jane Jackson. In the back, among the food supplies, she enjoys a grunting tussle with the customers. When a slob of a mental hospital attendant asks her to come away with him, he clinches the deal by offering, "I might even marry you." She has been married twice, both time to bums and bemoans, "I never even had a kid." Not even a high school graduate, Jimmie Jane is described by her lover as "kind of dumb, but with great jugs." Abetted by Hammersmith, who is presumably the Devil, her lover, Billy, becomes rich and famous; and Jimmie Jane begins to use her head, though the lover wants her to cook more, keep her mouth shut and not think. Remembering where she worked before, knowing that to Billy she is still just a dumb waitress, she is disappointed in the way things have turned out and in desperation gets herself pregnant by Hammersmith, and proclaims "I am the biggest mother of all time!"

1975   *Alice Doesn't Live Here Anymore*   ELLEN BURSTYN
        WB   Martin Scorsese

        Return To Macon County   ROBIN MATTSON
        AIP   Richard Compton

WRITER

Hollywood produced some biographies of women writers. Otherwise, with the fictional writers there is not much sense in the films of what a writer's life is like, or what it means to be involved in the creative process and balance that with personal relationships.

| 1930 | *Midnight Mystery* | BETTY COMPSON |
| | SU | George B. Seitz | |

| | *Strictly Modern* | DOROTHY MACKAILL |
| | FN | William A. Seiter | |

| 1933 | *When Ladies Meet* | MYRNA LOY |
| | MGM | Harry Beaumont | |

| 1934 | *The Barretts of Wimpole Street* | NORMA SHEARER |
| | MGM | Sidney Franklin | |

| | *Green Eyes* | SHIRLEY GREY |
| | CHESTERF | Richard Thorpe | |

| | *I Believed In You* | ROSEMARY AMES |
| | TCF | Irving Cummings | |

| 1936 | *The Ex-Mrs. Bradford* | JEAN ARTHUR |
| | RKO | Stephen Roberts | |

| | *High Tension* | GLENDA FARRELL |
| | TCF | Allan Dwan | |

| | *Mad Holiday* | ELISSA LANDI |
| | MGM | George B. Seitz | |

| | *Make Way For A Lady* | GERTRUDE MICHAEL |
| | RKO | David Burton | |

| | *Theodora Goes Wild* | IRENE DUNNE |
| | COL | Richard Boleslavsk | |

1937	*You Can't Have Everything*	ALICE FAYE
	TCF Norman Taurog	

1938	*The Call of the Yukon*	BEVERLY ROBERTS
	REP B. Reeves Eason	

	The Hollywood Stadium Mystery	EVELYN VENABLE
	REP David Howard	

1939	*It's A Wonderful World*	CLAUDETTE COLBERT
	MGM W. S. Van Dyke II	

1940	*Curtain Call*	BARBARA READ
	RKO Frank Woodruff	

	The Doctor Takes A Wife	LORETTA YOUNG
	COL Alexander Hall	

	Ellery Queen, Master Detective	MARGARET LINDSAY
	COL Kurt Neumann	

1941	*When Ladies Meet*	JOAN CRAWFORD
	MGM Robert Z. Leonard	

1942	*Mr. Celebrity*	DORIS DAY
	PRC William Beaudine	

	My Sister Eileen	ROSALIND RUSSELL
	COL Norman Taurog	

Russell loses her job on the Columbus newspaper and decides to try her luck as a writer in New York, despite her father's plea that she could always go back to teaching in Columbus. But she wants a career and refuses to sit around until some "local dope" decides to marry her. Her first efforts at selling a story to a magazine are unsuccessful, but an editor likes her work and encourages her to write about what she has experienced. There is one scene with her pounding furiously on her typewriter, and eventually this story is published and is a hit. Russell gives very little thought to men because it is always her pretty, blonde younger sister they are after; but the editor falls in love with her and her confidence in her writing and herself as a woman is established.

1943	*Mystery Broadcast*	RUTH TERRY
	REP George Sherman	

Old Acquaintance   BETTE DAVIS
WB   Vincent Sherman

Another writer ostensibly uninterested in men, Kit
(Davis) concentrates on her books. Millie (Miriam
Hopkins) is jealous of Kit's success as an author, but
remarks, "Being just a woman and a housewife has its
compensations." Still, to compete with Kit she writes
romance novels with popular appeal, and outsells her
friend's more critically acclaimed work. Millie's
pursuit of a career ruins her marriage, and she moans,
"I thought I had everything--a home, and a husband,
and a career; but they say you can lose yourself in
your work." Kit, ever loyal to her disloyal friend,
rejects the love of Millie's husband. Millie has
urged Kit to marry ("You're going to be a very lonely
old lady one day"), but when Kit finally does decide
to marry a younger suitor, he turns around and marries
Millie's daughter. Neither woman is lonely, but
connected to one another. For Millie, her many books
are small comfort despite the thrill of success; for
Kit, there is a philosophical acceptance of the fact
that she has at least accomplished something.

1944   *Brazil*   VIRGINIA BRUCE
       REP   Joseph Santley

1945   *A Song To Remember*   MERLE OBERON
       COL   Charles Vidor

"No one knows this human jungle better than I. No one
ever fought more bitterly to survive. To have some
talent and ambition, and to be a woman, in masculine
eyes something slightly better than a head of cattle.
I buried them, wrote behind a man's name, and wore
trousers to remind them I was their equal. It cost
the woman something to do it. There was the reward to
remember. I ruled my own life. What I set out to do
I did. Because I had talent and was a woman, I put
the woman behind me and wore men's clothes, to show
them I was as moral as they were. Even in the face of
contempt and slander." This is a terrific feminist
speech. Unfortunately, the context in which George
Sand utters it ruins its effectiveness. With this
statement Sand becomes even more of villain than she
has already seemed in this biography of Chopin. She
has already been presented as a woman with a mind of
her own, something very scary to the men who know her.
She is a writer of "books that shock the world" and

has "rules of conduct for herself." She has chosen to take a man's name and wear trousers because she was afraid they would not take a woman novelist seriously. Chopin's teacher refers to her as "the man who is a woman" and considers her debased. When first seen, Sand is wearing her customary gentleman's attire, but when she and Chopin travel to Majorca she wears a woman's coat and her trademark, a man's top hat. She wears gorgeous feminine attire in the salons of Paris, but generally wears pants at home. She takes control of Chopin's life and his genius, but she does not let their love affair interfere with her writing. Because she is tough, Hollywood considers that she must be evil, and her refusal to interrupt sitting for her portrait to go comfort the dying Chopin is presented as the ultimate in heartlessness. While Sand's biographers would undoubtedly find some truth in this portrayal, the woman's vulnerability and sensitivity are not shown. This is a very heavy-handed hatchet job on a woman who dared to be a non-conformist.

Over 21		IRENE DUNNE
COL	Charles Vidor	
Pan-Americana		AUDREY LONG
RKO	John H. Auer	
1946	*Devotion*	IDA LUPINO
	WB Curtis Bernhardt	
	Genius At Work	ANN JEFFREYS
	RKO Leslie Goodwins	
	Home Sweet Homicide	PEGGY ANN GARNER
	TCF Lloyd Bacon	
	Without Reservations	CLAUDETTE COLBERT
	RKO Mervyn LeRoy	
1947	*The Ghost And Mrs. Muir*	GENE TIERNEY
	TCF Joseph Mankiewicz	
	Linda Be Good	ELYSE KNOX
	PRC Frank McDonald	
	Violence	NANCY COLEMAN
	MONO Jack Bernhard	

1948	*Bungalow 13* TCF Edward L. Cahn	MARGARET HAMILTON
	The Luck Of The Irish TCF Henry Koster	ANNE BAXTER
	The Snake Pit TCF Anatole Litvak	OLIVIA DE HAVILLAND
1949	*The Great Sinner* MGM Robert Siodmak	AVA GARDNER
	A Letter To Three Wives TCF Joseph Mankiewicz	ANN SOTHERN
1952	*The Lady Says No* UA Frank Ross	JOAN CAULFIELD
	Sudden Fear RKO David Miller	JOAN CRAWFORD
1955	*Jungle Moon Men* COL Charles S. Gould	JEAN BYRON
	My Sister Eileen COL Richard Quine	BETTY GARRETT
1957	*Flight To Hong Kong* UA Joseph M. Newman	BARBARA RUSH
1958	*Kathy O* UI Jack Sher	JAN STERLING
	Maracaibo PARA Cornel Wilde	JEAN WALLACE
1959	*The Bat* AA Crane Wilbur	AGNES MOOREHEAD
1961	*Return To Peyton Place* TCF Jose Ferrer	CAROL LYNLEY
1962	*Who's Got The Action?* PARA Daniel Mann	LANA TURNER

Turner is a writer of romance novels who works at home
and tries out her novels' plots on her maid.   To
create a proper creative mood, she types in a bathtub
full of bubbles.   The plot of the film, however, does

not focus on her writing but rather on her becoming a
bookie in order to cure her husband of betting on the
horses. She gets in trouble with the mob and then
tries to convince the head of the mob to go into the
publishing business and publish her books. By film's
end she is, incredibly, painting plates which she
expects to sell through a mail order business.

1966	*Grand Prix*		EVA MARIE SAINT
	MGM	John Frankenheimer	
	The Swinger		ANN-MARGRET
	PARA	George Sidney	
1967	*Don't Just Stand There*		BARBARA RHOADES
	UNIV	Ron Winston	
1969	*Thank You All Very Much*		ELEANOR BRON
	COL	Waris Hussein	
1970	*C. C. And Company*		ANN-MARGRET
	AE	Seymour Robbie	
1971	*Believe In Me*		JACQUELINE BISSET
	MGM	Stuart Hagmann	
1973	*The Way We Were*		BARBRA STREISAND
	COL	Sydney Pollack	

In this pastiche purporting to portray the development
of an American Jewish radical and the trauma of the
McCarthy period, Streisand has several jobs in college
and, by her own count, eleven jobs during World War
II. Her primary job before marriage is writing for a
radio station, and after she marries and accompanies
her writer-husband to Hollywood, she writes synopses
of novels for screenplay consideration. But her main
activity is haranguing friends and strangers on street
corners about political and social injustice.

ACTRESS INDEX

MOVIE INDEX

446 Working Women on the Hollywood Screen